Content-Based Instruction in Primary and Secondary School Settings

Edited by Dorit Kaufman and JoAnn Crandall

Case Studies in TESOL Practice Series

Jill Burton, Series Editor

Teachers of English to Speakers of Other Languages, Inc.

Typeset in Berkeley and Belwe
by Capitol Communication Systems, Inc., Crofton, Maryland USA
Printed by United Graphics Incorporated, Mattoon, Illinois, USA
Indexed by Coughlin Indexing Services, Annapolis, Maryland USA

Teachers of English to Speakers of Other Languages, Inc.
700 South Washington Street, Suite 200
Alexandria, Virginia 22314 USA
Tel 703-836-0774 • Fax 703-836-6447 • E-mail tesol@tesol.org • http://www.tesol.org/

Director of Publishing: Paul Gibbs
Managing Editor: Marilyn Kupetz
Copy Editor: Marcella F. Weiner
Cover Design: Capitol Communication Systems, Inc.

ISBN 1931185174
Library of Congress Control No. 2004098607

Table of Contents

Acknowledgments

We wish to acknowledge several colleagues whose commitment and generous contribution of time, effort, experience, and wisdom have greatly enhanced this volume: Jill Burton, Colleen Grisham, Marilyn Kupetz, and Marcella Weiner.

We dedicate this volume to our TESOL colleagues and students whose inspiration, enthusiasm, and dedication contributed to advancing the profession and to Arie Kaufman and Joe Keyerleber for their unwavering love and support.

Series Editor's Preface

The Case Studies in TESOL Practice series offers innovative and effective examples of practice from the point of view of the practitioner. The series brings together from around the world communities of practitioners who have reflected and written on particular aspects of their teaching. Each volume in the series covers one specialized teaching focus.

◈ CASE STUDIES

Why a TESOL series focusing on case studies of teaching practice?

Much has been written about case studies and where they fit in a mainstream research tradition (e.g., Nunan, 1992; Stake, 1995; Yin, 1994). Perhaps more importantly, case studies also constitute a public recognition of the value of teachers' reflection on their practice and constitute a new form of teacher research—or teacher valuing. Case studies support teachers in valuing the uniqueness of their classes, learning from them, and showing how their experience and knowledge can be made accessible to other practitioners in simple, but disciplined ways. They are particularly suited to practitioners who want to understand and solve teaching problems in their own contexts.

These case studies are written by practitioners who are able to portray real experience by providing detailed descriptions of teaching practice. These qualities invest the cases with teacher credibility, and make them convincing and professionally interesting. The cases also represent multiple views and offer immediate solutions, thus providing perspective on the issues and examples of useful approaches. Informative by nature, they can provide an initial database for further, sustained research. Accessible to wider audiences than many traditional research reports, however, case studies have democratic appeal.

◈ HOW THIS SERIES CAN BE USED

The case studies lend themselves to pre- and in-service teacher education. Because the context of each case is described in detail, it is easy for readers to compare the cases with and evaluate them against their own circumstances. To respond to the wide range of language environments in which TESOL functions, cases have been selected from EFL, ESL, and bilingual education settings around the world.

The 12 or so case studies in each volume are easy to follow. Teacher writers describe their teaching context and analyze its distinctive features: the particular demands of their context, the issues they have encountered, how they have effectively addressed the issues, what they have learned. Each case study also offers readers practical suggestions—developed from teaching experience—to adapt and apply to their own teaching.

Already published or in preparation are volumes on

- academic writing programs
- action research
- assessment practices
- bilingual education
- community partnerships
- content-based language instruction
- distance learning
- English for specific purposes
- gender and TESOL
- grammar teaching in teacher education
- interaction and language learning
- international teaching assistants
- journal writing
- literature in language learning and learning
- mainstreaming
- teacher education
- teaching English as a foreign language in primary schools
- teaching English from a global perspective
- teaching literature
- technology in the classroom

◈ THIS VOLUME

For teachers, this volume offers a range of creative ways to link learning English with the subjects students study at school. Content-based instruction, a widely respected approach in TESOL, is here extended successfully to implementing ESOL standards-based teaching, subject team and school partnerships, and professional development.

Jill Burton
University of South Australia, Adelaide

CHAPTER 1

Standards- and Content-Based Instruction: Transforming Language Education in Primary and Secondary Schools

Dorit Kaufman and JoAnn (Jodi) Crandall

❖ INTRODUCTION

The unprecedented spread of English throughout the world in recent years has resulted in its major role and high prestige in the academic, cultural, and political landscape of a growing number of countries (Crystal, 1995, 1997; Fishman, Cooper, & Conrad, 1977; McArthur, 1998, 2002). The mandates to teach English in earlier and earlier grades, combined with a growing exposure to the English language through television, newspapers, popular culture, tourism, travel, and the Internet, have further increased the importance of the language. In many countries, English has become the second language of academia, requiring students to be proficient enough to be able to read a large amount of textual material in English or even to participate in discussions or make oral presentations in English at international conferences. Pervasive use of English in electronic communication in all academic areas has further underscored the need for high proficiency and literacy development in English across age groups, thereby having a significant impact on the profession of English language education in English as a foreign language (EFL) contexts.

Similarly, in the United States, as well as in other English-speaking countries such as Australia, Canada, Great Britain, and New Zealand, the growing ethnolinguistic diversity in educational contexts combined with recent educational reforms have considerably transformed language education for English language learners. In the United States, increased emphasis on language across the curriculum (American Association for the Advancement of Science, 1998, 2001; National Research Council, 1996) and the growing number of English language learners in all classrooms have underscored the need for teachers in all disciplines to be able to address the specialized linguistic and academic needs of English language learners. Indeed, teacher education professional standards across subject areas have incorporated the preparation of teachers for teaching in educational settings that have become increasingly more diverse.

At the same time, the emergence of content-based instruction (CBI) as a paradigm in language education (Brinton, Snow, & Wesche, 1989; Chamot & O'Malley, 1994; Crandall, 1987, 1993; Mohan, 1986; Short, 1993; Snow, Met, & Genesee, 1989; Stoller, 2004) and its implementation across educational contexts

(Crandall & Kaufman, 2002; Mohan, Leung, & Davison, 2001; Snow & Brinton, 1997) have radically changed the role of language teachers and the language curriculum in primary and secondary school settings and in postsecondary contexts. CBI has increasingly grounded language teaching in academic content across disciplines and has changed the focus from teaching language in isolation to its integration with disciplinary content in primary, secondary, and tertiary contexts in the United States and abroad. Furthermore, new state, national, and professional standards have also affected language education in their emphasis on performance-based evidence and accountability in primary and secondary schools and in teacher education programs. The standards have underscored quality of education to ensure academic success and higher achievement for all students, including English language learners.

The growing importance of English as an international language, the diversification of demographics in academic institutions, and increased emphasis on performance-based accountability and ongoing program improvement have expanded the impact and visibility of language educators and have greatly enhanced their professional role within the school and the community (Clegg, 1996). Understandably, this has helped to highlight the particular strengths that language teachers bring to educational settings and the significance of the quality of teacher education programs that prepare them for their greatly expanded role. The importance of CBI as an educational paradigm was underscored by research findings that identified several areas of concern; for example, the poor performance of English language learners in academic areas that was attributed in part to the specialized language of the academic disciplines, for instance, mathematics (Cocking & Mestre, 1988; Crandall, Dale, Rhodes, & Spanos, 1990; Cuevas, 1984) and social studies (Short, 1993). This highlighted one of the challenges for CBI—the lack of expertise among language teachers both in the content areas and in the discipline-specific pedagogy within which language teaching is embedded (Kaufman, 2004). The TESOL standards for teacher education programs (TESOL, 2002) have addressed this issue by emphasizing the melding of a strong linguistic foundation for teacher candidates with a solid grounding in the respective disciplines of the core curriculum. The theme of preparing English for speakers of other languages (ESOL) teacher candidates who are able to provide access to the core curriculum across content areas for primary and secondary school students is reiterated across the standards. The standards advance the position that teacher education programs must prepare ESOL teacher candidates who understand and are able to

- construct learning environments that support ESOL students' language and literacy development and content-area achievement (Domain 1—Language)

- construct learning environments that support ESOL students' cultural identities, language and literacy development, and content-area achievement (Domain 2—Culture)

- know, understand, and use standards-based practices and strategies related to planning, implementing, and managing ESL and content instruction (Domain 3—Planning, Implementing, and Managing Instruction)

- collaborate with their colleagues across disciplines and serve as a resource to all staff . . . to improve learning for all ESOL students (Domain 5—Professionalism) (TESOL, 2002)

The TESOL standards underscore the importance of expanded pedagogical content knowledge (Shulman, 1986, 1987) that, in the case of CBI, combines knowledge of linguistics, language acquisition, and language pedagogy with the content knowledge and the specialized pedagogy of the social and natural sciences disciplines. Partnerships and joint activities among ESOL and other content-area teacher preparation programs can facilitate the attainment of greater awareness and acquisition of instructional skills in these areas. The advent of CBI has made the content from other disciplines an integral part of language teaching, and the pedagogical approaches that are prevalent in the respective disciplines within which language teaching is embedded are also becoming part of the CBI classroom experience. For instance, constructivism, an approach grounded in the cognitive developmental theory of Piaget (1970) and in the sociocultural theory of Vygotsky (1978), has been a dominant pedagogical paradigm in mathematics and science education for several decades and has also affected language learning research and pedagogy (Freeman & Johnson, 1998; Hall, 2002; Johnson, 2000; Johnson & Golombek, 2003; Kaufman, 1996, 2000; Ko, Schallert, & Walters, 2003; Lantolf & Appel, 1994; McGroarty, 1998; Murrell, 2001; Prabhu, 1996). Embedding of content in language teaching and the focus on standards-based education will likely strengthen integration of pedagogical approaches such as constructivism in language teacher education (Kaufman, 2004).

The challenge for language teacher education programs is to prepare candidates whose pedagogical content knowledge includes linguistic-based pedagogy with content-based pedagogy of science, mathematics, and social studies. Such preparation includes the construction of deeper understandings of linguistics and mathematical and scientific concepts to enhance the design of learning environments that support students' cultural identities, language and literacy development, and academic achievement. An additional challenge is the preparation of teachers in all subject areas to address the needs of English language learners. Although the standards for these disciplines, set by their respective professional associations, discuss issues of differentiated instruction or teaching all learners, to date there has been little research or curriculum development from within these disciplines that guides teachers in accommodating linguistic and cultural diversity in their instruction. What may be required is an approach such as that used, for example, in California or Florida, where all primary and secondary school teachers are required to complete a program that includes language and literacy development, intercultural communication, and the integration of language and content instruction.

The importance of combining content and pedagogical content knowledge in the preparation of qualified teachers has also been given increased attention in national and professional standards and in scholarly work across disciplines (Darling-Hammond, 2001; Interstate New Teacher Assessment and Support Consortium [INTASC], 1992, 2002; National Board for Professional Teaching Standards, 1991; National Council for Accreditation of Teacher Education, 2001b; National Council of Teachers of Mathematics, 2000; National Research Council/National Science Foundation, 1996; TESOL, 2002; Wang & Walberg, 2001). The emphasis on strengthening pedagogical content knowledge is further evidenced in the recent melding of the pedagogically focused 1992 Interstate New Teacher Assessment and Support Consortium (INTASC) standards for teacher candidates with the discipline-based standards. One example is the redesigned set of standards—a collaborative project of INTASC with the National Science Teachers Association—that has resulted in new integrated standards for science teacher candidates (INTASC, 2002). Similar initiatives are underway as additional disciplines integrate their professional disciplines with the national INTASC standards that emphasize pedagogy.

◈ MAJOR THEMES IN THE CONTENT-BASED INSTRUCTION CASE STUDIES

Standards-driven curriculum development, enhanced interdisciplinary collaboration in language teaching, and reflection and assessment in professional development are highlighted across all case studies showcased in this volume. Although the major themes described here are interwoven throughout the volume, some chapters give greater emphasis to one or the other of these and have been arranged accordingly. The major themes are

- partnerships and constructivist notions in CBI
- reflection and inquiry in CBI professional development
- standards-based CBI curriculum, assessment, and professional development

Partnerships and Constructivist Notions in Content-Based Instruction

Collaborative partnerships have played a key role in transitioning language teaching and learning to a CBI paradigm (Crandall, 1998b; Kaufman, 1997; Kaufman & Grennon Brooks, 1996). The authors in this volume, who represent state education departments, universities, or schools in the United States and in other countries, describe a range of professional endeavors and a multiplicity of collaborative initiatives that have emerged within schools and between schools and tertiary institutions in response to the new standards and changing paradigms. These joint projects that include primary and secondary school faculty and administrators, teacher candidates, teacher educators, and representatives from state education departments and national professional organizations underscore the increased role of all stakeholders in the educational process. Some examples of these include a school-university project that placed upper-intermediate English language learners in mainstream social studies classrooms designed especially to meet the needs of linguistically and academically diverse students (chapter 2: Bunch, Lotan, Valdés, & Cohen), a whole-school intervention project that included teacher supervisors and teachers in the design of a content-based EFL curriculum (chapter 3: Jakar), a schoolwide partnership in an EFL context to identify required English language functions and assign the teaching of these to ESOL and other content teachers (chapter 4: Hurst & Davison), collaborative partnership between an ESOL teacher with teachers across the curriculum in the teaching of beginning English language learners in a middle school (chapter 5: Bernache, Galinat, & Jimenez), and a joint exploration by practicing teachers and teacher learners of Vygotsky's (1978) zone of proximal development (chapter 6: Gordon). These case studies display collaboration that is multifaceted and includes interpersonal, interdisciplinary, and cross-institutional initiatives.

Reflection and Inquiry in Content-Based Instruction Professional Development

In recent years there has been increased attention to teachers' self-image as emerging professionals and to their developmental discourse about the process of becoming a professional (Edge, 2002). A critical reflective stance on practice, performance-based accountability, increased diversity, and enhanced technological proficiency has become an integral part of the process of state, national, and professional accreditation. Educational reform has stimulated inquiry and reflection, review of existing organizational structures and curricular content, and increased clinical experiences in teacher education programs (Williams, 2000). Through the TESOL (2002) standards and the accreditation process, CBI has become central to curriculum reform and has been infused into institutional and program conceptual frameworks. Development of CBI learning modules has engaged participants in reflective inquiry and discourse within and across disciplines. Educators have collaboratively redesigned curriculum and learning experiences and alternative assessment approaches for improving learning and teaching for English language learners. Reflection and inquiry have become central to professional development and to joint inquiry with primary and secondary school professionals as exemplified in many of the case studies. Some examples include a joint inquiry between teacher educators and primary and secondary school teachers through a Professional Development School model (chapter 7: Dubetz, Abreu, Alegria, Casado, & Díaz), the infusion of language into a social studies class to encourage reflection and better understanding of cultural issues in current events (chapter 8: Olsen & Belnap), reflective practice as central to helping language teachers move from traditional language teaching approaches to more content-based approaches in an elementary EFL program (chapter 9: Díaz-Maggioli & Burbaquis-Vinson), and reflective communication between the subject specialist and language specialist that raises interpersonal and interdisciplinary challenges as new understandings of each other's disciplinary foci emerge (chapter 10: Arkoudis).

Standards- and Content-Based Instruction Curriculum, Assessment, and Professional Development

The transition to standards-based curriculum development requires a paradigm shift in teacher education. The increasing importance of standards in designing and implementing CBI curriculum, developing effective assessment systems, and providing appropriate professional development is central to many of the chapters. Some examples include the development of a standards-based assessment initiative in collaboration with the state education department to prepare teachers to integrate the state's content standards into their language instruction (chapter 11: Gottlieb & Boals); a collaborative curriculum mapping process using state curriculum frameworks and assessment to transform a grammar-based high school ESOL curriculum to a content-based curriculum that articulates with and serves as a bridge to the mainstream curriculum across subject areas and grade levels (chapter 12: De Jong &

Grieci); and a sustained theme-based CBI program at a junior high school aligned with district, state, and TESOL standards to provide a basis for a range of experiences for English language learners that include academic/formal and social/informal language (chapter 13: Bigelow, Ranney, & Hebble).

Technological advances have led to the proliferation of new technologies for educational contexts and have opened new possibilities for classroom learning and professional development. Computer, video, and wireless technologies have expanded the notion of community of learners beyond local communities into global electronic learning communities. New technologies have greatly enhanced student achievement and teacher learning (Beatty, 2003; Bransford, Brown, & Cocking, 2000; Perkins, Schwartz, West, & Wiske, 1995; Warschauer, Shetzer, & Meloni, 2000). Universities have drawn on the new technologies to expand their role in professional development beyond the local region. Through online and distance learning, universities combine distance technologies with interpersonal face-to-face communication in working groups and community of learners to design programs for in-service teachers from all disciplines, regardless of geographical location. Teemant (chapter 14) describes a distance-learning program in which CBI plays an important role and is integrated throughout the program and instruction guide for the teachers. An important feature of this professional development program is the combination of distance and on-site approaches and the use of specially trained on-site ESOL/bilingual facilitators.

◈ CONCLUSION

CBI has emerged in recent years as a pedagogical anchor to language education and has opened new opportunities for integration of interdisciplinary collaborative approaches for language teaching and learning. The current emphasis on standards-based accreditation and resulting reconceptualization of teacher education programs will likely further expand the horizons of language pedagogy by bringing constructivist approaches to the foreground in CBI and language teacher education and by opening new avenues for linguistic and interdisciplinary classroom-based research.

This volume reflects the diversity of CBI paradigms that are prevalent in primary and secondary schools and collaborative partnerships that have emerged within and across institutions and disciplines. These underscore the dramatic shift that has taken place in the field of language education and highlight the new challenges that have emerged in recent years in the preparation of teacher candidates for their reconceptualized role. Such preparation is no longer discipline-specific but extends beyond the field of linguistics and language education to other social and natural sciences and their respective pedagogies. In the coming years, the pedagogical content knowledge of language teachers will likely integrate epistemological notions that underpin the disciplines within which language teaching and learning is embedded.

◈ CONTRIBUTORS

Dorit Kaufman is director of the professional education program at Stony Brook University, State University of New York (SUNY), in the United States. Her research interests include native language attrition and narrative development in children, teacher education, content-based instruction, and constructivist pedagogy. She received the R. Neil Appleby Outstanding Teacher Educator Award and the SUNY President's/Chancellor's Award for Excellence in Teaching.

Jodi Crandall directs the interdisciplinary PhD program in Language, Literacy, and Culture and codirects the MA Program in ESOL/Bilingual Education at the University of Maryland, Baltimore County, in the United States. She has written extensively on content-based instruction from the perspective of research, program or materials development, and teacher education and on adult ESOL and literacy.

PART 1

Partnerships and Contructivist Notions in Content-Based Instruction

CHAPTER 2

Keeping Content at the Heart of Content-Based Instruction: Access and Support for Transitional English Learners

George C. Bunch, Rachel A. Lotan, Guadalupe Valdés, and Elizabeth G. Cohen

◈ INTRODUCTION

Manuel, Diego, Julia, and Laura, designated by their school as transitional limited English proficient (LEP), were seventh-grade students in mainstream world history classes at Gerona Middle School in Garden City, California. As part of a collaborative university-school project during the 2000–2001 academic year, these and other transitional students at Gerona studied in mainstream classrooms where the curriculum, classroom organization, instruction, and teacher preparation were designed to meet the needs of linguistically and academically diverse students.

We begin this case study by describing what students were able to do in English at the end of their last social studies unit of the school year, entitled "Challenging the Authority of Institutions: The Reformation." We present excerpts of essays in which students demonstrate content learned, link that content to the central ideas of the unit, and write effective persuasive essays. Through the activities of this unit, students came to understand and write about how the Reformation, a sweeping social, political, cultural, and religious movement, challenged the authority of the medieval church in Renaissance Europe. Creating essays such as the ones excerpted in this chapter represents a significant accomplishment for academically underprepared English learners such as Manuel, Diego, Julia, and Laura. After discussing the essays, we describe the classroom conditions that allowed the students to accomplish what they did.

In their essays, students were asked to imagine that they lived during the Reformation and to persuade members of their families either to join or to oppose Martin Luther and his supporters in their campaign against the church. Students were given explicit guidelines, had the opportunity to work on their writing in class and at home, and were allowed access to texts and materials used during the unit. The writing in this chapter represents students' initial drafts. We will take up the issue of students' writing errors after considering their success in demonstrating content learning and effective persuasive writing.

Using what he has learned about social and religious protest during the Reformation, Manuel adroitly marshals evidence to support his position that his family should join Martin Luther in the fight against corruption, including the unreasonable and unfair sale of indulgences, the burdensome taxes levied on the poor, and the dishonest selling of influential positions in the church:

> Family I believe that Martin Luther's beieves are good. Some people think that Martin Luther's way of teaching is wrong but I think that they are the one that are wrong. Martin Luther believe's that the church is currupted and I Also believe that. Three ways that the church is currupted is because the saling of indugences; it keep all the taxes Money, and the saling of positions on the church . . .
> Family one way that the church is currupted is because the saling of Indulgences. Luther believes that the church can't forgive the peaple that only god can forgive your sins. Another thing that Luther said about the saling of Indulgences is that not all the peaple could buy the Indulgences. So not all the peaple got their sins forgiven. I also believe that the saling of indungences is bad because its discrimination for poor people. I think that you should believe that only god can forgive your sins . . .
> I believe that Martin Luther theaching are good and the church is wrong. Family I think that you should goin Martin Luther. I gave you three good reason to going hin and nat to goin the church because is currupted.
> —Manuel

Diego renders a sharper attack, characterizing the church's practices as an affront to the poor:

> The institusen that I am chalange ing is the church. Because they are thaking the money away from the peastens. I support Martin Luther . . .
> Like the indulgenses the Pope was liying about that and wen he said if you bye them you will be able to go to heven and god will forgive your siens and well the people was bing them and the pap will be kipping the money in his pocket and he will west it on some thing.
> —Diego

While acknowledging that members of her family might still hold onto traditional beliefs, Julia appeals to the most fundamental wishes of parents for the future of their children:

> We should challenge the Church because I beilieve that the pope selling indulgences is wrong. I know many of you beilieve what the pope says, but let me tell you why I believe what Martin Luther says.
> . . . We should Follow the teachings of Martin Luther and think about our freedom. We need to think about how we will feel being peasants for many years and the children, how do you think they will feel being oppressed by the lords. These are some reasons I believe we should challenge the church.
> —Julia

Laura includes what she has learned about the Peasants' Rebellion of 1524–1525, a movement designed to loosen the stranglehold of feudal lords upon their tenants. Along with her own words, she paraphrases original language from the pronouncement of the peasants' goals in the *Twelve Articles*, one of the primary documents studied (see Figure 1):

> The second argument is about peasants freedom. Peasants should have the right to be free. The peasants have the right to wish to be so. Just because they

were the lowest class, that dosent mean they don't have their rights. Peasants weren't allowed to fish. The noble have appropriated all the woods to themselves alone. The peasants would fight to get wood, water, fire, to fish, and to build their own houses

—Laura

In addition to discussing specific charges made against the church during the Reformation, in other parts of their essays students cite further relevant historical information: how the printing press, a new technology, allowed for the rapid spread of ideas and for the newly translated Bible to be read by and to the masses, and how political cartoons were a new means of waging social and political protest in

---

Unit: The Reformation

CHALLENGING THE AUTHORITY OF INSTITUTIONS

**Activity 3: The *Twelve Articles* and the Peasants' Rebellion of 1524-25
Resource Card**

Luther's challenging the authority of the Roman Catholic Church coincided with challenging the authority of other institutions. Many peasants, discontented with their poverty, began to openly challenge the authority of the Church and lords over their earnings. Inspired by the ideas and actions of Martin Luther, the peasants led a rebellion in 1524-25. They pronounced their goals in the *Twelve Articles*. Below follow a few of the *Twelve Articles*.	*Peasants challenged the Church*
The Second Article - Since the right tithe is established in the Old Testament and fulfilled in the New, we are ready and willing to pay the fair tithe of grain, but it should be done properly. The Word of God plainly provides that it should be given to God and passed on to his own. If it is to be given to a minister, we will in the future collect the tithe through our church elders sufficient for the livelihood of the minister and his family. The remainder shall be given to the poor of the place.	*What should be done with the donations*
The Third Article - It has been the custom for men to hold us as their own property, which is pitiable enough considering that Christ has redeemed and purchased us without exception. Accordingly, it is consistent with Scripture that we should be free and wish to be so.	*Why peasants should be free*
The Fourth Article - In the fourth place it has been the custom that no poor man was allowed to catch venison or wild fowl, or fish in flowing water, which seems to us quite unbrotherly and selfish....Accordingly, if a man holds possession of waters , he has purchased the right to use those waters.	*One right demanded by the peasants*
The Fifth Article - In the fifth place, we are aggrieved in the matter of wood-cutting, for our noble folk have appropriated all the woods to themselves alone...It should be free to every member of the community to help himself to such firewood as he needs in his home.	*Another right demanded*
The Seventh Article - Seventh, we will not hereafter allow ourselves to be farther oppressed by our lords. What the lords possess is to be held according to the agreement between the lord and the peasant.	*Another right demanded*

FIGURE 1. Sample Resource Card: *Twelve Articles* and the Peasants' Rebellion Activity (Copyright © Program for Complex Instruction/Stanford University School of Education, undated. Used by permission.)

subversive ways. Beyond a display of discrete content items, the students' essays also make connections between their assignment and the essential question of the unit: How do individuals and groups challenge the authority of institutions? Diego's essay, for example, clearly makes the connection between following Martin Luther and engaging in social change: "The institusen that I am chalange ing is the church. I support Martin Luther."

The students also show an understanding of the elements of a persuasive essay. They begin with a clear statement of position, unambiguously asserting whether they support Martin Luther or not. They understand that the genre calls for providing evidence to support one's position. They display an awareness that it is advantageous to anticipate counterarguments in a debate, in this case the threat of excommunication or the popularity of maintaining the status quo. Students effectively use rhetorical strategies appropriate for persuading a particular audience. Manuel, for example, begins and ends his essay with a direct appeal to his audience. Julia also uses a direct appeal, poignantly connecting with her audience: "I know many of you beilieve what the pope says, but let me tell you why I believe what Martin Luther says."

Students also use content-specific vocabulary correctly and precisely. They write about peasants, lords, and popes; corruption, beliefs, and excommunication; and tithes, church positions, and the sale of indulgences. Like social scientists, they write about challenging the authority of institutions and using tax money justly, and they examine religious beliefs regarding the forgiveness of sins.

The preceding analysis, emphasizing students' ability to display content learning and write persuasively, differs markedly from an error analysis, which might initially claim that these students lack the writing skills needed to succeed in school. Even an error analysis, however, reveals the emergence of grammatical morphology in the writing of these students. They mark regular verbs for tense and aspect, use irregular verb forms, choose correct pronouns, and use modals correctly. Many problems involve mechanical errors in spelling, punctuation, and capitalization that have not yet been attended to in these initial drafts. Because they are writers in the process of acquiring English, students also demonstrate some transfer from their native Spanish. For example, Manuel writes about not joining the church "because is currupted," deleting the required pronoun *it*, as would be correct in Spanish. More common than these second language issues are instances of transfer from standard and nonstandard spoken English into the written essays, a move not entirely surprising in an assignment that asks students to persuade their family to take a stand. Diego's prose, for example, becomes more lucid when one imagines him speaking out loud, in an informal conversation with natural pauses:

> Like the indulgenses/ the Pope was liying about that/ and wen he said if you bye them you will be able to go to heven/ and god will forgive your siens/ and well the people was bing them/ and the pap will be kipping the money in his pocket/ and he will west it on some thing.

It is essential that English learners, like other students, develop strategies for minimizing mechanical and grammatical errors and that they learn how academic writing differs from oral discourse. However, focusing on errors alone eclipses both the sophisticated content students have learned and their evolving effectiveness in demonstrating that learning.

✦ CONTEXT

The unit on the Reformation, for which students wrote the essays excerpted here, was the last of four units completed in six Gerona Middle School classrooms that were using complex instruction. Complex instruction is a pedagogical approach specifically designed to promote student achievement in academically and linguistically heterogeneous classrooms (Cohen & Lotan, 1997).[1] In complex instruction classrooms, all students work in groups of mixed academic and linguistic backgrounds as they tackle open-ended tasks that require contributions from students with many different kinds of intellectual abilities. Using complex instruction, these Gerona teachers incorporated the following features, which will be discussed in more detail later in this case study, in their classrooms:

- creating group-worthy tasks
- offering textual support for struggling readers and writers
- demystifying academic language for social studies
- providing additional time and support during writing assignments
- delegating authority to students
- facilitating peer support
- treating status problems

Each complex instruction unit followed several days of more traditional social studies instruction, including teacher minilectures and work with mainstream textbooks, in which students previewed some of the historical context relevant to the unit.

Gerona Middle School is located in a medium-sized city near California's central coast. Three-quarters of the student body identifies itself as Latino, and more than half of the students at the school are designated English learners. Among Gerona's Latino students are first- and second-generation immigrants along with those whose families have lived in California for generations. Most students at Gerona are poor; a majority of the student body qualifies for free or reduced lunch. Although there are at Gerona a few middle-class students who speak English as their predominant language, the town's economic and ethnic segregation limits the number of speakers fluent in prestige varieties of English and those experienced in using English for academic purposes.

Based on standardized tests, language assessments, and teacher recommendations, personnel at Gerona have traditionally designated those at the intermediate or upper level of English proficiency as transitional LEP. Prior to the university/school intervention described in this study, school policy deemed these students to be beyond the need of English for speakers of other languages (ESOL) classes but still in need of sheltered content instruction and, therefore, separated from mainstream peers and grade-level curriculum. One of the major interventions of the project was to move students previously designated as transitional into the new, specially designed mainstream classrooms that used complex instruction.

---

[1] For more information on complex instruction, see http://www.complexinstruction.org.

The social studies teachers whose classrooms we describe in this case study had previous training and experience using complex instruction. Two language arts teachers with experience in complex instruction also participated in the study. One of them had experience teaching ESOL, and both communicated with the social studies teachers as part of grade-level "families" at the school. At the university, the project team consisted of educational scholars and graduate research assistants whose combined expertise included teaching experience in secondary schools; developing curriculum; providing professional development to teachers; and conducting research in academically and linguistically diverse classrooms, schools, and communities. To prepare for the inclusion of transitional students in mainstream classrooms, the social studies and language arts teachers participated in a week-long summer institute sponsored by the university/school coalition. In the workshop, teachers, school personnel, and the university team discussed the goals of the intervention, features of the curriculum designed to meet the needs of linguistically diverse students, and specific strategies for academic language development. Throughout the school year, the university team provided follow-up workshops and support in the classrooms.

❖ DESCRIPTION

Over the course of the 2-week Reformation unit, Manuel, Diego, Julia, and Laura each worked in a different small group of four or five students to complete all four activities in the unit. Each heterogeneous group included monolingual English speakers, students formerly classified as LEP, and other transitional students. During a given class period, each group worked on a different task. For example, on a typical day Manuel and his group might interpret authentic political cartoons from the time of the Reformation (see Figure 2) and then design their own political cartoon challenging the authority of a current institution.

In the same classroom at the same time, Diego's group would read excerpts from Martin Luther's *Ninety-Five Theses* and create a skit dramatizing the conflict between Luther and Pope Leo X. Meanwhile, Julia's group would study the Peasants' Rebellion of 1524–1525, read the demands stated in the *Twelve Articles* (see Figure 1), and then create a "peasants' manifesto" using words and images to persuade an audience during the Reformation. Finally, Laura and her group would analyze mechanical diagrams of the printing press and pictorial representations of the printing process to make a physical model of the machine out of everyday materials the teacher had collected. For each of these activities, students were provided with an activity card with a set of discussion questions, a description of the task, and evaluation criteria (see Figure 3); resource cards consisting of the primary sources; and a question with which to write an individual report at the conclusion of the activity (see Figure 4).

The multimedia products—models, skits, posters, and cartoons—were the most visible manifestations of students' work in the groups. But the groups were also responsible for connecting their products to a social and historical context by answering the discussion questions and linking the particular activity to the big idea of the unit. In their presentations, students reported on the preparation of their group product and how their discussion was related to that central concept. After each activity, each student wrote a paragraph-length report and, upon completion of each unit, an essay such as the ones excerpted previously. Group presentations

FIGURE 2. Sample Resource Card: "Art as a Weapon" Activity (Copyright © Program for Complex Instruction/Stanford University School of Education, undated. Used by permission.)

served as opportunities for students to learn from each other and for the teacher to lead an intellectually challenging discussion. Any given day of presentations consisted of reports on all four different activities. Students had the opportunity to (a) preview how a different group tackled an activity they would soon encounter or (b) compare and contrast the ways in which a different group completed an activity they had done several days before. Therefore, students had recursive opportunities both to grapple with the big idea and to use language for academic purposes.

Despite being categorized by the school as LEP and perceived as academic underachievers, English learners engaged in content- and language-rich activities

---

Unit: The Reformation

CHALLENGING THE AUTHORITY OF INSTITUTIONS
Activity 2: Martin Luther's *Ninety-five Theses*
Activity Card

As a group, read the *Resource Card* and discuss the questions below.

1. What did Martin Luther object to? What phrases does Martin Luther use in his letter that shows his respect for the Church? What phrases does Martin Luther use to question the Church's practices?

2. How did the Pope respond to Martin Luther's actions? Identify specific expressions and words that show how the Pope felt about Martin Luther.

3. How did Martin Luther's actions challenge the authority of the church?

• • •

As a group, create a skit that dramatizes the conflict between Martin Luther and Pope Leo X. Use words and expressions from the texts on the *Resource Card*. One person should play the role of Martin Luther. And one should be Pope Leo X. The remaining members should be characters who must decide whom to follow (either Martin Luther or Pope Leo X). Present your skit to the class.

> *Evaluation Criteria*
> • Martin Luther and Pope Leo X use persuasive language to argue their perspectives
> • Skit shows the conflict between the two sides
> • The skit ends with the other characters stating their reasons for following either Martin Luther or Pope Leo X

FIGURE 3. Sample Activity Card: Luther's *Ninety-Five Theses* (Copyright © Program for Complex Instruction/Stanford University School of Education, undated. Used by permission.)

that required communication with English-speaking peers; they addressed the themes of the unit repeatedly in substantively different ways to gain solid conceptual understanding. Students were expected to think deeply about both historical details and essential questions of the discipline. They interpreted primary sources and puzzled over the meaning of authentic historical artifacts; they posed questions, argued, and negotiated to conceive, plan, construct, and evaluate their projects; and they wrote about what they learned. They were also required to report and to present what they had accomplished to their peers.

Students were not expected, however, to negotiate such a challenging curriculum alone or without support. The following features of the curriculum, the classroom organization, and the teachers' instructional interventions were designed to provide optimal support for students in these diverse classrooms without watering down either the language or the content of the unit.

Name: _____   **Unit: The Reformation**

CHALLENGING THE AUTHORITY OF INSTITUTIONS
Activity 4: The Printing Press
Individual Report

How did the invention of the printing press bring about the spread of the Reformation?

Evaluation Criteria

- Answer discusses the benefits of this invention
- Answer discusses how the printing press changed the way information was disseminated
- Answer explains why this was an effective way to challenge institutions

---

FIGURE 4. Sample Individual Report Assignment: Printing Press Activity (Copyright © Program for Complex Instruction/Stanford University School of Education, undated. Used by permission.)

Group-Worthy Tasks

The activities of the Reformation unit, like those of other complex instruction units, use specific design principles that ensure that tasks are demanding and intricate so they cannot be adequately completed by an individual student alone during the limited time of a regular class period. These are "group-worthy" tasks (Lotan, 2003). They are open ended and require complex problem solving around discipline-based, intellectually important content. Using multiple representations (e.g., visuals, models, diagrams) of the historical information enables students to access the task in multiple ways. By requiring products that rely on their different abilities, skills, and repertoire of problem-solving strategies, students have opportunities to display different dimensions of their intellectual competence. The learning tasks also include specific criteria for the evaluation of the group product. Responding to these criteria, students become self-critical and able to assess the quality of their own group product. Finally, creating a sophisticated group product requires positive interdependence and completing the individual report ensures individual accountability.

Textual Support for Struggling Readers and Writers

Reading and interpreting primary sources made considerable demands on most students, but particularly on struggling readers and language learners. To provide support, notations were added in the margins of the resource cards. These notations were intended not to summarize the content, thereby reducing reasons for students to grapple with it, but rather to guide students into the original text by highlighting where particularly relevant information could be found or what the nature of the content was (see Figure 1).

Demystification of Academic Language for Social Studies

Students with limited experience using language for academic purposes often do not understand expectations that teachers take for granted. At Gerona, teachers made the essential features of an academic *explanation* and *persuasion* explicit (see Figure 5). In addition, teachers developed rubrics to help students organize their writing. For the persuasive essay, for example, the rubric outlined one way a five-paragraph essay could be structured, emphasizing a clear thesis statement, refuting counterarguments, and connecting the essay to the big idea of the unit. Teachers discussed model essays with students and led the class as a whole in writing a sample introductory paragraph, eliciting suggestions while serving as scribe. At the beginning of the year, for both individual reports and the unit essay, teachers gave students sentence starters that provided extensive scaffolding for their writing. As the year progressed, these supports were gradually reduced so that by the final unit, students were composing their own sentences and paragraphs, assisted instead by marginal guidelines and the rubric.

Additional Time and Support During Writing Assignments

Just as scholarly writers do, students were allowed to use available resources: resource cards, notes, the textbook, and their groups' product. For their unit essay, students used their previously completed individual reports that included teacher feedback following evaluation criteria provided (see Figure 4). Although it was made clear that their writing was to be their own, students were allowed to consult with each other or the teacher to share ideas. Given the constraints of short class periods, students were given as much time as possible in class to write. For individual reports,

---

Persuading

(while speaking OR writing)

To **PERSUADE** is to

    state a position and attempt to get others to agree.

When we **PERSUADE**, we

- take into consideration the beliefs and opinions of our audience
- include sufficient support for our opinions
- respond to the other side of the argument

To **PERSUADE** effectively, we use the following techniques:

- providing reasons for our argument
- stating facts
- giving examples
- appealing to the emotions of the audience
- presenting the argument against our position and pointing out the weaknesses of that argument

---

FIGURE 5. Classroom Guidelines for Effective Persuasion

students had 5 minutes at the end of each period to begin to write their reports before taking them home for homework, thus allowing students time to understand the assignment, begin a response, and ask questions. Students had at least one entire class period to work on their unit essay and were allowed to take their work home. With the support of their language arts teachers, students were also given one language arts period to work on their social studies essays.

Teachers' Delegation of Authority

To foster talking and working together, teachers delegated authority to groups. Rather than telling students what to do, teachers understood that their most important job in managing the classroom was to hold students responsible for their own and their group's learning. Teachers were encouraged not to hover over groups but rather to intervene only when absolutely necessary. To illustrate, students in one group at Gerona grappled with a complex political cartoon depicting Tetzel's sale of indulgences (see Figure 2). Especially confusing to the students was how the image related to the caption "As soon as the coin in the coffer rings, the soul into heaven springs." Instead of doing the group's job for them by giving his own interpretation of the cartoon, the teacher simply took a coin out of his pocket, dropped it on the table, and asked, "What does this sound like?" This intervention was enough to redirect the students' attention, without limiting their opportunity to use language to interpret the cartoon themselves: One student immediately said, "Oh, they're putting money in the box! The monk is selling indulgences!" Students were then able to continue discussing and further interpreting the cartoon.

Peer Support

Working in heterogeneous groups, Manuel and the others interacted with peers with more experience using English for academic purposes. These classmates at times read particularly challenging resource cards out loud, defined unfamiliar vocabulary, or suggested a specific phrase. Students in these classes were encouraged to provide and seek help when necessary. In fact, two of the norms emphasized throughout the year were to ask for help and to assist when asked. Collaboration took a variety of forms. In the activity on the Peasants' Rebellion, for example, students in one group took turns reading each of the *Twelve Articles* included on the resource cards. After each student read, the group collectively tried to paraphrase the original language into more understandable prose before moving on to creating their own peasants' manifesto.

Working in groups can be challenging for all seventh graders, and even more so for language minority students who might be unfamiliar with norms for group interaction in U.S. schools. Students learned and practiced how to be aware of each other's needs, to explain without doing the work for others, and to be accountable to the group, in addition to fulfilling one's individual responsibilities—in short, how to serve as academic and linguistic resources for one another. Norms of collaboration and cooperation were introduced to the students through a series of skill-building exercises at the beginning of the academic year (Cohen, 1994). In addition, students were assigned specific roles to play in each group (Cohen, 1994). For example, the facilitator saw to it that the group moved along in its work, stayed on task, and that everyone understood the task. The materials manager identified and procured the materials needed to build or to prepare the group product. The reporter organized the group's presentation to the class at the end of the work period. The harmonizer was responsible for the group's social and emotional well-being. All students played all the roles on a rotating basis. These cooperative norms and roles supported productive interactions among group members. Research has shown that individual participation and the process of talking and working together produce learning gains on these open-ended group tasks (Cohen & Lotan, 1997).

Treatment of Status Problems

One of the most serious problems of cooperative learning is domination by some and no participation by others. Cohen (1994) has called this a "status problem." High-status students who participate more learn more, whereas low-status students who participate less learn less. If untreated, status problems can widen the achievement gap between high-status and low-status students.

In complex instruction classrooms, teachers use specific strategies called status treatments to equalize participation (Cohen, 1994). These are practical interventions for teachers that will boost the participation of low-status students and prevent the domination of other students in the group. For example, in introducing one round of activities, a teacher pointed out that to analyze blueprints and to build a printing press requires many different intellectual abilities, such as the ability to plan ahead and anticipate stages of construction, mechanical ingenuity, inventiveness, and the ability to see a three-dimensional object in a two-dimensional picture. The teacher also emphasized to students that although no one will be good at all of these abilities, everyone will be good at one of them. This strategy, called a multiple-abilities treatment, widened the students' conception of what it meant to be "smart" and established the relevance of these abilities to the successful completion of the task. Students began to realize that those group members who they considered high-status students might not be good at all the abilities and that the contributions of those who were perceived as low-status students might be vital to the group. Assigning competence, a second strategy, was a teacher's public recognition of a specific and relevant intellectual contribution made by a low-status student. Such recognition changed students' expectations of the contribution of that low-status student to group success.

◈ DISTINGUISHING FEATURES

The goals of the approach described in this study were to keep rigorous social studies content at the heart of instruction, provide support for diverse learners, and assist in the academic language development of all students. These goals are consistent with other approaches to K–12 content-based instruction and sheltered instruction (see Crandall, 1993, 1997; Grabe & Stoller, 1997; Murphy & Stoller, 2001). However, too often sheltered instruction results in segregated settings and less academically rigorous curriculum (Valdés, 2001). The curriculum and instruction described here were designed to avoid those problems.

First, the thrust of the intervention consisted of expanding, not contracting, the type of content and language available to English learners. The main texts of primary source documents were not altered, nor were expectations for finished products.

Students were expected to participate in groups with mainstream peers, and teachers were prepared to hold students from a variety of language backgrounds accountable and to treat status problems when necessary. Students used mainstream textbooks (with peer support) in understanding the information in those textbooks.

Second, content and language teachers supported English learners with the help of curriculum materials developed at the university. The approach therefore attempted to avoid two common pitfalls regarding the content of content-based instruction: the need for ESOL teachers to create content curriculum around unfamiliar subject matter, and the need for ESOL or content-area teachers to adapt for English learners a comprehensive, mainstream curriculum not designed with the needs of linguistically diverse learners in mind.

Finally, the approach represents an explicit strategy for creating conditions for the development of academic language (see Bunch, Abram, Lotan, & Valdés, 2001). Academic language, as we define it, is not solely the amassing of sophisticated linguistic features associated with a particular register, such as complex syntax or vocabulary items, although these may indeed be important. As evident in this case study, we conceive of academic language as consisting of a variety of features necessary for engaging in a particular academic task effectively. Thus, students were challenged to write like academics, supported in this endeavor by explicit guidelines, models, and lots of practice and feedback, and not penalized for features of second language use that were a natural part of their second language acquisition.

As in most middle schools, bringing about these changes in instruction was not an easy task. Traditional, short class periods reduced the time available for students to complete their group tasks and begin to prepare their individual reports. Pressures on teachers and students to prepare for standardized tests limited the school's time, focus, and enthusiasm. Sometimes teachers inadvertently denied students the opportunity to use language to grapple with content on their own by intervening in the groups too often and for too long. The number of peer models fluent in prestige varieties of English and experienced in using it for academic purposes was limited because of the city's economic and ethnic segregation. Finally, in a school consistently criticized for low academic achievement and behavioral problems, teachers and students alike battled against low morale throughout the school year. In light of the challenges and problems, however, we were encouraged by the quality of the student writing described in this chapter.

◈ PRACTICAL IDEAS

It is not an easy task to design and deliver instruction that maintains language-rich, academically rigorous curriculum while incorporating support for English learners to access that curriculum. We offer the following suggestions for teachers and others attempting to do so.

Challenge Students With Rigorous Content and Language

Experiment with ways to ratchet up, not down, the curriculum available to English learners. As demonstrated by Laura, Julia, Diego, and Manuel, under the right conditions, English learners can do the difficult work of social studies, and they can use English persuasively to convey what they have learned.

Find Ways to Support Students as They Tackle
Challenging Content and Language

At Gerona, support was offered by facilitating access to peers and providing textual supports (e.g., marginal notations, sufficient time, the opportunity to revise work with feedback). Students were also provided with explicit evaluation criteria and other kinds of guidance for their multimedia products, their oral presentations, and their written assignments. The goal was to "let students in on the secret" through modeling, highlighting, practicing, and evaluating students' use of targeted aspects of academic language within the context of learning academic content.

Create Opportunities for English Learners to Interact
With Peers at Higher Levels of English Proficiency

Even in classes with limited linguistic diversity, teachers can work toward facilitating contact between students at different language proficiency levels. As discussed in this chapter, such efforts may include having students discuss and practice some of the challenging aspects of group work, assigning specific student roles, and reminding students of all of the intellectual abilities necessary for the completion of a particular task.

Remember That English Learners Will Write and
Sound Differently From Native English Speakers

We believe that the goal is not to compare English learners with native speakers but rather to focus on (a) how well students have understood the content they are expected to learn and (b) how they are developing in their ability to use English effectively to demonstrate that understanding. Effective assessment, therefore, may require separate measures for content and language.

◈ CONCLUSION

All students face the central challenges of social studies: to "develop a core of basic knowledge and ways of thinking drawn from many academic disciplines, learn how to analyze their own and others' opinions on important issues, and become motivated to participate in civic and community life as active, informed citizens" (National Council for the Social Studies, 1994, p. vii). English learners, however, face additional obstacles. They are often denied the opportunity to access the knowledge and ways of thinking outlined in the social studies standards, either because they are placed in mainstream classes that offer little support for their needs as English learners or because they remain segregated from mainstream curriculum for long periods of time. In addition, English learners' attempts to demonstrate what they have learned and are able to do may be judged more on linguistic accuracy than on the social studies ideas with which they are grappling. From a language learning perspective, English learners can become caught in a vicious circle: They may not be allowed access to the real content and language of social studies until they master a certain level of English proficiency, and yet it is the access to authentic language models from teachers, texts, and English-speaking peers, along with the opportunity to interact with them, that is needed to develop both language and content (Valdés,

2001). In this case study, we have offered one equitable alternative that keeps content at the heart of content-based instruction, allows English learners to access that content, and provides support for them to do so.

◈ CONTRIBUTORS

George C. Bunch, a former ESOL and sheltered social studies teacher, recently completed a PhD in educational linguistics at Stanford University and is now assistant professor of education at the University of California, Santa Cruz, in the United States.

A former ESOL teacher, Rachel A. Lotan is associate professor (teaching) at Stanford University and director of the Stanford Teacher Education Program.

Guadalupe Valdés is the Bonnie Katz Tenenbaum Professor of Education and a professor of Spanish and Portuguese at Stanford University.

Elizabeth G. Cohen is a professor emerita of education and sociology at Stanford University.

CHAPTER 3

Pickles, Proverbs, and Play: Finding Out About Ourselves and Others

Valerie S. Jakar

◈ INTRODUCTION

The seasons, children's rights, road safety, Jerusalem, the environment, soups, games that Grandpa played, pickles, proverbs, and Ramadan. What do all of these terms have in common? Lest the reader waste time trying to find associations and commonalities, I will reveal that they were all topics chosen for English as a foreign language (EFL) instruction for classes in Grades 2–9 in a pilot project for which local folklore was a focal area of interest.

In some cases, the topics were chosen for use in schoolwide projects, whereas, in others, they were investigated in year (grade) groups or in individual classes. But how were the topics selected? How were they taught? And what were the outcomes? Why was content-based instruction (CBI) introduced in an EFL program for elementary and junior high (preparatory) students? In this case study, I address these questions as well as present and analyze specific examples of project-based units of work, the significant elements of which have now become established in the curriculum of the involved schools.

◈ CONTEXT

Many education authorities in non-English-speaking countries are insisting that school children begin learning English at the elementary-school level. Such is the case for our focal group of Arabic-speaking children who, at the age of 6 or 7, begin EFL classes in first grade while learning to read and write classical (literary) Arabic. They receive EFL lessons four to five times weekly until they reach high school.

A Holistic Intervention Project

It was with this group of learners and their teachers, in six schools with a population of more than 3,000 students, that we, a university-based team of teacher-supervisors, became involved. This 3-year program, known as the Holistic Schools Intervention Project, was sponsored by the Jerusalem Municipality Education Authority (part of the Israel Ministry of Education) whose goal was to raise the educational achievement in the area by providing professional development opportunities to all Grade 1–9 teachers involved in the six schools (Olshtain, 2002). The schools were chosen from more than 40 public elementary and junior high schools in East Jerusalem and villages close by, where the majority of students come from large families with low socioeconomic status. We sought first to raise teachers' awareness of pedagogical possibilities in the core subjects (mathematics, literacy, reading skills, and EFL) and then to assist them in developing practical skills in curriculum development while exploring ways to integrate the subjects of study and collaborating to develop curriculum initiatives.

In a learner-centered language curriculum, the topics addressed (or used as a vehicle for language instruction) are geared toward the learner's interests and body of world knowledge. Textbook writers strive to suit the content to their projected populations but perceptions of who their learners are and what these learners can relate to are often far from the reality. Such was the case for our project group. In these schools, where class size ranges from 26 to 40 students, two series of foreign-produced textbooks (one for Grades 1–6 and one for the junior high grades) have been used for many years as the sole materials for English classes, constituting the only exposure to English. Although the students live in semirural areas close to the city, they rarely get the chance to engage in independent learning, through seeking out, for instance, native speakers of English or by reading authentic material in the streets or by visiting cinemas that show English-speaking movies.

Recently, books of stories, both trade books and EFL special materials, were introduced into the lower grades of the project's schools. This was part of a literacy drive that was initiated by an enlightened teacher adviser who was convinced of the strength of real stories to demonstrate the power of love, hope, heroism, and faith. (Bettelheim, 1976; Ghosn, 1998). Nevertheless, overall, the program of study continues to be determined by the content of archaic textbooks that are neither learner oriented nor socioculturally appropriate to the population. These structurally based textbooks contain a disparate variety of topics, with language points featured intermittently, bearing little relation to commonly accepted findings in acquisition studies or current practice in language pedagogy.

◈ DESCRIPTION

Program of In-Service Education for Teachers

In a situation such as this, with the limited English input available, teachers must be extremely resourceful if they want their students to engage in communicative, meaningful language learning that will stand them in good stead for their future development. Therefore, the EFL specialists in the teacher-supervisor team introduced a program by means of in-service education for teachers (InSET) that was followed by individual counseling. The program offered ideas for compensatory, pedagogical practice to enhance the underdeveloped curriculum that was viewed by the teachers as being essentially the content (texts and the language exercises) of the required textbook. The style of teaching was, for the most part, consistent with the precepts of the textbook, using the traditional mode of "chalk and talk," a teacher-fronted, lock-step approach, with much repetition, recitation, and unprepared reading aloud by the students. Every teacher in the program was a native Arabic speaker, with just three individuals having been educated, in part, in an English-speaking environment. The teachers reported that although they attempt to use English in the classroom as much as they can, few use it for more than 40% of the lesson time.

Early on in our program of InSET, we introduced the 30 teachers to the idea of humanistic language education (Moskowitz, 1978) and reading for understanding. As a preliminary task, these teachers adapted a well-known folk story—which has versions in both Hebrew and Arabic—into an English narrative that could then be used in class at a range of levels (Olshtain, 2002).

Shortly after this exposure to ways of addressing a text that engage one's emotions as well as one's cognitive resources, the teachers' group had a guest speaker, an anthropologist specializing in folklore studies for children of diverse nationalities (Lichman, 2002). He demonstrated how one could bring together children and their families from a number of communities, who may well have experienced conflict in the past, in the pursuit of celebrating their own cultures by sharing them with others. He showed how the various groups learned more about themselves and their own families and local communities by interacting peacefully, face-to-face, while sharing the richness of their own cultures and learning about other cultures. The language of communication in the reported encounters was usually the native tongue, be it Amharic, Hebrew, Arabic, or Russian, with translators and interpreters assisting the process. Our InSET teachers were enchanted to see a display of dolls made in the traditional manner by both children and their parents. They also witnessed a video recording of a get-together of children, parents, and grandparents in a newly built mosque, where groups presented traditional songs and foods used for the seasonal festive occasions of Ramadan, Hanukkah, and Christmas.

The subsequent in-service program for the English teachers in the Holistic Schools Project was devoted to the principles of project work and CBI. New to the teachers was the notion of task-based language learning, where students pursue an interest or subject of their choice, in an in-depth manner, while acquiring new language competence and possibly new learning skills and strategies. That the learning is achieved by experiential means, in a series of processes (cf. Legutke & Thomas, 1991), was difficult for the teachers to accept, having for so long been accustomed to the traditional styles of teaching. We, as members of the teacher-supervisor team, presented examples of CBI to orient the teachers to this less-than-traditional approach. Then, we presented the ideas of Snow, Met, and Genesee (1989), who showed how we can build a conceptual framework for foreign language learners, and Mohan (1986). Mohan's significant contribution was his focus on graphic organizers, which generate language use even if they are simple diagrams or charts (cf. Kagan, 1998). This concept was introduced to the teachers who had never before encountered the use of anything else but straightforward text in the English classroom. It was stressed that the subject matter and the language learning were equal partners; that neither was neglected in favor of the other (cf. Stoller, 2002).

We gave the participants examples of CBI projects developed by teachers in similar situations, for example, the chess project (Bawab & Jakar, 2001) where sixth-grade boys not only learned (or taught others) to play chess, in English, but also learned about the history of chess, the language of battle, and the notion of strategy. A further example given to the teachers was the "watching the moon" project (Roberts, 1999), which entailed the use of regular journal entries to document the phases of the moon, as well as weather and seasonal changes. In the Roberts project, students in early grades used a minimal amount of English in their writing but supplemented the language with illustrations. Students in higher grades used more English and added graphic organizers of various types (e.g., charts, graphs, diagrams). This topic was particularly pertinent to the work of the InSET group who would, soon after, prepare for the month of Ramadan, in which the movements of the moon play an important part.

Later, InSET dealt with evaluation and assessment, the heterogeneous class and attention to learning difficulties, and the use of the concept of multiple intelligences (Gardner, 1993) in language teaching (Berman, 2001; Christison, 1996). Following the stimulating presentation given by the expert in local folklore previously described and explanation and demonstration of CBI in practice, the English teachers were inspired to accept a challenge: to develop curriculum units that focused on local issues but used English as the medium of instruction wherever possible. They discussed the range of topics that could be entertained in the framework of folklore: elements of life and tradition that are representative of one's local culture. The topics that the teachers found attractive included clothing, food, farming implements and utensils used for food preparation, songs, rituals and celebrations, ways and means of staying healthy, toys, games, rhymes, riddles, and proverbs. Small groups of teachers brainstormed to explore and analyze the project possibilities and then mind-mapped their conclusions. These mind maps (cf. Kagan, 1998), presented and shared, formed the basis of the curriculum goals that each teacher developed.

Thus, the teachers embarked on an adventure in pedagogy and in humanistic education. But where did the English language learning enter the scene? How could one justify the learning about and sharing of ethnic traditions in anything but one's own language?

Why English?

The teachers had been introduced to anthropology and had looked at ways of researching and maintaining ethnic identity through the preservation and celebration of what was their own. They had been shown ways of teaching English with a communicative, humanistic approach. During the InSET, they were also exposed to ways of teaching about global issues, in particular, to the work of international groups who strive for peace among nations (e.g., UNICEF) and, more specifically, the welfare and rights of children. They became more aware of issues that are important for all learners but are not generally taught in their schools. It was suggested that by working in English—or at least by producing a final product where only English would be used—students could communicate with students in other regions. The teachers could take advantage of the need for language instruction to have *some* element of content, and so introduce topics that may be beneficial to students although absent from the regular curriculum. Furthermore, students who could use the language well for conversational communication, or who could create a visual representation of their topic in the form of a tourist's guidebook or an advertising poster, could act as ambassadors or representatives of their school, their village, or local area when entertaining visitors and dignitaries who were not Arabic speakers. Teachers were reminded that, while learning more about these topics, the students would be practicing their reading, writing, and speaking in meaningful ways. The students would be, and were, the owners of the knowledge and information that was to be imparted; their self-esteem and their pride in their local community could only be enhanced. The teachers were convinced, and they accepted the challenge (Crandall, 1998a).

For most of the teachers in our program, the first venture into the world of CBI had been the early experience in our Holistic Project program when they first introduced projects on Ramadan (see Practical Ideas) that was celebrated, at the time, a third of the way through the academic year. In groups, according to the grades they were teaching (in this case, Grades 3–9 were involved), they discussed the appropriate topics that they could address with their particular classes and then brainstormed ideas on three focal issues: language practice (vocabulary items to be presented; structures or idiomatic uses to be reviewed), study skills practice, and topic presentation. They reviewed the types of tasks or products they wished to see as outcomes of their projects (cf. Goodrich, Hatch, Wiatrowski, & Unger, 1996) and collaboratively worked on the feasibility of effecting their plans. This process was a daunting experience for many teachers. Never before had they been concerned with creating curriculum. They were encouraged to start small, with just two lessons based on materials and ideas for learning activities that would yield a product of which the students would be proud.

The results of this pilot project were such that the Ramadan project has now become a regular part of the English language curriculum. The preparation procedures that were used for the Ramadan project became the basic model of preparatory procedures for subsequent projects. The notion of *brainstorming,* new to most of the teachers, yielded many positive outcomes. Ideas for teaching, materials production, exercises, and activities were shared, critiqued, and refined. Although certain grade-level teachers decided to work independently from their colleagues, all teachers benefited from the sharing and the critiques, learning much more about what is done in other grades than ever before. The model that evolved was used for other projects. Since the initial project, schools have had presentation days exhibiting work on the environment, a healthy body and a healthy mind, road safety, the seasons, and the olive (see Practical Ideas).

Constraints and Responses

At the preparation stage, each school group of teachers spent time discussing possibilities. The teachers established that their efforts might be constrained by the norms of the individual schools and their policies. They would, for example, have limited time to engage in their projects because of examinations and special holidays. For the sake of stability and classroom management, they needed to incorporate some material from the textbooks. In some schools, the resources were minimal, with no access to electronic communication systems. Thus, the teachers were required to exploit the local knowledge, expertise, and resources to a high degree. What better way to do this than to explore the folklore of the participants, the students themselves?

What follows is a description of one of the projects. This is an adaptation of a report made by two teachers who participated in the program.[1]

Games people played *A project for Grades 2, 3, and 4*

We talked in class, in Arabic, about the games they play in the playground (yard), and the games that they play when the weather is too hot or too wet

---

[1] The account is a compilation of teachers' reports given at the InSET post-project evaluation.

to be outside. We (the teachers) wrote some key words in Arabic and English on the board in random fashion. We reviewed the words, the Arabic was erased, and then we put the words into lists (categories) according to the students' decisions. There were words such as *jump, hop, catch, throw, in, out, count, stones, win, lose, sing, cheer.*

We elicited the names of the most popular games and types of activities and wrote those on the board in English characters only, with an English/American cultural equivalent where possible (skipping, jump rope, hop-scotch, marbles, jacks, red rover, five stones). If there was a rhyme or chant that went with the game, the students recited it. The students were asked to think about whether their grandparents played the same games when they were children. They were told to ask their elders (grandparents, uncles, aunts, and parents) about skipping or jumping games they used to play outside, with stones or fruit pits, coins, and courts marked out on the ground (we were hinting at "hopscotch" or "X" as it is known here). They were given a worksheet on which they were to write—in Arabic—about the games they heard about.

Before the next lesson, we prepared and displayed posters containing the previously featured words. We added some vocabulary connected with playing games. Then the students presented examples they had brought to school or talked about the games their elders played. They compared rules with each other. They were shown a rule sheet for a familiar game. Some students made up their own rule sheets. We began to use the phrases *you can, you cannot,* and *you must.* The students were encouraged to try to use some of the words they had seen in the first lesson. We taught the students some basic vocabulary about turn-taking and game-playing: *It's your turn, It's my turn, You are the winner, I won,* and *Who is next?*

We thanked the students for asking at home, and we talked about how it felt to be doing the homework in such a "strange" way. In the last lesson, one of the groups practiced counting in English and then went out to the playground to play hopscotch or jump rope. The school principal was delighted. Her students were enjoying their English lessons! The students were told to try to use English only. They found it difficult but enjoyed trying. The other groups made posters about chosen games, drawing diagrams and composing rules (we helped them). They were all reminded to sign their names on the posters and to add "with help from (name of elder who they asked)." The posters were displayed in the corridors. The students were extremely proud of their work, as were their parents when they saw that the elders' names were included too.

After that project, we went back to the textbook, but the students often asked for another project, so we plan to do another one in the next few weeks. Sometimes we notice the students playing their usual games but using some English terms.

Outcomes

Naturally, not every project went as planned or was declared a success. The teachers expended a great deal of energy in preparing materials, planning lessons, finding and adapting appropriate language exercises, and organizing displays. Their efforts were not always rewarded with enthusiasm, signs of achievement in language production or in content awareness, or acknowledgment from their principal or supervisor. For some, the problem lay in the choice of topic or homework activity: The topic was too sophisticated for the target age group, or it was not possible to carry out the investigation activity. Two teachers felt they could not relinquish the power of providing the text for whatever class they were giving, so they were burdened with extra preparation while their students felt customarily uninvolved in the preparation of texts. The resulting presentations of their classes reflected the students' lack of enthusiasm and self-determination: Copied texts (from Internet sources and books) constituted the placards prepared for display.

Nevertheless, the overall feeling was one of achievement. Teachers resolved to include at least two projects in their future annual curriculum. They had learned teaching strategies that they were able to apply to their regular classes, and they had gained insights into how and what learners learn when they are engaged in meaningful tasks. They had learned how to use graphic organizers, for process and for products, and how to exploit the graphic organizers to generate language use. Professional development had taken place during the InSET. The collaborative experience gained by developing the project units together became a norm for most of the teachers. They had become fully aware of how effective collaborative work can be. Furthermore, while the teachers were in conference, or participating in the InSET, they were using English, listening to it, reading materials in English, and writing it. They were maintaining their proficiency levels, something which many nonnative-English-speaking teachers are unable to effect because of pressures of work or the unavailability of the opportunities to use English outside the classroom (Jakar, 2002).

At the post-project teachers' meeting, it was agreed that certain issues had to be discussed because some pupils' needs were not being fulfilled and some teachers' principles were not being upheld. Taking the students' needs first, the teachers noted that those with learning difficulties, or simply weaker-than-average students, had not participated in the language production activities. They were either intimidated or not capable of answering the questions. However, the teachers observed that when it came to practical activities that involved interviewing people at home or speaking to some elders and bringing in the data, the weaker students did as well as their peers. The issue of attention to weaker learners had been raised in the context of the CBI project, but it had far-reaching implications. The teachers became aware of these learning difficulties and were concerned about how to treat them. They would pursue this topic in the next round of InSET.

The teachers' principles became a controversial issue that was widely discussed. It related to the use of the first language (L1) in the classroom for discussion and vocabulary building but English for presentation. The teachers claimed that they preferred not to use Arabic in the English lessons, although soon after the teachers made this statement, they acknowledged that each and every one of the group used the L1 for certain activities, whether it was for the students' comfort or for the teacher's management skills. It was pointed out that language awareness, including awareness of one's own language, is a hot topic in current thinking.[2]

---

[2] The new English curriculum for Israeli schools (Spolsky, et al., 2001) includes a standard for language appreciation and awareness that involves consideration of the differences between English and the native language.

What did the students gain from the experience? They certainly gained a sense of worth and value. They were each experts in their own fields. Their elders were the experts in their cultures, and the students were the transmitters of the information to a wider world. They were in command of the content of the English lessons. Some took the opportunity to use a computer. Thus, they gained practice in resourcing information—in English. They gained confidence in their ability to speak to an audience in English, to present their own work, and to write meaningfully in their notebooks. They were taught some reading strategies and learned new games and new and old stories; they learned much more about their own backgrounds and even about family relationships. They gained pride in their heritage and improved their self-esteem.

What did the teachers gain? They gained much the same as the students, although with a different level of intensity. The English departments were held in high esteem for producing materials and displays and for their collaborative work within the school and together with the entire English teachers' group. They were able to liaise with teachers of other subjects, and in some cases this liaison formed the basis of an interdisciplinary venture.

◈ DISTINGUISHING FEATURES

The following features distinguish our model of curriculum intervention from the customary foreign language in elementary schools (FLES) programs to which the students are usually exposed.

Most obviously, this venture did not involve the use of language textbooks nor were the chosen topics selected from the standard school curriculum, as in a "content-enriched" curriculum of the FLES type. Rather, the EFL teacher prompted and outlined the topics, but the students themselves expanded on the topics. In some cases, the topics were generated by students' discussions. The ideas and materials came from the students and from other sources (such as the Internet).

Some of the recommended activities (see Practical Ideas) that were successful may be frowned upon by communicative language proponents because they hark back to ancient pedagogic practice. Be that as it may, they serve to raise the students' language awareness (Andrews, 1993), and they enable the teacher to discover the students' understandings of the English phonological system. The recommended procedure for the proverbs projects evolved from a collaborative meeting of the teachers during one InSET session. It consisted of a series of lessons using rote learning as well as giving the students the opportunity to practice encoding.

Despite the lack of similarity with conventional language instruction programs, the model and the implementation of the model have proven to be successful in creating and delivering language learning achievement. The use of graphic organizers has become part of the students' learning styles (as well as part of the teachers' competence). The notion of a relevant (and sometimes tangible) task to be performed acts as a powerful motivator, with scope for sustaining interest and activity beyond the prescribed framework of the task. The involvement of family further enhances the students' motivation, although as students progress into adolescence they become more self-centered and less likely to want to remain within the family circle.

The model could be said to resemble the theme-based approach (cf. Pally, 1999) in that the teacher extracts or creates language activities that follow naturally from the content ideas. The content is in no way the sustained content of the higher level schools and universities, with a curriculum organized by the teacher of the discipline and an adjunct program of language study provided by the EFL teacher (Stoller, 2002), although there is scope for this in the future as the English teachers have been building an admirable rapport with their colleagues in the other disciplines.

In the spirit of the holistic movement, EFL teaching is bringing together a broad range of interests, facilitating participation across the curriculum. A variety of topics exemplify this phenomenon, but one in particular was found to be all (or almost all) encompassing: the pickles project. It should be pointed out that vegetable and fruit preservation and conservation is common practice in all Middle Eastern countries and has been for thousands of years. Each family has its traditional recipes and methods of preparing, containing, and preserving pickles. Along with the traditions go stories, rituals, anecdotes, memories of times past, and associations with geographical and historical phenomena. In addition, the scientific aspects related to the preparation of the pickles—of growth and development, chemical change, natural and artificial effects on elements—and the aesthetic aspects of pickles, make for a particularly fertile topic. Add to this the long-abiding popularity of the olive, a frequently pickled item, with all its connotations and associations (with the Bible, with the resources that it provides), its multifarious uses, coupled with its symbolism as a sign of peace, and the curriculum is almost overcrowded (see Practical Ideas for ideas on making pickles).[3]

◈ PRACTICAL IDEAS

This section offers some ideas that were used by the teachers in the planning and implementation stages. The individual items featured were selected as representative of the teachers' practice, with particular reference to the topics of Ramadan, proverbs, and pickles.

Identify Topics Popular With Teachers and Students

These topics could include children's games, dances, festivals, folktales, games (inside and out), health and nutrition in our traditional society, olives, pickles, proverbs, rhymes, sweet foods, taking care of our environment, toys, and weddings.

In the Holistic Schools Project, the teachers focused on one, or more, of different Ramadan topics, including

- phases of the moon
- the teachings of Mohammed
- the Five Pillars of faith
- decorations for the festival
- traditional clothing and adornments
- special food, fasting, and nutrition
- songs and poetry

---

[3] In other climates or cultures, the same popularity may be attributed to nuts or tea.

- the special schedule for Ramadan and how this affects everyday routines and habits
- how different ethnic groups celebrate Ramadan
- stories of past practice (e.g., the lamplighter)
- special implements, utensils, and other objects (artifacts)
- Mecca and the visit to Mecca (the hajji)

Display the Products of the Project (the Ideas and Activities)

Figure 1 (below) illustrates ideas on how to display students' projects.

Include Similar Components in Every Lesson or in a Series of Lessons

These components could include

- attention to a language feature with some activity to reinforce the learning process
- attention to a study skill
- an introduction to the new topic
- an orientation and brainstorming event
- a requirement that students bring data (information or real objects) from home to share and investigate
- individual or collective presentation of what was learned by means of display, entertainment, or production of a document for the purposes of evaluation and assessment, as well as student satisfaction with a job completed
- some manipulation, description, or analysis of the data collected
- a subsequent mapping of information or ideas

Display artifacts; traditional foods; "little books" made by students on particular topics; posters on the Five Pillars; short dramatic sketches based on the stories told by parents and grandparents; charts on daily schedules, phases of the moon, and nutrition.

Prepare a poster

The word **Ramadan,** or some other word that holds significance for the students, written down the side of the paper with words or sentences flowing from each of the letters of the word.

OR

Using each letter of the word RAMADAN as an initial letter, a list of names of students in the class is written. They each become the opening of a sentence.

OR

Each letter is the initial letter of a feeling or an adjective connected with Ramadan and the practice and worship that is special for the occasion.

FIGURE 1. Ramadan Activities

"Pickles are fertile"

A project on pickles can involve the science teachers to investigate natural resources and growth factors of the vegetables and fruit, the effects of pickling (chemical reactions), flavors, tastes, and constituents. It can involve the geography teacher to investigate what gets pickled, when, where, and why. What are the best areas, climates, and conditions for growth?

Tasks for a final product (writing and presentation) can include recipes, process description, commentaries on demonstrations, advertising posters, party menus, poetry, documentation of family stories, or factual information presented in attractive ways (e.g., booklets, posters, Web sites).

Creative writers and thinkers can create a set of cartoon characters called "The Pickles." Have the characters interact (the dialogue can be represented in bubbles or in captions under each frame) in familiar situations.

FIGURE 2. Interdisciplinary Unit on Pickles

Involve Other Teachers and Other Disciplines in the Unit

Figure 2 (above) is an example of an interdisciplinary project on pickles.

In an interdisciplinary unit, it is important not to neglect the language learning skills, which includes use of vocabulary, description of process, questioning skills, spoken presentation skills, and reading strategies.

Use a Single Topic for a Series of Learning Sessions

Figure 3 shows a series of learning lessons on using L1 proverbs to explore translation and transliteration. This could be a unit of work for four lessons or more.

◈ CONCLUSION

It was and is my conviction that language is best learned in context and in the context of use, in meaningful situations, which is why we implemented the CBI approach in this program. To make the language use meaningful, one inevitably turns to the content of the language learning enterprise. In the case of our program for a group of schools where the required materials for EFL pedagogy were considered less than stimulating, we chose an area of content that we felt would be of interest to most students. The topic of folklore lends itself to work with all age groups, and our belief that all the students would view it favorably was supported. They were able to look at their own heritage, through the eyes and ears of an English speaker, and by so doing, learned more about themselves and their peers. They heard the stories their grandparents told and the memories of childhood recalled by their parents. They learned why they eat certain foods on particular occasions, what ideas appealed to the senses, and about the history of their families. They learned about agriculture, putting today's work in a different context, and were encouraged to think critically about the modern world (their world) and the worlds that have passed.

The teachers are still required to use the assigned textbook, but they have become more discerning since the project. Their attitudes to curriculum development have become far more dynamic and productive. They focus on what they

---

1. In Class

- The teacher:

  a. gives examples (in L1) of proverbs and discusses meanings with the class

  b. elicits more proverbs, according to topics

  c. writes up a chosen proverb (in L1), considering its topic and its application

  d. transliterates the chosen proverb

  e. translates the proverb into English: first, the literal translation, then the English equivalent, if one exists (here the teacher discusses the application of the proverb, the real meaning or moral lesson derived)

2. At Home

- Students' first homework assignment:

  a. to investigate and collect proverbs

  b. to write them down (in L1)

  c. to check their meanings and applications

  d. to note who told them each proverb

3. In Class

- The teacher:

  a. elicits proverbs brought by the students (the students present their findings)

  b. notes the prevalent topics; students discuss meanings and applications

  c. choosing one example, as a model for students' further work, proceeds through stages 1c–1e

The students each choose one of their own examples and follow the procedures 1c–1e in their notebooks or files. They enlist the help of the teacher if they cannot translate the proverb or discover an English equivalent. Working in pairs or groups of three or four, they may make a collection of proverbs on particular topics.

4. In Class

Students prepare a presentation (as in the teacher's model), with illustrations, dramatization, interpretation, recitation; they may choose to create a game or puzzle. If a book is prepared, there should be a title page and a contents page. In every case, the students should acknowledge the contributors.

FIGURE 3. Making Proverbs Work

believe the students will be interested in and have already developed new units based on the literature content of one textbook unit. They use the outline procedures as a skeleton plan but are already drawing up further projects. They are now the teacher-leaders in their groups, and it is hoped that some of them will become teacher advisers and curriculum coordinators, at which point the cycle can begin again.

◈ ACKNOWLEDGMENTS

My thanks go to the following InSET participants for their contributions to the preparation of this case study: Mona Shehade, Lana Bazbaz, Khulud Abdunrahman,

Huda Abuzaid, Shireen Bawab, Haifa Mashni, Einaam Oraib Safi, Huda Jaber, Sabri Kais, Mai Nahour, Josephine Zakkak, and Riham Hidmiih.

◈ CONTRIBUTOR

Valerie S. Jakar has been an ESOL teacher for more than 30 years. She holds a PhD in educational linguistics from the University of Pennsylvania, in the United States. Her professional interests have moved from curriculum development to professional development for teachers. She is now concerned with issues of social responsibility as they affect the language classroom and its learners.

CHAPTER 4

Collaborating on the Curriculum: Focus on Secondary ESOL

Donna Hurst and Chris Davison

◈ INTRODUCTION

On-the-job training and support for the integration of language and content teaching in English-medium schools have long been promoted in the TESOL field. However, most approaches have tended to focus on methods and techniques to use in the mainstream classroom or on the analysis of the linguistic demands of the content areas. There has been much less attention to the development of collaborative curriculum structures to support the long-term work of English for speakers of other languages (ESOL) and content teachers in schools. This chapter presents one innovative approach to the development of more effective collaboration between ESOL and content teachers that focuses on the curriculum, rather than just on teaching materials, methodology, or teacher roles.

In the mid-1990s, International School Bangkok (ISB), a large K–12 English-medium international school serving a growing population of speakers of English as a second or additional language, adopted a sheltered immersion model of ESOL provision. In the sheltered immersion model, ESOL students were immersed in mainstream classrooms for the majority of the time while continuing to receive ESOL instruction through elective options and/or in-class support. The program has been gradually refined over the years to incorporate a much stronger focus on the development of an inclusive and collaborative curriculum and assessment system. The current aims of teachers and administrators at all grade levels are to (a) expedite second language acquisition; (b) maintain high academic standards for all students; (c) maintain ongoing teacher in-service, appropriate scheduling, and student-teacher ratios; (d) provide equal access to the full curriculum, and (e) develop cross-cultural awareness and understanding. Hence, ESOL and mainstream teachers are expected to work together to ensure that all students can understand and use the language and content of the core curriculum (English, social studies, and science) as well as participate in classroom activities. In addition, all teachers are expected to apply instructional strategies that make language meaningful and understandable, thus facilitating language development. These expectations have been formalized as an explicit standard in the school's formal professional evaluation program; that is, competent professionals will ensure all students learn through language that is accessible to them.

The targets for ongoing teacher in-service at ISB are determined at the start of each school year and are derived from the annual evaluation of the school strategic plan. Teachers set annual professional development goals relative to these targets, and this works in tandem with the existing standards. For example, *differentiating instruction,* one of main targets for the 2002–2004 school years, dictated the content of the school in-service programs with all teachers being expected to

- maintain high academic standards, use strategies for effective interaction, and demonstrate that the language of the classroom is meaningful and understandable

- have all students learn reading strategies and use the writing process across the curriculum

- demonstrate student understanding through a variety of assessments

- demonstrate cross-cultural understanding and knowledge of second language acquisition

Within this framework, ESOL and content teachers collaborate and agree on curriculum outcomes and assessments. In other words, all ISB teachers are language teachers to some degree. The challenge lies in assessing and setting language development goals for ESOL students in two very diverse contexts: the ESOL classroom and the core classrooms. The design and implementation of collaborative curriculum structures have gradually evolved to reflect this shared responsibility.

Both authors of this chapter were involved in this process from the beginning— Donna Hurst as the ESOL specialist in the high school and Chris Davison as consultant to the project from 1998 onwards.

◈ CONTEXT

ISB is an English-medium K–12 school offering both U.S. high school and international baccalaureate (IB) diplomas. The Grades 9–12 ESOL students, mostly Japanese (approximately 25%) as well as Thai, Taiwanese, Korean, and Europeans, are especially challenged by the rigors of the curriculum and the high academic standards. Most high school teachers are recruited overseas from the United States or the United Kingdom and are highly qualified. Both students and teachers represent a range of international experiences and cultural backgrounds. The mainstream classrooms include students from more than 50 countries, 18% of which are students receiving ESOL support; the rest are nativelike speakers of English with strong literacy and motivation to continue their studies in higher education. Only about 20% are native English speakers, primarily from the United States, the United Kingdom, Australia, and New Zealand.

At ISB, ESOL students are mainstreamed from the primary grades, are included in all middle school core classes (with additional ESOL instruction provided), and participate in the full range of course offerings in the high school with one or two ESOL classes in place of electives, depending on the student's English-language proficiency. Students with little or no English can enroll as complete beginners up to Grade 6 but must also demonstrate good academic achievement and literacy in their primary language. Those entering middle and high school must, in addition, demonstrate English proficiency at basic levels. This leaves quite a formidable challenge for classroom teachers who are required to teach content to all students without compromising standards, and at the same time, continuously assess and develop English language knowledge and skills across the curriculum. In the high school, in Grades 9–12, ESOL faculty support the core curriculum areas only; that is, English 9–12; history and sciences in Grades 9–10; and the graduation requirements in Grades 11–12: Thai South East Asia and Senior Seminar, a graduation requirement based on the IB Theory of Knowledge. The following description of the collaborative curriculum structure at ISB is based on the high school ESOL program, although most of the agreements and many of the practices occur throughout K–12.

◈ DESCRIPTION

When the mainstream curriculum was first being overhauled and standardized (see Appendix A), ISB ESOL teachers recommended including the language implications for each unit being taught. Developing common curriculum outcomes in all content areas and mapping the language outcomes required in each unit and at each level proceeded concurrently, which was, in retrospect, a key factor in establishing the effectiveness of the ISB initiative. Language is not seen as a separate issue but as an integral component of curriculum planning. Thus, in developing any unit, teachers begin with the general outcomes and from these identify specific outcomes, illustrative examples (or activities along with strategies), language implications, assessments, and resources. Language implications are therefore an integral part of all units at all grade levels. ESOL teachers and core teachers negotiate these implications as a part of the collaborative curriculum development process. For planning, teaching and assessing purposes, the K–12 ESL Curriculum Committee for ISB has classified these language implications into five elements: language functions, text types, vocabulary, language features, and cultural understandings.

The social and academic functions of the mainstream classroom are the first and most fundamental elements of the development of this collaborative curriculum. Adapting the TESOL standards (TESOL, 1997) and drawing on the work of Finocchiaro and Brumfit (1983), Mohan (1986), and Yalden (1983), the K–12 ESL Curriculum Committee identified the functions most appropriate to the ISB curricula (see Figure 1). The social macrofunctions include the expressive, interactional, and directive functions, and the academic macrofunctions include the functions of classification, principles, evaluation, description, sequence, choice, and imagination. Although not exhaustive, these represent the main functions ISB students are expected to control in any mainstream classroom. In English 10, for example, the assessment "Individual oral participation with teacher and written commentary in journal" suggests the social-expressive function along with the academic function of *principles*. In Modern World History 10, the students must complete a Venn diagram graphic organizer comparing the Hitler and Mussolini regimes. Here *principles* and *description,* the microfunction being compare/contrast, are involved. These functions were relatively easy to identify and because they focused on doing things with language, they were relatively accessible and transparent to the content teachers.

The second type of language implication is oral and written text types (see Appendix B), divided into narrative, recount, informative report, procedure, explanation, description, persuasion/argument, discussion, exposition, multiple texts, summaries/notes, newspaper report, diary/reflection, poems, and letters. It was often quite complicated to identify the exact language being targeted within these text

I. SOCIAL FUNCTIONS

A. EXPRESSION

expressing, clarifying, or arranging one's ideas, thoughts, or feelings
Examples: ability, wishes/hopes, fear/worry, likes/dislikes, surprise/disbelief, satisfaction/dissatisfaction

expressing modality
Examples: possibility, certainty, necessity/needs, wants, obligation

B. INTERACTION

establishing and maintaining desirable social and working relationships
Examples: greetings, invitations, thanks, initiating, leave-taking, apologies, permission, promises, excuses

C. DIRECTION

attempting to influence the actions of others
Examples: advice/suggestions, requests/offers, persuasion, commands, corrections, approval/disapproval

questioning/inquiring

giving directions, instructing

II. ACADEMIC FUNCTIONS

A. CLASSIFICATION

understanding, applying, or developing concepts, definitions, and classifications

using operational definitions

B. PRINCIPLES

explaining

predicting

interpreting data, inferring, and drawing conclusions

formulating, testing, and establishing hypotheses

understanding, applying, or developing generalizations
Examples: cause/effect, means/ends, rules, strategies, results, analysis, synthesis

summarizing

paraphrasing

C. EVALUATION

evaluating, judging, ranking

appreciating, criticizing

forming, expressing, and justifying preferences and opinions

recommending

understanding, analyzing, and deciding on goals, values, policies, and evaluation criteria

Continued on page 45

D. DESCRIPTION

    reporting, identifying, and observing

    naming

    comparing/contrasting

    describing

E. SEQUENCE

    sequencing objects, ideas, or events

    recounting

    narrating

    relaying steps in a process

F. CHOICE

    making decisions

    negotiating/arguing

    expressing/inquiring about intentions

    expressing personal opinions

G. IMAGINATION

    discussing literature/arts

    expanding ideas suggested by others or by a piece of literature, art, or music

    creating rhymes, poetry, stories, or plays

    recombining familiar dialogues/passages creatively

    suggesting original beginnings/endings to dialogues/stories

    solving problems/mysteries

FIGURE 1. Functions of the Mainstream Classroom

types. Sometimes it was easier to work backwards and identify the various text and sentence-level patterns of language needed to complete specific curriculum-based tasks. Through collaboration, teachers determined how the core teachers would approach the development of these text types in their classrooms as well as the extent to which students needed to practice these smaller bits in context in the ESOL classroom. It was most effective to make agreements as to the specific language of these text types and reinforce them across the core curricula.

The third element of language implications, vocabulary, is divided into two categories: the technical or topic-specific vocabulary of the classroom and the academic (ESOL-needed) vocabulary. Classroom teachers were most comfortable with describing and assessing topic-specific vocabulary. More work was often needed to identify the academic language that was essential for communicating and exploring key concepts but which was often treated by teachers as assumed knowledge.

Language features is the fourth element of the language implications, divided into grammar, structure, pronunciation, and style. This element is best taught and assessed in the ESOL and English classrooms, as it requires a fair degree of technical knowledge about language, but it is still important to discuss and include it on the common curriculum pro forma to gradually sensitize all teachers to these kind of specific language issues.

Cultural understandings, the fifth and final element of the language implications, includes students' prior knowledge, shared understandings, links between culture and subject matter, key concepts and identity, comparisons of groups and subject, and students' ability to demonstrate their own knowledge. Once explicitly identified through the collaborative curriculum planning process, these aspects were easily incorporated into the daily routines and assessment processes of every core classroom.

The collaborative curriculum planning process is more cyclical than linear. The first step is usually to analyze the core curriculum units in terms of functions to see what functions are emphasized and where there are gaps. This will then help to identify what should be assessed, by whom, and where. The Curriculum Audit—Spectrum Analysis (see Appendix C for an example) shows the results of this effort. It is clear, for example, that the microfunction of expressing ideas/thoughts/feelings is emphasized in most core courses. Such cross-curricular functions are taught and assessed in ESOL as well as in the core classroom. Other functions that are particular to one content area will be taught and assessed in that class, with ESOL teachers providing support.

The ESOL curriculum template is then aligned with that of the mainstream template (see Appendix D for an example), except for the addition of language learning strategies. After much discussion on where to place strategies, it was decided to match language-learning strategies to the specific outcomes for the ESOL curriculum and have classroom teachers encourage the use of learning strategies in general as part of their illustrative examples appropriate to their outcomes. In this way, ESOL students can apply an array of strategies for different purposes, including cognitive, metacognitive, and social-affective strategies (see Appendix E for a description of these strategies). The ESOL general outcomes include both social and academic English and lead to the specific outcomes that are derived from the identified functions of the core curriculum. These specific outcomes determine the illustrative examples, language learning strategies, assessments, and resources used in the ESOL classroom to target language items not covered in the core curriculum (see Appendix D for a sample ESOL curriculum template).

In attempting to detail the illustrative examples, language learning strategies, and assessments, however, it was somewhat belatedly realized that the broad picture—the spectrum analysis of functions—was necessary but not sufficient for the specific analysis required for lesson planning. Hence, the language implications pro forma (see Appendix F for an example) was created, specifying the language implications for each unit as well as the teacher roles, resources, and so on. Sometimes the teachers were able to streamline the process by combining certain units together. For example, the specific outcomes in the English poetry units were grouped across Grades 9–12, and the common core functions, text types, topic-specific vocabulary (i.e., literary terms and poetic devices), and some general language features identified. The academic vocabulary, cultural understandings, and the remainder of language features were then specified in relation to each poem and/or theme. The same was also done with other literary genres in English. The specific outcomes of the sciences, as well as the other core course, however, were too disparate, so a unit-by-unit analysis of each core course was undertaken.

This collaborative planning enables teachers to sit down comfortably to write realistic outcomes and assessments targeting what ESOL students need for their language development as well as for their academic success, that is, developing a valid and workable collaborative curriculum. Equally or even more important, however, is the quality of the language learning and assessments that take place in the core classroom as a result of this collaboration and the agreements that are explicitly stated in the curricula. The last box on the Language Implications Analysis Worksheet (as shown in Appendix F) is the key to the collaborative curriculum working effectively—the "Assessed by" box. Who is responsible for teaching and assessing a particular language item—the core teacher, the ESOL teacher, or perhaps someone else? To arrive at this decision, the ESOL and core teams must negotiate. This requires dedicated times set up at the start of each semester and supported by the administration. In the high school, the ESOL teachers are integral members of the core teams. There are 85-minute blocks on a rotation schedule that enable teams to coplan at least once a rotation. For example, one of the ESOL teachers coplans, or "teams," with English 10 and Modern World History 10 teachers, another ESOL teacher meets with English 9 and World Civilization 9, and the teacher most comfortable with the sciences sits on the Science 9 and 10 teams.

On team meeting day, teachers bring their templates and worksheets with the goal being to complete the "Assessed by" box. Planning discussions focus on best classroom practices and where to make appropriate accommodations. This can involve topics such as approaches to differentiating instruction and assessments; coteaching; the use of graphic organizers, outlines, or cooperative learning strategies; effective inductive methods; the explicit teaching of language and cultural understandings; and the need for all students to understand the language of the classroom. Such discussion leads to questions such as: Who modifies texts where appropriate? Who develops supplemental materials? Who creates text/lecture outlines? Who gives vocabulary practice? Where should native-language texts be used? How should reference materials be used in the core classroom? Who should oversee the writing process? And in terms of assessments, who modifies the tests? Is formal grading postponed and for how long? What finally ends up in the "Assessed by" box as a result of this cyclical and dialogic process and the agreements made about language implications are the decisions about who, what, how, when, and where to assess, which then sets the broad directions for teaching and learning.

◈ DISTINGUISHING FEATURES

The distinguishing features of the curriculum collaboration at ISB include its emphasis on explicit attention to ESOL development as an integral part of the curriculum and assessment planning processes, the negotiation of a shared understanding of ESOL and mainstream teachers' roles/responsibilities (see chapter 10 in this volume), and the development of a supportive climate for ongoing cross-curricular collaboration and evaluation. The implementation of common curriculum planning pro formas and processes, including the establishment of systematic mechanisms for monitoring, evaluation, and feedback, has been the glue that binds everything else together. Each of these distinguishing features will be briefly outlined in turn.

Explicit Attention to ESOL Development Across the Curriculum

The creation of the various documents to address ESOL development across the curriculum is perhaps one of the most important and distinctive elements underlying the success of a collaborative curriculum (Arkoudis & Davison, 2002). The documents have given teachers a common language to discuss ESOL students' needs across the curriculum and have highlighted very effectively obvious gaps in language development. Explicitly evaluating lessons on an ongoing basis as teachers work together on student learning has helped meet the different goals of both language and content teachers. The documents have allowed teachers to identify and evaluate English language input as well as systematically and explicitly teach English language skills to ESOL students to make the outcomes of the core curriculum appropriate and achievable.

Shared Understanding of ESOL and Mainstream Teachers' Roles Responsibilities

The development of the collaborative planning pro formas and processes has also helped to establish a clear sense of complementary roles and responsibilities. All teachers are expected to meet the language and learning needs of ESOL students in their classes, regardless of students' length of residence or language proficiency. At the same time, the ESOL teacher is seen as a curriculum specialist, not simply a source of "technical" assistance (Davison, 2001). The documents also help ESOL teachers to achieve a major objective of sheltered immersion; that is, to provide support for mainstream teachers through collaborative planning and "on the job" in-service programs. At both the whole-school level and at the classroom level, the ESOL teacher is involved in and informs the planning, implementation, and evaluation of all the core learning areas.

Supportive Climate for Ongoing Cross-Curricular Collaboration and Evaluation

The final key to the success of the collaborative curriculum is the ongoing support and local in-service opportunities offered by the administration for both ESOL and core teachers involved. One of us (Chris Davison) developed a number of programs over the years to provide teachers with key concepts and understanding about second language and appropriate classroom practices. The school actively promoted and participated in these programs, demonstrating the administration's concern that mainstream teachers not only develop strategies for making subject matter learning accessible but also take responsibility for language development. Concurrent with this professional development was the team planning of curriculum and common assessments that provided for that important professional dialogue necessary to improve classroom practice, to ensure student learning, and to accommodate ever-changing needs.

That said, ESOL collaboration was not always sought by other subject departments in the early stages of developing curriculum, with ESOL issues often belatedly raised at the lesson-planning stage. Thus, the content curriculum, rather than the learners' stage of ESOL acquisition, tended to dominate the language focus initially, making the whole process of developing integrated curriculum more time consuming. Another problem was that subject teachers at senior levels were often less willing to integrate ESOL strategies and content into mainstream curriculum because they feared it would "slow down" topics, thereby jeopardizing coverage of key content. However, attitudes appear to be changing as both ESOL and mainstream teachers get more used to collaborating and making their objectives more explicit.

◈ PRACTICAL IDEAS

A collaborative curriculum in a sheltered immersion context requires the support and commitment from the various stakeholders involved. The following are some practical recommendations and strategies for the various key stakeholders.

School Administrators

- Ensure that teaching standards are in place whereby teachers work toward developing expertise in making language accessible for all students in content classrooms.
- Budget for in-service programs dedicated to maintaining high standards and to meeting language needs of all students.
- Budget for appropriate staffing and class sizes to allow for no more than one-third "high-needs" students per class.
- Communicate goals with community members on an ongoing, consistent basis.

Content and ESOL Teachers

- Establish a professional community allowing for genuine ongoing professional dialogue.
- Identify and develop a shared purpose.
- Establish an agreed protocol and meeting agendas.
- Define the language implications for each unit taught.
- Come to agreement on
  — who modifies texts where appropriate?
  — who develops supplemental materials?
  — who creates text/lecture outlines?
  — who gives vocabulary practice?
  — where to use native-language texts?
- Determine for assessments
  — who modifies tests?
  — who selects appropriate reference materials for class?
  — who oversees the writing process?
  — which learning strategies are taught where?
  — where is language development realistically going to be assessed?
  — when and how is formal grading to occur (and to what extent can it be postponed)?

- Consider coteaching options.
- Follow through on agreements based on curriculum analysis (who teaches what?).
- Assess agreed language implications.
- Keep data on student achievement to evidence successes.
- Communicate with and set out to educate and report to parents on an ongoing, consistent basis.

Content Teachers

- Be willing to modify classroom practice and make appropriate accommodations incorporating best practices.
- Differentiate instruction: process and product (assessments).
- Use advanced organizers, outlines, and so on for direct instruction.
- Use cooperative learning strategies.
- Use effective inductive approaches to learning.
- Have students identify and apply learning strategies.
- Ensure all students can work independently and participate effectively.
- Teach language and cultural understandings explicitly where appropriate.

ESOL Teachers

- Support the content teachers' risk-taking.
- Communicate student needs.
- Realize content teachers are also differentiating for students with high levels of English language proficiency.
- Teach students language learning strategies and metacognition.
- Teach language systematically and meaningfully within an immersion context.

Curriculum Leaders

- Establish action plans for all involved in the curriculum revision process.
- Encourage peer coaching and reflection as part of the school culture.
- Encourage teachers to evaluate and revise lessons on a daily basis to be able to meet students' needs and changing conditions.
- Ensure common assessments are an integral part of all curriculum areas.
- Encourage teachers to seek out and apply best practices.
- Plan with administrators in implementing realistic, applicable, and timely in-service programs to include the basics of second language acquisition, cross-cultural understanding, and best practices.

- Utilize the expertise of the faculty in in-service programs without over-burdening teachers.
- Consider implementing a language policy across the curriculum.

◈ CONCLUSION

The rewards of bridging the gap between core and ESOL classrooms can only benefit ESOL learners. We know that our work is not a destination but rather a journey. At ISB, teachers have taken on a new set of challenges, and perhaps surprisingly, have found these challenges energizing rather than debilitating. They have discovered the curriculum to be the cornerstone to successful collaboration. ESOL teachers used to be anxious about why they were collaborating—it seemed hit and miss, was often unfulfilling, and lacked follow-through and change. ESOL teachers often found themselves caught up with day-to-day crisis management at the expense of much-needed professional dialogues. Now ESOL teachers have a purpose and a sense of continuity—curriculum agreements based on solid outcomes. The interdependency of the ISB faculty, from teachers to administrators, has led to positive change. The high standards set by teachers has led to the school explicitly defining and disseminating those standards for the wider school community, giving all teachers a stronger sense of pride in their work and an understanding of what it means to be part of an ESOL community.

◈ ACKNOWLEDGMENTS

We would like to express our sincerest thanks to the ISB ESOL teams and high school classroom teachers who have participated in the sheltered immersion model program since 1995. The ISB initiative would also not have happened without the invaluable support and encouragement of the Deputy Head of School (Learning), Dr. Deborah Welch, as well as that of the Head of School, Dr. Bill Gerritz, and the supportive administration at all division levels. We would also like to acknowledge the contribution made to this chapter by the Grade 10 ESOL teacher, Karen Reau, who developed some of the appendices.

◈ CONTRIBUTORS

Donna Hurst has worked as an ESOL educator for the past 14 years at International School Bangkok (ISB). Before that, she worked in international K–12 schools in Saudi Arabia and Colombia, as well as in public schools in the United States, including Osborn School District in Phoenix, Arizona, and Jefferson County Schools outside Denver, Colorado. She presented ISB's work on ESOL curriculum at the TESOL Convention in Salt Lake City in 2002.

Chris Davison is an associate professor in English language education in the Faculty of Education, University of Hong Kong. She has published widely in the area of mainstreaming and ESOL issues and has carried out extensive consultancy work on mainstreaming in schools in the Asian-Pacific region, including Australia, Japan, Taiwan, Laos, China, Singapore, Hong Kong, Thailand, Vietnam, Indonesia, and the Philippines. She has been a consultant to ISB since 1998.

◈ APPENDIX A: CURRICULUM TEMPLATE (DESCRIPTION OF CATEGORIES)

Exit Outcome Cross-Reference

General Outcomes	Specific Outcomes	Illustrative Examples	Language Implications	Assessments	Resources/Technology
A broad statement specifying what a student should know (knowledge) and be able to do (skills) relative to academic areas. General outcomes need to be in alignment K–12. Most content areas have a range of 8 to 12 general outcomes. General outcomes are known by many names in other countries and school systems. Some examples are standards, goals, essential learnings, general learner expectations, proficiencies, vital results, and overall expectations.	A specific outcome translates a general outcome into a measurable statement of what a student should know and be able to do according to grade, age, or developmental level. The assessments are directly tied to the specific outcomes. Not every specific outcome needs to be assessed, but the most important ones do. Specific outcomes can be combined for assessment, such as in a project.	Sample activities or tasks that demonstrate and elaborate on the general and specific outcomes. They are important in conveying the richness, breadth, and depth intended in the outcomes. The sample tasks and activities should connect logically with the outcomes. They should also address a variety of learning styles. In addition to activities, many teachers include focus questions for the unit in this area.	Given the specific outcomes of the unit, what does the language look like? What are the linguistic and cultural implications of the language of the unit? Where are the learners relative to the language expectations? What strategies will assist in making this language accessible? For example, vocabulary words can be listed, text types noted (narrative, lab report, report, etc.) and skills (classifying, comparing and contrasting, judging, etc.) identified that may require special teaching strategies. Strategies such as advance organizers, cooperative groups, and so forth can be listed.	Any method used to collect evidence of, report, and record progress toward desired learning outcomes. The assessment ties directly to the specific outcomes. If the outcomes states what a student should know and be able to do, the assessment offers the evidence that a student can demonstrate the knowledge and skills. Consider the use of paper-and-pencil tests (e.g., multiple choice, true/false, matching, short answer, essay).	Software, books, media, and support materials that connect logically with the relevant outcomes. Library media and technology staff and specialist teachers are important resources for assistance in this area.

Continued on p. 53

General Outcomes	Specific Outcomes	Illustrative Examples	Language Implications	Assessments	Resources/Technology
	How do you know that a specific outcome is a good specific outcome? • It should be a clear, specific statement of what a student should know and be able to do. • It should meet/ exceed the standards of curricula from other schools. • It should be measurable and observable. • It should contain content meaningful for today's world. • It should be an expectation for all students.		For cultural implications, the unit can be reviewed according to what would make the content more accessible to someone from a different cultural background.	Consider the use of performance tasks (e.g., projects, dramatic and musical performances, formal oral presentations, labs, simulations, maps, demonstrations, charts, models, portfolios, research papers, displays, journals, illustrations, timelines, media presentations, computer programs). Consider the use of oral communication (e.g., interviews, debates, panel discussions).	

◈ APPENDIX B: BASIC TEXT TYPES

Text type	Typical text structures	Typical language features	Examples from subject areas
Narrative *Purpose:* to entertain *Focus:* sequential specific events	• orientation • initiating events • complications • resolution	• defined characters • descriptive language • dialogue • usually past tense	English: stories History: a biography
Recount *Purpose:* to retell events *Focus:* sequential specific events	• orientation • events in time order • reorientation (optional) • evaluation (optional)	• time markers (later, after, before, etc.) • action verbs • simple past tense • specific participants	Mathematics: recount the steps involved in a math problem-solving activity Science: the method (what we did) section of a science report English: a journal of the events in a past holiday or excursion
Informative Report *Purpose:* to classify and describe a class of things *Focus:* general things	• generalization or classification • description • summary (optional)	• generalized participants • impersonal objective language • timeless present • subject-specific vocabulary	Science: an informative essay on volcanoes Health: an informative essay on common allergies
Procedure *Purpose:* to describe how to do things *Focus:* sequential general events	• goal • materials • method • evaluation	• detailed factual description • imperatives (draw a line, heat the water) • time markers (after, until, as soon as) • timeless present	Science: how to make an electrical circuit Technology: instructions on how to operate a computer or other device
Explanation *Purpose:* to explain phenomena *Focus:* general things, explains how or why events happen	• define phenomenon • explanation sequence	• generalized, nonhuman participants • cause and effect relationships • passive voice (is caused by) • timeless present (soil is)	Science: an explanation of the water cycle Health: an explanation of how digestion operates

Continued on p. 55

Text type	Typical text structures	Typical language features	Examples from subject areas
Description *Purpose:* to describe a place, person, thing, event, situation *Focus:* describe the context or backdrop for an event, provide a visual image	• to describe a particular thing or person • precise • to define in depth	• similes and metaphors • use of is, had, with • relative clauses	English: description of a scene Science: description of the earth's crust
Persuasion/Argument (one side of an argument) *Purpose:* to present and justify a particular point of view *Focus:* argument for one position	• major point of view (thesis) • arguments • reiteration	• language of cause and effect • modality (may, might, conditional sentences, etc.) • transitions linking ideas (however, while, nevertheless)	English, Social Studies: a letter to the editor arguing for improved public transportation
Discussion *Purpose:* to explore an issue in depth *Focus:* arguments for and against	• statement of the issue • arguments for and against • recommendations	• generally uses present tense to express opinions • language of cause and effect • modality (may, might, conditional sentences, etc.)	All subjects: response to issues (the advantages/disadvantages of solar power); research paper
Exposition *Purpose:* to explore a topic in depth *Focus:* presentation, interpretation, and/or analysis of different aspects of a topic	• cause and effect • compare and contrast • definition	• literary present tense • language of cause and effect • language of compare and contrast • transitions	English: literary analysis Social Studies: an essay comparing and contrasting the lives and teaching of Buddha and Christ
More complex texts **Multiple texts** (combining mixtures of the above text types) *Purpose:* These texts will have two or more purposes. At secondary level most factual texts involve mixtures of text types	• likely to follow one text type predominantly	• features change to reflect the text type operating	All subjects: an informative report on the earth's crust may move from a description of the composition of the earth's crust to an explanation of how tectonic plates move

Continued on p. 56

Text type	Typical text structures	Typical language features	Examples from subject areas
Summaries/Notes *Purpose:* to reflect the main points of an article in a quickly accessible form	• varies depending on the purpose of the summary and structure of the original text	• dot points or note form • subheadings with notes clustered underneath • usually short or incomplete sentences	All subjects: • notes taken on a topic under investigation • summary of a newspaper article
Newspaper Report *Purpose:* to inform (the public) of events *Focus:* specific "factual" events	• headline, byline, lead • next most important information • consequences or further developments (optional)	• time markers (yesterday; on July 29, about 8:45 a.m.) • past tense • headline in present or passive • direct speech	English: a newspaper report about a real or imaginary event Social Studies: a newspaper report about a current or historical event (Greek magazine)
Diary/Reflection *Purpose:* to record experiences, impressions on ideas, or to inform; may be for self or for future wider audience	• paragraphs organized under dates or days of the week • entries not necessarily linked	• personal participants • often informal, interpersonal, free-flowing, close to spoken English • may contain features of a range of basic text types	English, Social Studies: • diary of a key historical figure • diary of an immigrant at Ellis Island • diary of a fictitious character • personal diary
Poems *Purpose:* to entertain, to share experiences, reflections, and emotions	• varies	• often incomplete sentences • very precise, economical choice of words • use of descriptive imagery • often with an identifiable rhythm	English: haiku, diamante, and cinquain poems, poems using the letters of a student's name
Letters *Purpose:* • argument (see Persuasion/ Argument) • personal to share experiences and information; to maintain relationships	• greetings • orientation • points/experiences/ observations		

From State of Victoria Department of Education (1997).

APPENDIX C: CURRICULUM AUDIT—SPECTRUM ANALYSIS

Language Functions	E9	E10	E11	E12	WC	MWH	TSEA	SS12	HLTH	PHYS	CHEM	BIO	ELW	Center
IA. Expressive														
1. expressing ideas/thoughts/feelings	✓	✓	✓	✓	✓	✓								9
2. expressing modality						✓							12	
IB. Interactional														
1. establishing/maintaining relationships													10	
IC. Directive														
1. seeking to influence others' actions								✓			✓		11	
2. questioning/inquiring							✓	✓			✓		9	
3. giving instructions/directions								✓			✓		9	
IIA. Classification														
1. understanding/applying/developing concepts/definitions/classifications					✓	✓	✓	✓			✓	✓	9	9–10
2. using operational definitions										✓				
IIB. Principles														
1. explaining					✓			✓			✓	✓		10
2. predicting													12	
3. interpreting data/drawing conclusions					✓			✓	✓		✓	✓		
4. forming/testing/establishing hypotheses					✓					✓	✓			
5. understanding/applying/developing generalizations	✓				✓			✓			✓	✓	9–12	
6. summarizing	✓						✓					✓	9	
7. paraphrasing		✓					✓	✓					10	

Continued on p. 58

Language Functions	E9	E10	E11	E12	WC	MWH	TSEA	SS12	HLTH	PHYS	CHEM	BIO	ELW	Center
IIC. Evaluation														
1. evaluating/judging/ranking		✓		✓		✓			✓				11	
2. appreciating/criticizing		✓	✓										11	9–10
3. forming/expressing/justifying preferences/opinions					✓			✓					10	
4. recommending	✓													9–10
5. deciding goals/values/policies and/or evaluation criteria														9–12
IID. Description														
1. reporting (identifying and observing)							✓		✓		✓	✓		
2. naming	✓	✓							✓		✓	✓		
3. comparing/contrasting things					✓	✓					✓	✓	9	9–12
4. describing						✓					✓	✓	11	9–12
IIE. Sequence														
1. sequencing objects/ideas/events													9	9–12
2. recounting														9–12
3. narrating													11	
4. relaying steps in a process										✓	✓	✓	9	9–12

Continued on p. 59

Language Functions	E9	E10	E11	E12	WC	MWH	TSEA	SS12	HLTH	PHYS	CHEM	BIO	ELW	Center
IIF. Choice														
1. making decisions														9–12
2. negotiating/arguing														9–12
3. expressing/inquiring about intentions														9–12
4. expressing personal opinions								✓						9–12
IIG. Imaginative														
1. discussing literature and arts			✓										9–12	9
2. expanding upon ideas of others			✓											9
3. creating rhymes/poetry/stories/plays	✓	✓												11
4. recombining familiar dialogues/passages														12
5. suggesting original beginning/endings														11
6. solving problems/mysteries											✓	✓		11

E9–12 = English 9–12
WC = World Civilization 9
MWH = Modern World History 10
TSEA = Thai Southeast Asia 11
SS12 = Senior Seminar 12
HLTH = Health 10

PHYS = Physics 9
CHEM = Chemistry 9
BIO = Biology 10
ELW = English Language Workshop 9–12
Center = English for Academic Purposes (Resource) Center 9–12

◈ APPENDIX D: SAMPLE ESOL CURRICULUM TEMPLATE—GR. 10 BIOLOGY

ESOL Curriculum (English for Academic Purposes [EAP]) Center and English Language Workshop [ELW]):

General Outcome: To use English to achieve academically in all content areas

Grade 10

Specific Outcome	*Illustrative Examples*	*Learning Strategies [See Appendix E]*	*Assessments*	*Language Implications*	*Resources*
Description (macrofunction)	**Describing Structure, Appearance, Position**				
	Activity for Content and/or ESOL Focus—Maintain an EAP vocabulary and grammar notebook for study and practice with target language features	**Cognitive Strategies** • resourcing • grouping • deducing/inducing • using imagery • using auditory representation	• Vocabulary notebook (adj/n/ v/prep to describe; academic vocabulary) • Vocabulary quiz • Grammar notebook (simple present tense)	**Language Features** *Adj/n/v to describe structure/ appearance* • a strand of, coil/wind around, a chunk of, twist like a staircase, resemble a double helix, pinch inward, condense/ compact, look like a rod, reel to opposite sides, be visible/invisible, form around, be joined by *V/prep to describe position* • align along, line up in, pair up with, move toward, at the poles, assemble, across, attach to, form between *Simple present tense*	**Link to . . .** ISB HS Biology Curriculum Unit 5: Cell Reproduction **Texts:** *Biology: Visualizing Life,* Chapter 6 (Biology class text) **Supplemental Text:** *Biology: An Everyday Experience,* Chapter 22 (EAP supplemental text)
	Information Gap Activity • pairs (back to back) • manipulatives or drawings • oral description using target language features	**Cognitive Strategies** • using imagery • using auditory Representation **Social-Affective Strategies** • questioning for clarification • cooperating	• Quiz: Describing structure, appearance, and position		**Text-Based Resources:** EAP Chapter 6 Text Outline/ Reading Guide Interactive audio CD program (language development reading comprehension) for *Biology: Visualizing Life* Instructional transparencies for *Biology: Visualizing Life*
	EAP Worksheet: Review of Cell Organelles	**Cognitive Strategies** • transferring • resourcing		**Topic-Specific and Academic Vocabulary** (See HS Biology Curriculum)	**Biology Classroom-Based Materials** EAP Biology class notes

Continued on p. 61

Specific Outcome	Illustrative Examples	Learning Strategies [See Appendix E]	Assessments	Language Implications	Resources
Principles (macrofunction)	**Understand, Apply, Develop Generalizations of Cause and Effect**				
	Activity for Content and/or ESOL Focus— Maintain an EAP vocabulary and grammar notebook for study and practice with target language features	**Cognitive Strategies** • resourcing • grouping • deducing/ inducing • using imagery • using auditory representation	• Vocabulary notebook (adverb clauses, academic vocabulary) • Vocabulary quiz	**Language Features** *Adverb clauses used to describe cause and effect relationships* • stimulate, trigger, enable, influence, contribute to, lead to, result in, be the result of	EAP annotated and/or highlighted biology labs/ activities EAP review guide for biology unit test **EAP Classroom-Based Materials** Vocabulary lists and puzzles EAP worksheets • The Cell Cycle **Online Resources** http://www.cellsalive.com /index.htm (beg. ESOL) http://avery.rutgers.edu (adv. ESOL)
	Class reading and discussion on cancer (cultural understandings)	**Cognitive Strategies** • resourcing • note-taking **Metacognitive Strategies** • self-monitoring **Social-Affective Strategies** • cooperating • questioning for clarification		*Simple present tense* **Topic-Specific and Academic Vocabulary** (See HS Biology Curriculum) **Cultural Understandings** • Genetic mutations are not always harmful • Cancer found in societies around the world	
	Text deconstruction of expository paragraphs of cause and effect	**Cognitive Strategies** • note-taking **Metacognitive Strategies** • advance organizing	• Quiz: Text deconstruction and identification of language of cause and effect	**Text Types** • multiple texts • summaries/ notes	
	Paragraph writing • expository ¶ of cause and effect (model writing process, inclusive of peer edit)	**Metacognitive Strategies** • organizational planning • self-evaluating	• Expository paragraph of cause and effect		

◈ APPENDIX E: LEARNING STRATEGIES

Cognitive Strategies

Cognitive strategies are those in which the learner interacts with the material to be learned by manipulating it mentally (as in making mental images or elaborating on previously acquired concepts or skills) or physically (as in grouping items to be learned in meaningful categories or taking notes on important information to be remembered).

Resourcing	Using target-language reference materials such as dictionaries, encyclopedias, or textbooks.
Grouping	Classifying words, terminology, or concepts according to their attributes.
Note-Taking	Writing down key words and concepts in abbreviated verbal, graphic, or numerical form during a listening or reading activity.
Summarizing	Making a mental or written summary of information gained through listening or reading.
Deducing/Inducing	Applying rules to understand or produce the second language, or making up rules based on language analysis.
Using Imagery	Using visual images (either mental or actual) to understand and remember new information.
Using Auditory Representation	Playing back in one's mind the sound of a word, phrase, or longer language sequence.
Elaborating	Relating new information to prior knowledge, relating different parts of new information to each other, or making meaningful personal associations to the new information.
Transferring	Using previous linguistic knowledge or prior skills to assist comprehension or production.
Inferencing	Using information in an oral or written text to guess meanings, predict outcomes, or complete missing parts.

Continued on p. 63

Metacognitive Strategies

Metacognitive strategies involve executive processes in planning for learning, monitoring one's comprehension and production, and evaluating how well one has achieved a learning objective.

Advance Organizing	Previewing the main ideas and concepts of the material to be learned, often by skimming the text for the organizing principle.
Organizational Planning	Planning the parts, sequence, main ideas, or language functions to be expressed orally or in writing.
Selectively Attending	Deciding in advance to attend to specific aspects of input, often by scanning for key words, concepts, and/or linguistic markers.
Self-Monitoring	Checking one's comprehension during listening or reading, or checking the accuracy and/or appropriateness of one's oral or written production while it is taking place.
Self-Evaluating	Judging how well one has accomplished a learning activity after it has been completed and setting new goals.

Social-Affective Strategies

Social-affective strategies are those in which the learner either interacts with another person in order to assist learning, as in cooperation or asking questions for clarification, or uses some kind of affective control to assist a learning task.

Questioning for Clarification	Eliciting from a teacher or peer additional explanation, rephrasing, examples, or verification.
Cooperating	Working together with peers to solve a problem, pool information, check a learning task, model a language activity, or get feedback from an oral presentation.
Self-Affirming (self-talk)	Using mental techniques that make one feel competent and confident to do the learning task.

Based on concepts from Chamot & O'Malley (1987).

❧ APPENDIX F: LANGUAGE IMPLICATIONS ANALYSIS WORKSHEET

Grade: Subject: Unit:

CONTENT SPECIFIC OUTCOMES (Outcomes from the core curriculum specific to each unit of study)	RESOURCES (Resources used in the core unit of study)
Gr. 9–12 Poetry	**Gr. 9–12 Poetry**
• know and be able to use literary terms	Poetry packets, selected poetry
• formulate personal understanding and interpretations	**Gr. 10 Biology**
• apply and adjust strategies for comprehending a variety of texts	*Text-based: Biology: Visualizing Life,* Chapter 6; Directed Reading; Chapter 6 Notes
Gr. 10 Biology	*Labs:* Mitosis (#15); Time for Mitosis (#16); Comparing Mitosis and Meiosis (#17); General Biology: Mitosis Lab
• define chromatin	*Online Resources:* The Biology Project/Cell Biology (Univ. of Arizona) Activity: Online Onion Root Tips
• describe the structure of a chromosome	
Gr. 10 Modern World History	**Gr. 10 Modern World History**
• explain conditions and motivations that contribute to conflict, cooperation, and interdependence among groups, societies, and nations	*World History* textbook (Chapter 23)

Continued on p. 65

LANGUAGE IMPLICATIONS ANALYSIS (AGREEMENTS MADE WITH ESOL TEACHER)

*1) Functions (examples cross-referenced from ESOL Curriculum)	*2) Text Types (cross-referenced from ESOL Curriculum)
EXPRESSIVE ☐ express feelings/clarify one's ideas OTHER: _____ INTERACTIONAL ☐ maintain social/work relationships OTHER: _____ DIRECTIVE ☐ give directions/question/instruct OTHER: _____ CLASSIFICATION ☐ define/classify/develop concepts OTHER: _____ PRINCIPLES ☐ explain/predict/generalize/infer/state cause & effect/analyze/synthesize/ summarize/paraphrase OTHER: _____ EVALUATION ☐ evaluate/judge/criticize/ analyze OTHER: _____ DESCRIPTION ☐ describe/compare/contrast/report/ name OTHER: _____ SEQUENCE ☐ sequence/narrate/relay steps in process OTHER: _____ CHOICE ☐ negotiate/argue/express opinion OTHER: _____ IMAGINATIVE ☐ discuss literature/create stories/ solve problems or mysteries OTHER: _____	☐ narrative (stories, biographies) ☐ recount (science method, math steps) ☐ informative report (health allergies) ☐ procedure (operating computer device) ☐ explanation (digestion process) ☐ description (describe a scene) ☐ argument/persuasion (letter to editor) ☐ discussion (letter to editor for an idea) ☐ exposition (cause/effect, compare/ contrast, definition) ☐ multiple texts (combination description/explanation, etc.) ☐ summary/notes ☐ newspaper report ☐ diary/reflection (of literature piece) ☐ poems ☐ letters

* Five elements of language implications to be considered in writing language implications on ISB's curriculum templates

Continued on p. 66

LANGUAGE IMPLICATIONS ANALYSIS (AGREEMENTS MADE WITH ESOL TEACHER)

*3) Vocabulary
 	
  a) **Topic Specific**
    (i.e., content/subject area vocabulary)
 	
  b) **Academic**
    (i.e., vocabulary ESOL students need to understand the lesson)
	*4) Language Features
	(grammar, structure, punctuation, style, etc.)
	
	(This is determined via oral/ written text analysis of readings and other assignments within the core courses.)

*5) Cultural Understandings **(Student prior knowledge, shared understandings, conveyance of different meanings, links between culture and subject matter, key concepts and identity, comparing groups and subject, and students being able to demonstrate their own knowledge)** **Gr. 9–12 Poetry** • Knowing that Western poets also romanticized war at certain times, especially World War I **Gr. 10 Biology** • Understanding deductive logic and its application **Gr. 10 Modern World History** • Understanding that imperialistic aims are viewed differently in different times by different countries	**Assessed by (Core Teacher/ESOL Teacher/Other)** **(This is where agreements between teachers are recorded.)** **Gr. 9–12 Poetry** *Core Teacher* • Outcomes, topic-specific vocabulary, cultural understandings • Language features: style effects, punctuation *ESOL Teacher* • Other language features **Gr. 10 Biology** *Core Teacher* • Outcomes; topic-specific vocabulary; cultural understandings *ESOL Teacher* • Academic vocabulary; reinforce topic-specific vocabulary; strategies; test preview **Gr. 10 Modern World History** *Core Teacher* • Outcomes, topic-specific vocabulary, cultural understandings, text type for compare/contrast (as part of essay assessment) *ESOL Teacher* • Academic vocabulary, functions and language features for compare/contrast

* Five elements of language implications to be considered in writing language implications on ISB's curriculum templates

CHAPTER 5

Coteaching in a Sheltered Model: Maximizing Content and Language Acquisition for Beginning-Level English Language Learners

Carolyn Bernache, Kathleen Galinat, and Sandra Jimenez

◈ INTRODUCTION

The current educational environment in the United States includes pressure to prepare increasingly larger numbers of English language learners to meet content standards and be prepared for mandated state and local assessments. Given these dynamics, the staff and administration of Buck Lodge Middle School, in Adelphi, Maryland, a suburb of Prince George's County, felt it was imperative to integrate content instruction into the initial levels of English language acquisition. Although many English for speakers of other languages (ESOL) programs incorporate elements of content instruction at the beginning level and many sheltered courses attempt to modify content instruction to overcome language barriers, based on our experience neither of these approaches was successful at maintaining consistent and authentic language acquisition and content instruction across the curriculum. Ultimately, we were looking for a program that would maximize student achievement. According to Crandall, Bernache, and Prager (1998), some of the features that characterize successful programs include:

- a scaffolded sequence of courses that integrates ESOL instruction with grade-level-appropriate content knowledge (this combination of materials may be presented either by a content teacher with ESOL training or in a coteaching model with a content teacher and an ESOL teacher working together)

- additional instructional time

- thematic or parallel instruction across the curriculum

- opportunities for individual attention

- opportunities to interact with spoken and written academic English at the appropriate level, with the level of English increasing in difficulty as students' language mastery progresses

- common planning time among all teachers working with beginning-level English language learners to foster interdisciplinary teaching and the development of thematic units that integrate students' learning across curricular areas

- sustained program of professional development

Currently, some programs place ESOL students in low-track classes with low-achieving native-English-speaking students. This practice offers "the fewest opportunities for student interaction and extended spoken or written discourse because teacher-centered instruction and individual seat work activities dominate class time" (Harper & Platt, 1998, p. 33). Without appropriate English language instruction, many beginning-level ESOL students become disengaged from, or at best passive participants, in mainstream content instruction (Harper & Platt, 1998). These students are often characterized as having behavior problems, special education disabilities, or being quiet and withdrawn. In other programs, beginning-level ESOL students are placed in mainstream classes where the number of students makes it difficult for teachers to implement strategies to meet ESOL students' needs. Typically, the verbal and instructional level in these classes is higher than the comprehension level of the beginning ESOL student. Yet another approach is to place beginning-level ESOL students into a sheltered content class designed to meet the needs of intermediate-level ESOL students. Although more ESOL strategies are incorporated, a significant disparity still exists between the verbal and instructional level of the class and the level of comprehension and oral production of the beginning-level students.

Like many other districts, Prince George's County is in the process of redesigning programs to better address the acquisition of oral and written academic English in mainstream or sheltered classes. For 4 years, Buck Lodge Middle School has piloted a cutting-edge program of cotaught sheltered instruction for beginning-level English language learners. The development of this program was framed on the features quoted from Crandall, Bernache, and Prager (1998). This pilot program provides beginning-level ESOL students with access to grade-level content material while maximizing opportunities for the development of basic interpersonal communication skills (BICS) as well as cognitive academic language proficiency skills (CALPS). Given the short time students spend in Buck Lodge's 2-year middle-school program, the priority of this program was to intensify integrated language acquisition and content instruction so that students could "catch up with their native-English-speaking peers in order to graduate before they reach the age limit for high school" (Peyton & Adger, 1999, p. 4).

In this chapter, we highlight the pilot program at Buck Lodge. We look at the educational context of Buck Lodge and articulate the rationale of the program, including project development, its design, the obstacles that had to be overcome, and the lessons learned. We also identify the distinguishing features of this program and culminate with a sample thematic unit.

◈ CONTEXT

Buck Lodge Middle School is recognized as one of the most diverse schools in Prince George's County, the 19th-largest school district in the nation. With approximately 900 students in seventh and eighth grades, more than 40 nationalities are represented and 80 languages are spoken at this school. Figure 1 indicates the ethnic diversity of the student population.

African American	Hispanic	Asian	Native American	Caucasian
51.2%	37%	5.8%	0.4%	5.6%

FIGURE 1. Ethnic Diversity of Student Population at Buck Lodge Middle School in 2000 (Data from *Maryland School Performance Program Report, 2000.*)

These percentages do not reflect the approximately 40% of all students classified as African American but who are actually foreign-born immigrants from African or Caribbean countries. Other characteristics of this student population include high levels of transience, totaling about 46% of all students. This results in high numbers of incoming beginning-level ESOL students throughout the school year. The school also has a high incidence of poverty: According to the *Maryland School Performance Program (MSPP) Report* (2000), 68% of students from this school participate in the free/reduced-price lunch program. About 10% of ESOL students at Buck Lodge and its feeder high-school populations have received 3 years or less of formalized education in their country, and 23% of beginning-level ESOL students have 0–3 years of formal schooling in their native country, thus requiring initial literacy and English language development at the same time. In addition to their language needs, these students' academic deficits require targeted and comprehensive interventions in order to be overcome.

The context from which this program developed was one in which beginning-level ESOL students were receiving 90 minutes of self-contained ESOL instruction per day. However, many content teachers at Buck Lodge were concerned with the large number of Ds and Es that these students were receiving in math, science, social studies, and reading. Additionally, behavior and attendance problems were higher among the students with 0–3 years of formal schooling in their native country. Teachers were concerned with the limited staff development provided to mainstream content teachers who were not familiar with strategies appropriate for the beginning-level ESOL students in their regular classes. Both ESOL and content teachers were frustrated by the lack of content texts and materials appropriate for the beginning-level English language learner.

As a result, the administration proposed the implementation of a cotaught sheltered model for limited formally schooled and beginning-level English language learners that paired an ESOL teacher with mainstream teachers to integrate language and literacy acquisition with grade-appropriate content delivery across the curriculum. The administrators and teachers identified the following factors as being critical to the success of the program: voluntary mainstream teacher participation, consistent and ongoing teacher training/staff development, use of grade-level appropriate curricula and support materials, and creative scheduling.

◈ DESCRIPTION

Program design began by assessing the needs of all beginning-level ESOL students. It was determined that these students ranged from those with no prior academic background who were unable to read, write, or do basic computations in their first language to those who may have had as many as 6 years of academic preparation but no English language proficiency. To accommodate the wide differences in first language literacy, these English language learners were grouped into two classes. One class, designated ESOL Level 1A, included those students who were determined to be "underschooled" in their first language (i.e., they had 3 years or less of formal education and/or marginal literacy skills). The other class, ESOL Level 1B, was for all other beginning-level English language learners.

When the program was implemented in the 1996–1997 school year, only one ESOL teacher was available to coteach the core content subjects (language arts, social studies, science, math, and health) with the non-ESOL-trained content teachers. The content teachers involved in the program taught both levels of ESOL students (Levels 1A and 1B) in their specific subject area. The schedule was designed to provide more assistance for the underschooled students (Level 1A). Although the ESOL teacher was not present in some of the Level 1B classes, the content teachers were already familiar with the lesson and the instructional strategies as modeled by and cotaught with the ESOL teacher in the Level 1A section. Figure 2 provides the daily schedules for Levels 1A and 1B students. Cotaught classes are indicated by bold print.

This schedule represents a typical day; however, if a content teacher saw a specific need for coteaching assistance during the Level 1B math, science, social studies, or health class, the ESOL teacher could modify his or her schedule to be available for that period.

With each class lasting 45 minutes, the Level 1A underschooled students received 3 hours and 45 minutes of integrated content and ESOL instruction daily. The Level 1B students received a minimum of 1 hour and 30 minutes of cotaught content and ESOL instruction. The content teacher in the Level 1B classes implemented the Level 1A strategies and materials that had been codeveloped with the ESOL teacher. This allowed the Level 1B students to receive 3 hours and 45 minutes of targeted language acquisition and content instruction. To further support the professional development of the teachers in the program and the implementation of ESOL strategies, the ESOL coteacher and content teachers shared a common lunch time and planning time. Additionally, the ESOL teacher attended all team meetings to address concerns about the progress of ESOL students.

All of the content teachers who volunteered to participate in this program had

ESOL Level 1A (underschooled)	ESOL Level 1B (all others)
Class 1 Language Arts	Class 1 Math
Class 2 Reading	Class 2 Science
Class 3 Math	Class 3 Health
Class 4 Science	Class 4 Social Studies
Class 5 Lunch	Class 5 Lunch
Class 6 Art/Music (Team Planning)	Class 6 Physical Education
Class 7 Social Studies	Class 7 Art/Music
Class 8 Health	**Class 8 Language Arts**
Class 9 Physical Education	**Class 9 Reading**

Note. Cotaught classes are indicated by bold print.

FIGURE 2. ESOL/Content Coteaching Schedule

more than 20 years of teaching experience; however, they had no formal ESOL training. To supply the needed ESOL pedagogy, these teachers participated in regularly scheduled training/staff development sessions provided by the ESOL coteacher. These sessions were conducted after school hours, and teachers received a stipend for attending. Topics addressed during these sessions had common application across the curriculum, such as the methodology of initial reading instruction through content materials. These staff development opportunities allowed teachers to self-reflect on the progress of the program and their students.

Both of the Level 1 classes had 12 students in September but increased to 26 by the beginning of the 4th quarter of the school year. The design of the program allowed the school to address the constant influx of beginning-level ESOL students. As a result of the increased amount of ESOL/content instruction, most students progressed in their language acquisition at an accelerated rate. As students' linguistic and academic skills increased, they were able to move to a higher level. Because of this upward mobility, appropriate placement was available for new students who arrived throughout the year. As new students arrived, a class was available that was appropriate for their academic and linguistic level. Instruction in the Level 1A class continued to target the needs of underschooled non-English-speaking students, and Level 1B was for non-English-speaking students with academic backgrounds in another language.

◈ DISTINGUISHING FEATURES

There are several aspects of the cotaught ESOL/content program in our district that distinguish it from other existing ESOL programs. First is the manner in which ESOL instruction is delivered to beginning-level English language learners. In this model, students receive content instruction from a mainstream content teacher who benefits from a variety of services provided by the ESOL teacher. These services include coteaching on a daily basis, coplanning, resource material support, and ongoing in-service training in appropriate ESOL strategies. Beginning-level ESOL students are not "pulled out" to receive ESOL instruction as a separate component of their academic day. Rather, English language acquisition is integrated into all content areas throughout the day. The ESOL teacher who travels with his or her students to their math, science, social studies, and language arts classes facilitates this process with the content teachers.

The second distinguishing feature of this program is the instructional materials used. Traditionally, sheltered ESOL courses rely on content trade materials that have been modified specifically for ESOL students and are presented by an ESOL teacher. However, in the coteaching model, the regular mainstream text and support materials are used with both the Level 1A students (0–3 years of schooling in their native language) as well as the Level 1B students within the first weeks of school. For example, the social studies and science teachers use the mainstream text to teach students to gather information from pictures, graphs, charts, and selected short readings. These readings may be from a sentence or two to several paragraphs in length. The language arts teacher introduces a variety of genres: biography, autobiography, poetry, as well as basic narrative writing and writing to inform by using selections from the mainstream curriculum. Trade and support materials, such as *Happy Birthday, Martin Luther King* (Marzollo, 1993) and selections on Columbus

Day and Kwanzaa, are used to provide authentic reading tasks related to holidays. The math teacher teaches basic math operations and introduces word problems, helping to reinforce reading skills that are being taught in the reading class. The math teacher first introduces the mainstream text as a source of basic practice problems and later to support topics such as graphing, probability, and percents and decimals. For the Level 1B students, use of the mainstream text is a greater part of the daily instruction from the outset. However, in both groups the goal is to use the mainstream texts as often as possible so that students become familiar with their formats and develop the academic reading skills needed to interact with grade-level materials and resources.

In addition to using mainstream texts, the ESOL and content teachers develop thematic support materials including warm-ups, short readings, cloze activities targeting content vocabulary, and follow-up activities highlighting the use of strategies designed to support multiple intelligences. This collaboration results in interdisciplinary thematic units across the curriculum that accelerates both linguistic acquisition and academic content mastery. As noted by Silver (1997), this type of teacher collaboration and interdisciplinary instruction is recommended to make secondary curriculum more comprehensible to limited English proficient learners. A consistent linguistic framework underlies instruction from one classroom to another. Vocabulary, grammatical structures, and basic academic content are framed and used in each of the core content classes. This systematic exposure to targeted linguistic and academic knowledge enhances both language and content acquisition.

A third distinguishing feature of this program is the integration of reading instruction to parallel content and language acquisition across the curriculum. Through the weekly team meetings and staff development sessions, each core content teacher is informed of which grammatical patterns and phonemic elements are being introduced in the reading/English/language arts (RELA) class. For example, during the first quarter, students in Levels 1A and 1B would be focusing on the present tense of the verb *to be* and regular present tense verbs, pronouns, and interrogatives used in declarative statements and questions. Phonemic awareness of beginning, ending, and medial consonants, as well as long vowel sounds signaled by silent *e*, would also be introduced. Therefore, daily reinforcing written and oral practice of these phonemic elements could be provided through math, science, social studies, and health classes. This meant that students received deliberate targeted linguistic instruction throughout their day, rather than only in a self-contained ESOL classroom, with little, if any, deliberate linguistic follow-up in other content-area classrooms.

The fourth distinguishing feature of this program is the direct correlation of in-service training to the needs of the mainstream teachers. As either the ESOL teacher or the mainstream content teachers perceived instructional questions and challenges, immediate support can be provided by formal or informal means. In some cases, the ESOL teacher provides immediate intervention. This intervention might be in the form of modeling, restating questions or clarifying content information for greater student understanding, or supplying written follow-up activities. In other cases, the in-service training can be provided during team meetings or after school. Figure 3 provides a partial list of topics for in-service training. See Bernache (1999) for a further discussion and explanation of the strategies in Figure 3, as well as outlines of the actual workshops.

- Knowing our beginning-level English language learners (cultural, historical, social awareness, what to expect from the beginning-level student, etc.)
- Developing phonemic awareness through content materials with strategies such as the *cloze spelling*
- Teaching the underlying academic literacy skills, such as tracking and visual discrimination
- Integrating vocabulary development techniques and strategies
- Interpreting behavioral clues (Is the student's skill level matching the task or assignment?)
- Modifying instruction based on skill proficiency (page density, question type, etc.)
- Developing appropriate performance tasks
- Assessing

FIGURE 3. In-Service Training Topics

◈ PRACTICAL IDEAS

Planning is the key to the integration of language acquisition and content features into instructional units. The following considerations assisted us in developing lesson plans:

- Select authentic content that is appropriate to the age and grade levels of students.
- Determine the key concepts to be presented (these should be limited to not more than five major concepts).
- Identify the key content vocabulary needed to acquire major concepts.
- Develop literacy and/or content objectives as appropriate.
- Present the content material using as many modalities as possible.
- Provide comprehensible text for students to read with teacher assistance.
- Allow students to reread the comprehensible text and respond to the comprehension questions.
- Provide opportunities for students to respond orally and in writing using complete sentences and then share their written answers.
- Assess students' progress toward meeting literacy and/or content objectives using oral, written, and/or alternative assessment methods.

Research indicates that thematic units across the content increase English language proficiency (Silver, 1997). This chapter's appendix provides one example of how second language acquisition and content can be integrated across the curriculum using a thematic unit.

◈ CONCLUSION

This case study has illustrated how beginning-level ESOL instruction can be integrated across the curriculum by using appropriate mainstream content and ESOL strategies that are delivered through a coteaching model by a content teacher and an ESOL teacher. To assist others with the implementation of this model, we have described the critical factors that need to be addressed, which include voluntary mainstream teacher participation, consistent and ongoing teacher training/staff development, the use of grade-level appropriate curricula and support materials, and creative scheduling. The appendix includes a sample unit, which balances language and content acquisition, to serve as a template for the creation of other cross-curricular thematic units. Because of the unique instructional delivery, the authentic nature of the instructional materials used, the integration of language acquisition and initial reading instruction across the curriculum, and the ongoing correlation of in-service training to meet the needs of the classroom teachers, the cotaught sheltered program at Buck Lodge addresses the challenge of supporting initial second language acquisition and grade-level appropriate academic content and skills by enabling content teachers and ESOL teachers to work as equal partners to meet the challenging academic needs of our beginning English language learners, even those with limited prior schooling or literacy.

◈ CONTRIBUTORS

Carolyn Bernache is an ESOL specialist at Langley Park McCormick Elementary School in Prince George's County, Maryland, in the United States. She is the author of *Gateway to Achievement in the Content Areas* (published by the National Textbook Company in 1994), a text for developing academic ESOL literacy. Her dissertation explores teacher perceptions of ESOL literacy students and how the effects of those perceptions impact instruction.

Kathleen Galinat has taught Grades 1–8 in Prince George's County for 30 years. She has received the Washington Post Distinguished Educational Leadership Award. She is a teacher and the language arts coordinator at Buck Lodge Middle School, in Maryland.

Sandra Jimenez is the principal of Langley Park McCormick Elementary School, in Maryland. She has taught at the elementary through university levels in ESOL and bilingual programs in the United States and other countries.

◈ APPENDIX: MARTIN LUTHER KING, JR.— BEGINNING-LEVEL ESOL THEMATIC UNIT

Boldfaced items indicate activities that are included in the pages following the chart.

Language Arts	Math	Social Studies	Science
• Introduction of core vocabulary (*leader, protest, speech, peaceful,* etc.)	• **Use of core vocabulary in word problems based on information from Dr. King's life**	• Use of the core vocabulary to create a timeline of Dr. King's life	• **Use of core vocabulary to describe Dr. King's non-violent strategies through the scientific method (the Montgomery Bus Boycott)**
• Presentation of Dr. King's life in a visual manner	• **Use of ordinal numbers and symbols to sequence the events in Dr. King's life**	• **Use of core vocabulary to create an accordion booklet, sequencing teacher-supplied sentence strips (students develop the illustrations for this booklet)**	
• **Presentation of Dr. King's life in a short, compre-hensible, teacher-made reading selection**			
• Presentation of grammatical concepts: nouns, verbs, contractions, etc.			
• Presentation of language mechanics			
• **Sequencing**			

Dr. Martin Luther King, Jr., Lesson Plan

Objectives: Students will be able to:

- practice tracking while reading a story about Dr. Martin Luther King, Jr.
- scan for information
- answer the five Ws orally and in writing using key content words
- review capitalization and end punctuation

Warm-Up: Students will be able to:

- write the spelling words in alphabetical order
- rewrite the sentences using capitalization and end-punctuation clues

Vocabulary	Alphabetical Order	Sentences
Protest		1. is leader. Martin Luther King a famous.
Leader	1.	
Speech		2. a famous He speech. Made
Peaceful	2.	
Famous		3. believed peaceful in He protests.
Believe	3.	

Introductory Activity: Using the visualizer or an overhead projector, the teacher will model reading the picture book *Happy Birthday, Martin Luther King* (Marzollo, 1993). After the students have heard the story and seen the pictures, the teacher will lead students through a picture walk of the book, asking questions such as, "Who do you see in the picture?" "Is Dr. King a boy?" "Do you see a bus?" etc.

Developmental Activity:

- *Provide comprehensible text for students to read with teacher assistance.*
- *Allow students to reread the comprehensible text and respond to oral comprehension questions.*

Viewing the text on the overhead projector (with the questions covered), students will read an adapted story about Dr. Martin Luther King, Jr. (included in the article entitled "Dr. Martin Luther King, Jr."). As each paragraph is finished, ask students the appropriate questions from the list (without uncovering the list) for students to find the answers in the text and read them aloud.

Guided Practice:

- *Identify key content vocabulary.*
- *Allow students to reread comprehensible text and respond to comprehension questions.*
- *Provide opportunities for students to respond orally and in writing using complete sentences and then share their written answers.*

Uncover the first question in the list. Read the question out loud (or have a student read it). Students will find the answer by scanning for information. They will read the answer aloud, and the teacher will record the answer on the overhead projector. Continue with other questions as needed.

Independent Activity:

- *Identify key content vocabulary.*
- *Allow students to reread comprehensible text and respond to comprehension questions.*
- *Provide opportunities for students to respond orally and in writing using complete sentences and then share their written answers.*
- *Assess students' progress toward meeting literacy and/or content objectives using oral, written, and/or alternative assessment methods.*

Distribute individual copies of the story and comprehension questions. Students will respond to the comprehension questions, using complete sentences with appropriate capitalization and end-punctuation conventions.

Assessment:

- *Assess students' progress toward meeting literacy and/or content objectives using oral, written, and/or alternative assessment methods.*

Using the following questions, assess students' responses:

- Did the student answer the questions correctly?
- Did the student use correct capitalization and end-punctuation marks?

Then have students share their responses by writing them on the overhead.

Closure:

- *Provide opportunities for students to respond orally in complete sentences.*
- *Assess students' progress toward meeting literacy and/or content objective.*

Using the written daily objective, students will be asked to summarize what they have learned and to evaluate their progress toward meeting the objective.

Developmental Activity—Questions to Be Used Orally

Dr. Martin Luther King, Jr.

Dr. Martin Luther King is a famous American. Dr. King was born on January 15, 1929. We celebrate his birthday on Monday, January _____. It is a holiday. There is no school.

Dr. Martin Luther King was a leader. He did not believe in violence. He believed in peaceful protests. Dr. King used peaceful protests to change bad laws. He wanted equality for black Americans. He made a very famous speech in Washington, DC. He said, "I have a dream" that all Americans will be able to live as brothers.

Dr. Martin Luther King was an important person. There are many schools named for him. There are many libraries named for him. There are many roads named for him.

Dr. Martin Luther King died in 1968. He was 39 years old.

1. When was Dr. Martin Luther King born?

    _____

2. When do we celebrate Dr. King's birthday?

    _____

3. Where did Dr. Martin Luther King make a famous speech?

    _____

4. Why are there schools, libraries, and roads named for Dr. King?

    _____

5. When did Dr. Martin Luther King die?

    _____

6. How old was Dr. Martin Luther King?

    _____

The remaining activities in this unit are examples of cross-curricular support materials for math, social studies, and science. These materials focus on grade-level appropriate content and critical vocabulary while reinforcing content knowledge, skill development, oral and written language acquisition, and higher level thinking. These materials take the content knowledge that is learned in language arts into other subject areas, providing a common foundation of vocabulary with which to manipulate content skills while strengthening oral and written communication skills.

The Montgomery Bus Boycott

Directions: Cut out the following sentences. Arrange the sentences in chronological order on your answer sheet. Label them with the words first, second, etc. Label them with the symbols 1st, 2nd, etc.

The police were unhappy with Dr. King.
The bus driver was unhappy with Rosa Parks.
The police arrested Rosa Parks.
After one year, black people could sit in any seat on a bus.
Rosa Parks got on a bus.
Rosa Parks sat in the front of the bus.
The bus driver called the police.
Dr. King told black people to walk to work.
Black people were unhappy.
Black people were happy.

THE MONTGOMERY BUS BOYCOTT ANSWER SHEET

Word	Symbol	Sentence
First	1st	Rosa Parks got on a bus.

Dr. Martin Luther King, Jr.: Thematic Unit Word Problems

Directions: Read and solve each of the following word problems.

1. Dr. Martin Luther King, Jr., was born in 1929. He died in 1968. How old was he when he died? Show your work.

2. Dr. King gave his "I Have a Dream" speech in Washington, DC, in 1963. How many years was this before he died? Show your work.

3. Approximately 250,000 people listened to Dr. King speak on August 28, 1963. If the crowd was made up of 15% children and 85% adults, how many children heard Dr. King's speech? How many adults heard his speech? Show your work.

Creating an Accordion Booklet

Directions: Cut a 12 x 18 inch sheet of drawing paper into two 6 x 18 inch pieces. Fold each strip, accordion style, so that each panel is 6 x 6 inches. Staple an end together with an end of the second strip. You should have a title page and six sections to draw and read about six events in sequence of Dr. King's life.

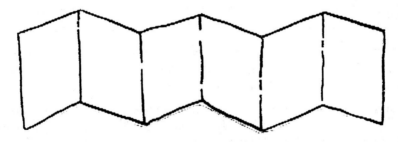

- Dr. Martin Luther King, Jr.

- Martin Luther King was born in Atlanta, Georgia, on January 15, 1929.

- Martin was a good student.

- Martin became a pastor (minister) at a church in Atlanta. He was called Reverend Martin Luther King, Jr.

- Dr. King gave his famous "I Have a Dream" speech in the summer of 1963 in Washington, DC. His dream was that people everywhere would learn to live together in peace.

- Martin Luther King was shot and killed (assassinated) in 1968. On his gravestone were the words, "Free at last, free at last! Thank God Almighty, I'm free at last."

- Because Martin Luther King worked so hard for freedom and helped change some laws, we honor him every year with a Martin Luther King Day.

Applying the Scientific Method

Problem: Martin Luther King, Jr., and Rosa Parks were examples of how people used peaceful methods to solve problems. Can people in the 21st century use these peaceful methods?

Hypothesis: I think that people in the 21st century can use peaceful methods to solve problems.

Procedure: Create a survey to pass out to other students in the community. The survey should resemble something as follows:

1. Have you ever gone to peer mediation? If yes, answer the following questions.

2. Was your problem resolved by going to peer mediation?

3. If your problem was not resolved, did people become violent?

Data/Results: Data should be organized in a table.

Solution to Problem	Number of Students
Resolved peacefully	
Resulted in violence	
Total number of students	

Results could be displayed in a bar graph or written out stating how many students resolved their problem peacefully versus how many did not.

Conclusion: There are peaceful methods of solving problems. The results in this experiment supported the hypothesis that predicted people in the 21st century could resolve problems peacefully. Through exploring the peaceful resolutions of peer mediation, it can be concluded that, like Dr. King and Ms. Parks, we can live together in peace.

CHAPTER 6

Working Together to Raise Content-Based Instruction Into the Zone of Proximal Development

Tatiana Gordon

◈ INTRODUCTION

This chapter describes a school-university partnership that was created to explore instructional implications of Vygotsky's language development theory (1934, 1956, 1978) and to apply this theory in the content-based English for speakers of other languages (ESOL) classroom. In the content-based instruction (CBI) classroom, where the process of developing learners' academic language skills takes center stage, principles of zone of proximal development (ZPD) pedagogy, such as teaching of *schooled concepts* (Gallimore & Tharp, 1990, p. 193), use of scaffolding and other cognitive tools for mediating learning (e.g., Clay & Cazden, 1990), or conceptualization of teaching as assisted performance (e.g., Moll, 1990) acquire crucial importance. Applying the Vygotskian language development paradigm in the CBI classroom is a challenging task because of the complexity inherent in planning (Bragger & Rice, 1998; Holten, 1997; Met, 1991, 1994) and implementing (Holten, 1997; Richards, Li, & Tang, 1998; Short, 1997) content-based lessons.

Continuing the work of educators who explore instructional implications of Vygotsky's developmental theory (Dixon-Kraus, 1996; Moll, 1990; Newman, Griffin, & Cole, 1989; Tharp & Gallimore, 1988), the partnership involves administrators, expert teachers, teacher educators, and teacher-learners in action research work focusing on the exploration of the ZPD instruction in the context of content-based language teaching. The partnership seeks to apply Vygotskian theory to practice and to develop an electronic pool of cognitively stimulating CBI activities for the benefit of all partnership participants.

◈ CONTEXT

Hofstra University is a private school with a student body of nearly 5,000 students. The TESOL Program, which is housed in the Department of Curriculum and Teaching of the university's School of Education and Allied Human Services, has two tracks. The preservice track is intended for uncertified students; the in-service track is intended for those who are already certified in an area other than TESOL.

The program's partner, the Nassau Board of Cooperative Educational Services (BOCES), is an agency that provides ESOL and bilingual instructional services to various schools in Long Island's Nassau County. Alongside with instructional services, BOCES provides staff development and curriculum development support to various Long Island school districts and offers technical assistance to districts when they solicit information concerning New York State Education Department mandates, laws, and regulations. Additionally, the agency assists districts in evaluating their ESOL/bilingual programs and provides recommendations for the enhancement of instruction and staff performance.

Hofstra's TESOL Program places special emphasis on CBI. The CBI model is a common thread that links both of the program's TESOL methodology classes (one of which focuses on the elementary-level learner; the other, on the secondary-level learner). Notably, in our program, most pedagogical issues are examined in relation to content-based language teaching. Whether teacher-learners explore curriculum planning, academic literacy development, or alternative assessment, they focus on the interface of these topics with the CBI model. For their observation and student teaching experiences, we seek to place teacher-learners in the schools that have a proven record of implementing effective content-based ESOL teaching. The compilation of electronic portfolios, a graduation requirement for this program, involves the development of content-based interdisciplinary thematic units for elementary- and secondary-level learners; portfolio submissions include various artifacts, including examples of student work produced in the content-based classroom.

◈ DESCRIPTION

The partnership was conceived when Hofstra's TESOL teacher educators and BOCES faculty and administrators were discussing major challenges related to the planning and implementation of effective CBI. During these conversations, it was pointed out that positioning CBI in the language learners' ZPD is one of the most demanding tasks with which the ESOL teacher is confronted.

ZPD-positioned instruction is conceptualized here as the kind of teaching that "awakens and rouses to life those functions which are in the stage of maturity" (Vygotsky, 1956, p. 278), or, in other words, the teaching positioned at the "cutting edge of the child's competencies" (Clay & Cazden, 1990, p. 218). It was this cognitively demanding instruction that we found to be particularly hard to ensure in the CBI classroom. In the course of our meetings, we identified the following two areas of challenge.

Lesson Planning

In the content-based classroom, one of the most onerous jobs relates to planning for learning objectives positioned in learners' ZPD. We noted that teacher-learners in particular had difficulty planning for instructional objectives that were cognitively stimulating. For instance, when developing an instructional unit on dinosaurs for third graders, a teacher-learner might choose to teach concrete lexical items such as *dinosaur* but neglect the exploration of related abstract concepts, such as *fossil* or *extinction.*

The difficulty that we experienced in planning for higher-order learning objectives in the CBI classroom is not surprising. The teacher working in the CBI classroom is expected to develop instructional objectives whose parameters are singularly intricate. The teacher needs to identify the content obligatory and the content-compatible vocabulary (Met, 1994), that is, target language items crucial for or related to describing given content. Moreover, she or he needs to be able to assess *both* the level of students' language proficiency *and* the nature of their needs in the content areas (Bragger & Rice, 1998) and subsequently develop a range of instructional objectives that are congruent with these disparate linguistic and academic needs. When discussing the challenge of addressing both learner content and language needs, Holten notes that teachers who work in the CBI classroom "find that lesson planning becomes something akin to juggling: they must teach the content of the unit, as well as reading, writing and listening skills" (1997, p. 382). In view of these challenges inherent in planning for CBI, it is not surprising that partnership participants, especially teacher-learners, were observed to experience difficulty in developing instructional objectives that were not only *linguistically feasible* but also *cognitively stimulating*. Learners' limited second language (L2) proficiency seems to have caused teacher-learners (and occasionally even expert teachers) to plan for content objectives positioned in the zone of learners' actual— rather than proximal—development.

Lesson Implementation

The second challenge that we identified affected the actual implementation of content-based lessons. Partnership participants spoke of the trying task of designing activities that would transport learners to the farthest limits of their ZPD. We discussed the difficulty inherent in contextualizing context-reduced vocabulary (Cummins, 1994) or engaging students in sustained and meaningful academic literacy tasks (Snow, 1997). We pointed out that we found it to be particularly hard to engage learners in cognitively substantive academic experiences that involve personally meaningful negotiation and application of academic language. Partnership participants referred to excessive reliance on duplicated materials and lack of in-depth exploration of the subject matter as especially prevalent in content-based classrooms taught by novices.

This challenge has been described by Richards, Li, and Tang (1998), who point out that inexperienced teachers who work in the CBI classroom tend to have difficulty in helping learners acquire "deeper understanding of the subject matter" and "integrating language learning with broader curricular goals" (pp. 99–100). Short describes the secondary-level CBI classroom where teaching is "still delivered through the teacher lecture-textbook reading mode" (1997, p. 215); Holten observes that students in the content-based courses tend to "dismiss the content as boring, inapplicable, and unsuited to their academic needs" (1997, p. 380).

Summarizing the challenges experienced when planning and implementing CBI, the partnership participants found themselves confronted with the following two action research questions:

- What can we do to position learning objectives of content-based lessons in the farthest reaches of learners' ZPD?

- What can we do to develop meaningful and engaging learning activities that transport learners to the farthest reaches of their ZPD?

Having formulated the action research agenda, we proceeded to familiarize ourselves with research pertaining to exploration of Vygotsky's developmental model and its instructional implications (Dixon-Krauss, 1996; Moll, 1990; Newman, Griffin, & Cole, 1989; Tharp & Gallimore, 1988; Vygotsky, 1934, 1978). These readings informed the partnership's mission as well as its subsequent action research efforts.

Before outlining our own work of linking developmental theory with content-based language instruction, I would like to point out that it seems fitting that ZPD theory was adopted by the partnership as a framework for the problem analysis. After all, the goal behind Vygotsky's work was to enhance educational practices in his own country, Russia. In Moll's words (1990, p. 2), Vygotsky "emphasized educational change as a practical objective of his psychology." As Moll points out, Vygotsky's aim was to "develop concrete solutions to problems in education" (p. 2).

◈ DISTINGUISHING FEATURES

Applying Language Development Theory to Practice

Language development theory provided the partnership with a unified, comprehensive analytical framework; even more important, the partnership deployed the theory as a tool for problem resolution. The following cornerstones of ZPD theory informed the partnership's action research efforts.

Scientific Concepts and Their Conscious Use

Researchers (e.g., Panofsky, John-Steiner, & Blackwell, 1990) contend that teaching theoretical knowledge or schooled concepts or scientific concepts (to use some of the phrases deployed to render the Russian phrase *nauchnoe ponyatie* in English) is a cornerstone objective of teaching within ZPD. Studies of language development argue that "there is a qualitative difference between the concrete spontaneous concepts and the more abstract scientific concepts" (Dixon-Krauss, 1996, p. 44). Vygotsky (1934, 1978) and other researchers of the ZPD paradigm (e.g., Clay & Cazden, 1990; Gallimore & Tharp, 1990) point out that scientific concepts are learned in contexts of formal schooling, where they are examined as systems and used in purposeful and conscious ways. Gallimore and Tharp speak of schooling that enables learners to "experience language as a system" (1990, p. 194); Clay and Cazden say that in the ZPD classroom, learners are engaged in the "conscious manipulation of signs" (1990, p. 220). Given the importance of the use of schooled language for ZPD teaching, our goal is to foster instructional practices where language learners explore scientific concepts, become aware of systematic interrelations between them, and get to use these concepts in a purposeful and conscious way.

Instruction as Assisted Performance

The central tenet of ZPD teaching theory is that intrapsychological processes are preceded and preconditioned by interpsychological processes and that language development "first appears on the social plane, and then on the psychological plane" (Vygotsky, 1981, p. 163, as cited in Wertsch, 1990, p. 113). In the ZPD classroom, teaching is conceptualized as a social activity—most importantly assistance—with teachers guiding learners through tasks that learners cannot perform unassisted. In the words of Tharp and Gallimore (1988, p. 21) in the ZPD classroom, "students cannot be left to learn on their own; teachers cannot be content to provide opportunities to learn and then assess outcomes; recitation must be de-emphasized; responsive, assisting interaction must become commonplace." The interactive aspect of assistance is important to researchers of the ZPD paradigm. As Gallimore and Tharp put it, in the ZPD classroom, "productive interactions occur in goal-directed activity settings which are jointly undertaken by apprentices and experts" (1990, p. 200). To account for the interdependence of the interpsychological and the intrapsychological in language development, we strive to promote CBI where L2 learner-L2 teacher collaboration and interaction become an inalienable part of the academic process.

Use of Cognitive Tools

In our work, we are profoundly influenced by another central tenet of Vygotskian theory that "higher mental functioning is mediated by tools and signs" (Wertsch, 1990, p. 114). In everyday life, individuals make use of tools that help them perform various jobs. In the ZPD classroom, teachers provide assistance by involving learners in the manipulation of cognitive tools that facilitate concept comprehension and task completion. Referred to in later studies by the name of *scaffolds* (Wood, Brunner, & Ross, 1976, as cited in Tharp & Gallimore, 1988), these cognitive tools are exemplified in modeling, graphic organizers, semantic maps, and other means of assistance provided by the teacher. Given the critical importance of cognitive tools for the acquisition of scientific language, our partnership seeks to explore their potential for the CBI classroom.

Interface Between Schooled and Everyday Concepts

Studies of language development further point out that conscious use of scientific concepts is enhanced if they are linked to everyday concepts. In the words of Gallimore and Tharp, teaching within the zone is rendered more effective if it provides "the interface between emergent school concepts and everyday concepts," if school discourse is not only "hooked by system to the whole system of meaning given by schooling" but also "hooked by sense to everyday concepts" (1990, pp. 194–195). Given this language development contingency, we strive to promote teaching where learners explore the interface between schooled concepts and everyday language.

Authentic Exploratory Activity

The partnership's goals are informed by the work of Vygotskians who argue that teaching in ZPD is not concerned with the development of skills and subskills (Moll, 1990); rather it is carried out within "whole activities" (p. 8). These activities are meaningful, authentic (Goodman & Goodman, 1990), and exploratory (Hedegaard, 1990). Consistent with these principles, we are interested in promoting the functional and meaningful use of language in the content-based classroom.

Collaborating to Reposition Instruction

With a view toward effecting change in our classroom practice and applying major principles of language development theory, the partnership adopted a model developed by the Kamehameha Elementary Education Program (KEEP) (Tharp &

Gallimore, 1988). KEEP is a research-based project initiated by a team of psychologists, linguists, and teachers committed to researching and implementing ZPD instruction. The efforts of the KEEP team were particularly relevant to the Hofstra-BOCES partnership's action research agenda, because the team was working with a language and cultural minority student population. The KEEP team developed and tested instruction enhancement strategies while working with ethnic minority students, including Hawaiian children in Honolulu, Navajo children in Arizona, and language minority students in Los Angeles. Observation and conferencing as well as workshops (two strategies developed by KEEP staff toward effecting change in classroom practice) were adopted by the Hofstra-BOCES partnership.

Strategy 1: Observation

The first step toward meeting the partnership objectives is made when teacher-learners observe expert teachers and discuss their classroom practices. To render the observation process more meaningful and focused (Day, 1990; Richards, 1998), we have been using an observation questionnaire (see Appendix A), specially designed to help teacher-learners develop analytical frameworks that grow out of Vygotsky's educational theory. The questionnaire attracts the observer's attention to the ways in which various principles of the ZPD theory are put to work in the expert teacher's classroom.

Before observations start, teacher-learners participate in training sessions where they are trained to focus their attention as well as collect and record data (Richards, 1998). While collecting data, teacher-learners are instructed to identify specific lesson elements (e.g., instances of assisted practice, use of cognitive tools) and also provide a narrative meant to capture the details of the lesson.

Strategy 2: Project Consultation

During the next stage of collaborative action research, partnership participants engage in project consultation work. Tharp and Gallimore (1988) use the term *project consultation* to describe the effort where expert teachers, novice teachers, and teacher educators form a team upon which "the entire group operates in joint productive activity for the purpose of solving a particular problem" (p. 127). According to Tharp and Gallimore, project consultation is "the most powerful model" (p. 127) of instruction enhancement, because it helps overcome teachers' social isolation, "the major barrier to change in teaching process" (p. 190). As Gallimore and Tharp point out, "teachers, like their students, have ZPDs" (1990, p. 190); by engaging novices and experts in mutual assistance, project consultation teams help promote teacher professional development.

Typically, the work of the project consultation team starts with a teacher-learner developing a draft of an instructional unit upon which the team joins forces to explore possible ways of modifying the unit to raise it into learners' ZPD. Equipped with a questionnaire (see Appendix B), which serves as a tool for ZPD enhancement, the team considers how the unit can be adjusted to account for more consistent exploration of schooled language, more opportunities of the use of assisted practice as mediated by scaffolding, and more personally meaningful and more authentic classroom activities.

Each party contributes its own perspective to action research work. Whereas novice teachers tend to stimulate discussions with innovative and bold instructional decisions, expert teachers are better equipped to judge which of these are more viable and effective with a given student population. Hofstra's library and media resources are a powerful resource for lesson preparation, helping all participants acquire more in-depth knowledge of content and serving as repositories of ideas for more authentic classroom experiences. This is how one of the novice teachers describes her work with the team in her post-action journal.

> I can't believe how my lesson turned out. I thought I would just teach a short history lesson [on Johnny Apple Seed] and ended up doing science experiments where kids proved the presence of iron in apples and analyzed the symbolism of apples in American culture. Children also wrote Thank You notes to Johnny Apple Seeds and got to use all the new words that they had learned in writing. . . . I think the unit is fun and it turned out really great. I learned a lot from working with my team.

The work of project consultation teams has its own challenges. BOCES is a relatively small agency, and its affiliated faculty are not available to work with every single student in Hofstra's TESOL Program. In the future, the program plans to institutionalize its collaborations with its partners in a number of other school districts.

Creating the Pool of ZPD-Positioned Lessons

The results of the project consultation team efforts are made available to all BOCES- and Hofstra-affiliated faculty. For the benefit of the partnership participants, an electronic site called "ESL Activities Portfolio" was created (Hofstra University TESL Program/Nassau BOCES, 2005). The site serves as a clearinghouse of content-based interdisciplinary lessons.

Each unit featured on the site is aligned with the TESOL standards; a special emphasis is placed on those standards that relate to language learners' mastery of academic language (TESOL, 1997). When submitting their materials to the electronic site, partnership participants provide lesson plans as well as scanned copies of visual and graphic materials that can be used to enhance a given lesson. Whenever possible, site contributors describe the ways in which learners can be engaged in assisted performance when a given lesson is being delivered and also provide sample scaffolds that can be deployed to help learners produce academic work within the zone of their proximal development.

Use of Schooled Language

To render CBI more cognitively challenging, members of project consultation teams elevate learning objectives of instructional units to higher cognitive levels by focusing them on the systemic analysis of target language concepts from the domains of natural and social sciences. For instance, a fourth-grade unit integrates literacy learning objectives with the exploration of abstract concepts, such as *sexism* and *racism*. The integration of cognitive and literacy objectives is ensured by the unit structure. In the course of the unit, learners first analyze some instances of racism and sexism in the U.S. history and find out about citizens' heroic efforts to challenge institutionalized sexism and racism. For instance, students read *When Marion Sang* (Ryan, 2002), the story of Marion Anderson's heroic life and work. Following the history lessons, learners read *Amazing Grace* (Hoffman & Binch, 2003) which tells about Grace, an African American girl who is eager to try out for the part of Peter Pan in the school's production but is discouraged by those of her peers who feel that a black girl cannot cope with the role. When reading the book, the teacher stops midway (before Grace's crisis has been resolved by the author) and produces an envelope that contains a letter. The letter, which has been written by the teacher for Grace, is addressed to ESOL students and runs as follows.

Dear Class:

My name is Grace. I am in third grade.
I have a problem and I need your advice.
Today, I found my class will be performing the
play Peter Pan. I want to play the main role,
because I love to act. One classmate told me I
shouldn't audition, because I am a girl. Another
told me I shouldn't audition, because I am
black. What do you think I should do? Please
give me your honest opinion.

Thank you,
Grace

Now it is up to language learners to write letters of response giving their advice to Grace. In writing their letters, students not only express their opinions as to how Grace should handle her dilemma but also support their arguments by citing historic examples where individuals prevailed over the odds of sexism and racism in their society.

Assisted Performance

The project consultation team seeks to make sure that content-based lessons include various provisions for teacher-learner interaction and collaboration, such as brain-storming, step-by-step instruction, or guided participation (Tharp & Gallimore, 1988). Of all forms of assisted performance, questioning is given special attention in site activities, with most lessons containing interactive query-based learning experiences where the teacher does not merely test concept recall but also engages students in the application and critical examination of newly discovered schooled language (Kauchak & Eggen, 1998). For instance, an instructional unit that focuses on the exploration of the Americas by Columbus culminates in a full-scope questioning activity. Designed in the spirit of the transformation multicultural education, the activity invites learners to consider various perspectives on the exploration of the New World by the Europeans. The questioning activity is made possible by the sequential structure of the unit, which opens with shared reading experiences where students explore the cultural richness of the pre-Columbian Americas. During subsequent activities, students learn major facts of Columbus's voyage and then read an authentic document, a page from Columbus's diary in which Native American tribes are described as lacking in culture, poor, and so on. Following this reading, the teacher conducts a questioning activity whereby learners are encouraged to consider different and possibly opposing perspectives on the discovery of the New World.

Use of Cognitive Tools and Scaffolding

The scaffolds featured on the electronic site include semantic maps, charts, and graphic organizers, which facilitate understanding of context-reduced vocabulary, as well as story maps, graphic organizers, and word banks, which help sustain, organize, and elaborate performance of academic literacy tasks (Boyle & Peregoy, 1990; Peregoy & Boyle, 1990). When creating and using scaffolds, we are particularly interested in exploring the significance of modeling as "a powerful means of assistance," because modeling—a quintessential form of scaffolding—enables the teacher to maintain "the highest reaches of behavioral complexity" (Gallimore & Tharp, 1990, p. 179). The efforts of project consultation teams have focused on creating and deploying various types of models. For instance, a lesson that focuses on the solar system includes a total physical response (TPR) activity where learners impersonate planets to illustrate the concepts of rotation and revolution. We are also interested in exploring the role of modeling in the area of literacy instruction. In another unit that focuses on African culture, the teacher engages the class in the exploration of the significance of the myths of creation. As the unit's culminating activity, learners are supposed to write their own creation myths. To model task performance, the teacher not only read published myths but also wrote and illustrated her own myth of creation called "Why we have hurricanes," about a dance-loving but irritable cobra that, when performing a whirling dance and being in a particularly irritable state of mind, was unable to stop its dancing and thus created the Earth's first hurricane.

Linking Schooled Language With Personal Experiences

The site also contains instructional activities especially designed to enable learners to link schooled concepts to their day-to-day lives. For instance, in a culminating activity that focuses on the examination of food groups, students become food critics. The student "food critics" are commissioned by *The New York Times* to write reviews of food served at their neighborhood restaurants. Students are asked to visit the restaurants and write about the nutritional value of their dishes. A science lesson, which focuses on molecular activity and the link between kinetic energy and heat, integrates a series of questions that invite learners to examine common phenomena that exemplify the interrelationship between heat and molecular movement observed in day-to-day life. Students consider why substances, such as sugar, dissolve faster in warm tea, why their hands feel warm when they rub them, why warm water evaporates faster than cold water, and so forth.

Authentic Tasks

Partnership participants ensure that activities developed by project consultation teams are authentic and whole. Language learners perform science experiments, legislate in "Kids' Congress," participate in "ESOL Olympiad" games, and so on. Because authenticity of literacy tasks that flow from science and social studies lessons is of particular importance to us, we try to make sure that literacy activities developed by partnership members are modeled on literacy genres that occur in real life. An instructional unit that focuses on the exploration of the water cycle culminates in an activity where learners are asked to envision themselves as meteorologists. The "meteorologists" get letters from school children from the states of Washington and

Nevada. The children wonder about the peculiarities of climates in their states: "How come it always rains in Washington?" "Why is it that it hardly ever rains in Nevada?" The meteorologists engage in the analysis of the geographic locations of the two states (i.e., proximity to water basins, proximity to the equator) and write answers to the queries of their correspondents. In a unit that focuses on the history of immigration, youngsters imagine themselves as 19th-century immigrants who have just disembarked from a steamship in the New York harbor. Finding themselves in Ellis Island's Great Hall, our 19th-century immigrants write letters home about the reasons for their immigration, the vicissitudes of cross-Atlantic journey, and their first impressions of America.

◈ PRACTICAL IDEAS

Establish a System of Learning Objectives

When planning ZPD-positioned CBI lessons, narrow down choices of content-obligatory and content-compatible objectives to those that form a coherent, interdependent, thematically organized system. Avoid choosing incidental target language items. Also, avoid focusing on concrete target language items that are easy to contextualize and comprehend and present no challenge to learners. Rather, focus on those abstract concepts and ideas that require elaborate scaffolding and assistance for their comprehension and use.

Make Scaffolding an Integral Part of Instruction

Because use of scaffolding is central to the success of a ZPD-positioned lesson, be sure to create a classroom culture where scaffolding is provided at all stages of the instructional process. Use TPR and role-play activities to facilitate concept comprehension; include syntactic, lexical, and semantic scaffolding to sustain literacy tasks. To ensure that language learners understand the overall purpose of scaffolding as well as the ways in which the use of individual scaffolds enables them to deal with specific challenges, allow ample instructional time for scaffold analysis. Encourage students to identify scaffolds that are relevant to their needs, with more proficient learners using fewer scaffolds. Once graphic and text-based scaffolds (such as graphic organizers and semantic maps) have been used, do not dispose of them. Rather, create a convenient filing and storing system for future use.

Provide Nonsupervisory Forms of Assistance

Establish a classroom culture that values goal-directed collaboration, not direction and evaluation. Provide various forms of assistance that can serve to facilitate task performance. Aside from offering your own help in response to challenges experienced by students, use collaborative groups where learners work with their more competent peers. Encourage language learners to seek help from their families, professionals, and community members.

Authenticate Instructional Activities

In developing activities, avoid those that emphasize discrete, atomistic skills and subskills. Rather, develop and implement whole, meaningful instructional activities that emerge from learners' real-life experiences. When developing literacy activities for the CBI classroom, coach learners in a variety of real-life genres. Try to come up with genres that have the potential to stir and sustain student interest. For instance, combine literacy activities with role-play during the course of which writers will assume roles of historians, natural scientists, policy makers, physicians, astronauts, book characters, and so on. Authenticate instructional activities further by encouraging students to use commercially or teacher-developed stationery, such as forms, letterhead, and pictures.

◈ CONCLUSION

Participants of the Hofstra-BOCES partnership have joined efforts to study the instructional implications of the ZPD theory for the content-based L2 classroom. Using instructional enhancement strategies, such as project consultation teams, participants explore the use of various facets of the Vygotskian paradigm, such as conscious and systematic use of schooled language, assisted performance, manipulation of cognitive tools, and development of authentic tasks to plan and implement content-based lessons positioned at the cutting edge of learners' ZPD.

One of the most challenging questions with which partnership participants are confronted is ascertaining whether a given CBI ESOL curriculum is positioned in the zone of students' proximal (rather than actual) development. This question probes not only the fit between the curriculum and learners' prior knowledge but also the given plan of study's potential to stimulate learners. At this point, partnership members have primarily relied on teacher observation for answering this question. It seems essential, however, that more finely tuned, reliable, and valid assessment tools be researched and designed to evaluate learner academic language competencies and establish whether existing curricula meet learners' needs in terms of challenge and stimulation.

◈ CONTRIBUTOR

Tatiana Gordon is an assistant professor at Hofstra University, in Long Island, New York, in the United States, where she coordinates the MS TESOL/Bilingual Program. She received her EdD in applied linguistics from Teachers College, Columbia University and was a recipient of the 1997 Fulbright Memorial Scholarship.

◈ APPENDIX A: OBSERVATION QUESTIONNAIRE

Upon observing the CBI lesson, answer the following questions.

1. What are the lesson's content-compatible lexical objectives? What abstract language is explored in the lesson?

    Describe _____

2. What instances of assisted performance (e.g., questioning, guided participation) occur during the lesson?

    Describe _____

3. What cognitive tools (e.g., scaffolds, semantic maps, graphic organizers) are deployed by the teacher to facilitate concept comprehension and task completion?

   Describe _____

4. What does the teacher do to help learners bridge schooled language with the language of their day-to-day lives?

   Describe _____

5. What does the teacher do to engage language learners in activities that are authentic and meaningful (e.g., simulations, role-play, hands-on experiments)?

   Describe _____

◈ APPENDIX B: LESSON ENHANCEMENT QUESTIONNAIRE

Answer the following questions to raise the CBI lesson into learners' ZPD.

1. How can the lesson's content-compatible lexical objectives be modified to account for the exploration of schooled language?

   Describe _____

2. How can the lesson be modified to include more instances of assisted performance (e.g., questioning, guided participation)?

   Describe _____

3. What cognitive tools (e.g., scaffolds, semantic maps, graphic organizers) can be deployed to facilitate concept comprehension?

   Describe _____

4. What cognitive tools (e.g., scaffolds, semantic maps, graphic organizers) can be deployed to engage learners in more sustained and lexically rich writing activities?

   Describe _____

5. How can the lesson be further modified to help learners bridge schooled language with the language of their day-to-day lives?

   Describe _____

6. What modifications can be made to render the lesson more authentic?

   Describe _____

PART 2

Reflection and Inquiry in Content-Based Instruction Professional Development

CHAPTER 7

Supporting Sheltered Instruction in a Bilingual Program Through a Professional Development School Partnership

Nancy Dubetz, Hilduara Abreu, Reina Alegria,
Mercedes Casado, and Asunción Díaz

◈ INTRODUCTION

In TESOL's position statement on bilingual education, the organization advocates for having "a strong, carefully integrated ESL component" in bilingual programs (TESOL, 1993, p. 1). In this chapter, we present a profile of effective English for speakers of other languages (ESOL) content instruction in a transitional bilingual program and the professional development model that has helped us learn how to provide this type of instruction to our English language learners (ELLs). We describe approaches we used to examine the relationship between children's literacy development in a first and second language and to provide sheltered social studies instruction in K–3 bilingual classrooms. To successfully engage in this work, we participated in a bilingual teacher study group over a 2-year period. In the next section, we explain how our efforts were supported by our participation in a special type of school/university partnership known as a professional development school (PDS) partnership.

◈ CONTEXT

Our bilingual teacher study group was one of several collaborative professional development activities that have taken place in a PDS partnership between an urban public elementary school, Public School 291, in the Bronx, New York, and an urban public university, Lehman College, City University of New York. A PDS is a long-term collaboration between a university and school that has four functions:

- promote student learning
- restructure educational roles and practices for both school-based and college-based faculty
- establish sites of best practice for the preparation of new teachers
- engage in inquiry to study changes in student learning (Holmes Group, 1990)

To engage in these functions, a number of material and human resources are allocated to the PDS. Partnering institutions each release a person to serve as a PDS liaison. In addition, teams of school and college faculty collaborate on a variety of projects including an annual PDS conference open to all PDS participants, fieldwork and student teaching supervision, and college and school program evaluation. The Lehman/PS 291 PDS involves college faculty from programs in early childhood, childhood education, and TESOL and teachers, paraprofessionals, and staff developers working with children at PS 291.

PS 291 is a K–4 school that opened in September 1995 in the University Heights section of the Bronx. The school is a Title I/PCEN (Pupil With Compensatory Educational Needs)[1] school consisting of 18 general education classes where the language of instruction is English and four where instruction is in Spanish and English. In addition, there are two bilingual special education classes. PS 291 shares a school building with two other public schools. There are 630 students at PS 291, which was designed to accommodate only 530 children. Ninety-four percent of the children are eligible for free lunch. Just under one third of the children are ELLs, and roughly two thirds of these children were being instructed in the K–3 transitional bilingual program during the 2 years we participated in a study group.

Located in the Bronx, Lehman College is a 4-year liberal arts college that offers a wide range of teacher and counselor preparation programs at undergraduate and graduate levels. During the academic year, four college courses are held on-site at PS 291 for part of the semester, and 10–15 student teachers complete their student teaching in classrooms at PS 291 each year. The teacher preparation programs that are linked to the PDS are programs designed to certify early childhood (birth–Grade 2) and childhood (Grades 1–6) teachers and to offer bilingual extensions for teacher candidates in these programs wishing to become bilingual teachers. In addition, Lehman's TESOL program uses the PDS to provide student teaching placements for candidates wishing to teach elementary ESOL. The two institutions shared compatible missions and were committed to investing PDS resources to engage in all four of the PDS functions.

◈ DESCRIPTION

The work profiled in this case study is the work of bilingual teachers, student teachers, and college faculty who participated in the bilingual teacher study group and who worked with children in the transitional bilingual program at PS 291. Transitional bilingual programs are designed to move children into English as quickly as possible. Because children do not receive ongoing support in their native language beyond the transitional program, it is critical that content taught in the native language is tied to content taught in English and that, over time, children are exposed to increasing amounts of content matter in English. At PS 291, all areas of the curriculum are taught in Spanish except for social studies in kindergarten and first grade. In second grade, children receive 3 days of language arts and science in

---

[1] Title I is a U.S. federally funded program that provides financial assistance through state educational agencies to public schools with high numbers or percentages of poor children to help ensure that all children meet challenging state academic content and student academic achievement standards.

Spanish and 2 days of language arts and science in English, 4 days of math in English and 1 in Spanish, and all social studies in English. By third grade, all areas of the curriculum are taught in English except for 2 periods of language arts and 2 of science.

Our bilingual teacher study group met twice monthly from October 2000 to May 2002 to discuss issues related to teaching ELLs in the bilingual program. Additional meeting time was allocated during citywide staff development days. The general education teachers, special education bilingual teachers, and Title VII[2] staff developer regularly attended the study-group meetings. Other individuals who attended periodically included the principal, assistant principal, literacy staff developer, bilingual paraprofessionals, and teacher candidates from the college during the time they were student teaching in the classrooms of the bilingual teachers.

The college PDS liaison facilitated the study-group meetings. She was responsible for typing an agenda for each meeting based on what the participants wanted to discuss, though study-group discussions can and did move away from the agenda. The PDS liaison provided resources on language acquisition when they applied to a particular concern that was being discussed in the study group. In addition, the college PDS liaison met with teachers individually periodically to identify specific concerns they had and to collect materials that teachers wanted to have copied for the study-group meetings.

Study-group meetings were organized around teachers' questions and concerns. In the first meeting of the study group each year, the teachers generated lists of questions and concerns. Over a 2-year period, we pursued two lines of inquiry: (a) assessing and teaching to promote literacy development in Spanish and English and (b) planning for sheltered content-based ESOL instruction. In the next section, we provide examples of the work that we did in our classrooms related to these two lines of inquiry.

◈ DISTINGUISHING FEATURES

As members of a study group, we examined a number of sheltered practices and shared practices that we were using in our classrooms. Study groups are referred to in the literature under several names: teacher study groups or support groups (Clair, 1998; Trueba, 1989), work groups (Biagetti, 2001), or more broadly described as professional development and inquiry groups (Clark, 2001). These groups share three characteristics. First, they are learning oriented. The purposes of the discussions that take place are driven by the concerns of the participants. Typically, teacher study groups focus on inquiry into issues around teaching practice and student learning. In our case, we were interested in improving our practice for our bilingual learners. Second, study groups are voluntary and structured for community building among the participants. Finally, study groups meet regularly over time to solve problems and build knowledge and to provide emotional support. These three

---

[2] Title VII was a U.S. federally funded program that provided financial assistance to educational institutions to ensure that limited English proficient children meet challenging state academic content and student academic achievement standards.

qualities make study groups fertile places for undertaking long-term experimentation with and conversation around practice. In the following paragraphs, we share some of the practices we have found to be effective with bilingual learners.

Assessing Biliteracy Development in a Bilingual Program

Like most bilingual programs, reading and writing are taught in two languages and the choice of language depends in part on the language dominance of the individual child. One of the greatest challenges facing bilingual teachers is to assess the strengths and needs of bilingual learners in two languages. As has been demonstrated elsewhere, bilingual children often demonstrate different levels of literacy ability when assessed in their native language and in their second language (Hurley & Tinajero, 2000). In the school district where we work, several literacy assessment instruments are available to help bilingual teachers gather information about their children's literacy development in Spanish and English. The *Developmental Reading Assessment* (Beaver, 1997) and its Spanish counterpart, *Evaluación del Desarrollo de la Lectura* [Developmental Reading Evaluation or Assessment] (Ruiz & Cuesta, 2000), consist of a running record of the child's reading followed by an interview with the child to assess comprehension. These instruments are most useful in planning for instruction once children begin to develop emergent literacy abilities. In addition, we use two other instruments to assess beginning readers and writers: the *Early Childhood Literacy Assessment System* (New York City Board of Education, 1998), which is designed to provide information to teachers of children in Grades K–2 in the areas of sight word knowledge, phonemic awareness, reading, and writing mechanics, and, to gather similar information in Spanish, we use the *Instrumento de Observación* [Observation Instrument] (Escamilla, Andrade, Basurto, & Ruiz, 1996). We also use information from observations of children's functioning in the classroom and prior knowledge of students' family language preferences. These instruments offer us insight into how a child is functioning in the two languages. Sometimes this information provides strong evidence that a child is more dominant in one language than another; however, in other cases, we get conflicting information about a child's language dominance, and this makes it difficult to determine whether to focus on literacy development in the native language or the second language. We used our study group as a place to develop a framework to compare information from different assessments in the two languages to make instructional decisions and share stories about our students.

As shown in Figure 1, by comparing the information provided by a variety of sources using the framework, we were able to discuss instructional implications for particular children. For example, when reviewing the writing of a bilingual third grader, it became evident that the child had mastered the use of simple sentence structures using the first person in both Spanish and English. Members of the study group recommended that the teacher offer models of other kinds of sentence structures to facilitate his use of more complex structures.

To use the framework to discuss every child would be too time consuming, but it provided a structure for study-group discussions around children who seemed to provide conflicting information regarding language dominance. Understanding language dominance is particularly important in our literacy instruction because we teach in both languages.

Name: _____ Grade_____ Date_____

Language Profile

Primary language at home?

Preferred language(s) in class?

Preferred language(s) with friends in class? Outside of class?

Language Use in Social Situations: Overall Oral Language Balance

Spanish   Mostly Spanish   Bilingual   Mostly English   English

$\longleftarrow\qquad\qquad\qquad\qquad\qquad\qquad\longrightarrow$

Language Use in Academic Situations: Overall Oral Language Balance

Spanish   Mostly Spanish   Bilingual   Mostly English   English

$\longleftarrow\qquad\qquad\qquad\qquad\qquad\qquad\longrightarrow$

LAB SCORES: Reading _____ Listening _____ Speaking _____ Writing _____

Number of years in the United States?

Number of years at school?

Number of years in bilingual program?

Preferred language(s) when selecting books independently?

Other important information?

Literacy Information for Dominant Language(s)

Strengths in Reading in Dominant Language • What can s/he already do? • What areas has s/he shown good progress in over time?	Evidence of Transfer?	Suggestions for Instruction
Strengths in Writing in Dominant Language • What can s/he already do? • What areas has s/he shown good progress in over time?	Evidence of Transfer?	Suggestions for Instruction

Areas in Reading in Dominant Language That Need Attention:	Suggestions for Instruction
Areas in Writing in Dominant Language That Need Attention:	Suggestions for Instruction

Continued on p. 100

Literacy Information for Second Language	
Reading • What can s/he already do? • What areas has s/he shown good progress in over time? • What are his/her needs?	Suggestions for Instruction
Writing • What can s/he already do? • What areas has s/he shown good progress in over time? • What are his/her areas of need?	Suggestions for Instruction

FIGURE 1. Study-Group Framework for Biliteracy Discussions

Preparing for Sheltered Social Studies Instruction in a Bilingual Program

After our study group had been meeting for approximately 4 months, we learned that the school district was going to mandate that social studies be taught entirely in English beginning the following September. When encountering a curriculum in English, we had to find ways to make content comprehensible to our bilingual learners and link what they were learning in English with the content and language they had developed in their native language. The second line of inquiry in our study group focused on enhancing content-based instruction (CBI) in social studies. Our study group began examining strategies for sheltered content instruction by first looking at grade-level social studies materials and the New York State social studies curriculum and evaluating them in terms of the kinds of challenges they would present to our ELLs. An adapted set of the criteria for evaluating content materials from *CALLA Handbook* (Chamot & O'Malley, 1994) was used to frame our early conversations. We discussed challenges related to new and known vocabulary, language structures, prerequisite knowledge needed to access the information, and the resources that we had available to us to support instruction. Our second step was to share with each other ESOL strategies we were already using. Once we had done this, we began to investigate strategies that support ESOL content instruction that were new to us. We reviewed (a) recommended approaches from *Making Content Comprehensible for English Language Learners: The SIOP Model* (Echevarria, Vogt, & Short, 2000); (b) strategies for promoting second language literacy from *The Teaching of Language Arts to Limited English Proficient/English Language Learners* (New York State Education Department, n.d.); and (c) learning strategies recommended by Chamot, Barnhardt, El-Dinary, and Robbins (1999). We explored a variety of ways to engage ELLs in actively learning content in their second language.

Linking Native Language Instruction to Content-Based ESOL Instruction Through Theme-Based Curriculum

Thematic teaching creates opportunities for bilingual children to build concepts and vocabulary through interaction, inquiry, and risk-taking, which are very important to learning (Kucer, Silva, & Delgado-Larocco, 1995). To teach thematically, bilingual teachers introduce concepts in the native language, which are reinforced through activities during ESOL instruction. By focusing on themes across the curriculum, children have opportunities to apply learned concepts and vocabulary in a variety of situations. To illustrate thematic curriculum planning, we offer the following example of a kindergarten social studies theme web (see Figure 2).

The topic of the kindergarten social studies curriculum in our state is "all about me" in which children are expected to develop concepts and vocabulary through the study of themselves and their families. The bilingual kindergarten teachers use a social studies topic such as families to plan for activities that integrate language arts, social studies, math, the arts, and science content. Some of these subjects, for example, native language arts, are taught in Spanish, whereas others, such as social studies, are taught in English. Figure 2 illustrates the thematic web about families developed collaboratively by the general and special education bilingual kindergarten teachers in our study group.

As can be seen in the curriculum web, the topic of families is studied across a variety of subjects and activities. Children in the kindergarten are Spanish-dominant and their introduction to literacy is in the native language. Literacy-based activities, which occur every morning during the literacy block (e.g., read alouds and shared readings) are conducted in Spanish. Teachers select a variety of books for these activities including books that relate to the social studies topic of families. Thus, children's first exposure to talking about families is done in their dominant language. In contrast, social studies texts are in English and focus on similar themes addressed in the books on and about families presented during native language arts. By using books that present concepts already introduced in the native language, teachers are able to focus their efforts during ESOL on building English vocabulary related to families (e.g., names of family members, what families need and want, and what families do together) while reinforcing concepts already introduced in the native language.

For example, one of the social studies standards children must meet is to come to understand the way people are unified by values, practices, beliefs, and traditions. Before children begin working with vocabulary in English around family members to begin their family portraits, teachers read aloud books in the native language such as *Yo Amo a Mi Familia* to generate ideas in the native language. During ESOL social studies, teachers focus on building English vocabulary through theme books and poetry in English, for example, *Families, Families*. Figure 3 offers a display of samples of children's work in which they must identify families' needs and wants and find pictures representing each category. Then, based on their individual projects, children looked for differences and similarities among families. This activity helps build vocabulary in the new language around each concept.

In thematic instruction, it is extremely important that the two languages are separated for instruction (Baker, 2001). For this reason, the teachers use different languages for instruction depending on the subject. In addition, they use red markers

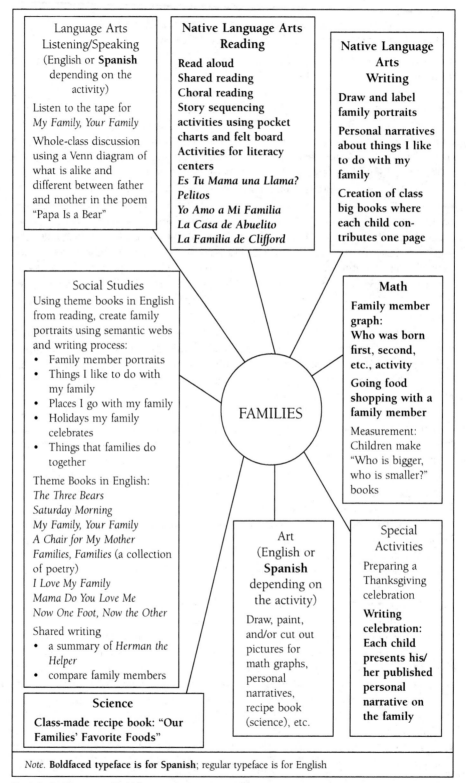

Language Arts Listening/Speaking (English or **Spanish** depending on the activity)

Listen to the tape for *My Family, Your Family*

Whole-class discussion using a Venn diagram of what is alike and different between father and mother in the poem "Papa Is a Bear"

Native Language Arts Reading

Read aloud
Shared reading
Choral reading
Story sequencing activities using pocket charts and felt board
Activities for literacy centers
Es Tu Mama una Llama?
Pelitos
Yo Amo a Mi Familia
La Casa de Abuelito
La Familia de Clifford

Native Language Arts Writing

Draw and label family portraits

Personal narratives about things I like to do with my family

Creation of class big books where each child contributes one page

Social Studies
Using theme books in English from reading, create family portraits using semantic webs and writing process:
• Family member portraits
• Things I like to do with my family
• Places I go with my family
• Holidays my family celebrates
• Things that families do together
Theme Books in English:
The Three Bears
Saturday Morning
My Family, Your Family
A Chair for My Mother
Families, Families (a collection of poetry)
I Love My Family
Mama Do You Love Me
Now One Foot, Now the Other
Shared writing
• a summary of *Herman the Helper*
• compare family members

Math

Family member graph:
Who was born first, second, etc., activity

Going food shopping with a family member

Measurement: Children make "Who is bigger, who is smaller?" books

FAMILIES

Art
(English or **Spanish** depending on the activity)

Draw, paint, and/or cut out pictures for math graphs, personal narratives, recipe book (science), etc.

Special Activities

Preparing a Thanksgiving celebration

Writing celebration: Each child presents his/ her published personal narrative on the family

Science

Class-made recipe book: "Our Families' Favorite Foods"

Note. **Boldfaced typeface is for Spanish**; regular typeface is for English

FIGURE 2. Thematic Web for Kindergarten Families Unit

for one language and black for the other when they write to help emergent readers and writers differentiate between the two languages. When teachers elicit ideas from children during ESOL, it is not uncommon that a child will provide an answer in Spanish. When this occurs, the teacher acknowledges the child's response in the native language and restates the response in English.

Scaffolding Grade-Level Content During ESOL Instruction

Grade-level content materials often pose challenges to bilingual learners because of their lack of background knowledge, vocabulary, and the learning strategies they need to make the information comprehensible. Teachers, therefore, must scaffold their instruction to build children's capacity to gain meaning from these materials. Scaffolding refers to both the instructional sequence that the teacher uses to engage children with the content (e.g., modeling followed by practicing) and the grouping structures they put in place during learning (e.g., moving from whole group to small groups and partners to independent work) (Echevarria, Vogt, & Short, 2000). The following description illustrates how scaffolding is used in the third-grade bilingual classroom.

The social studies focus for third grade is communities around the world. Some of the primary goals of this curriculum are (a) to understand what makes communities similar and different throughout the world; (b) to develop map reading skills; and (c) to describe primary source documents such as pictures, photographs,

FIGURE 3. Family Needs/Wants Display

and posters. The third-grade texts include a textbook entitled *Comparing Communities Level C* (Joyce & Erickson, 1987), an accompanying workbook, and a text entitled *Maps, Charts, Graphs: Communities* (Foreman & Allen, 1990). Because these materials are designed for native English speakers, the texts pose two major challenges to ELLs. First, only key social studies concepts are highlighted and defined. Words and language structures that may be familiar to English-speaking third graders pose challenges to ELLs. Second, the texts include multiple-choice and fill-in-the-blank questions to assess comprehension, which require an understanding of both common vocabulary as well as specialized vocabulary and language structures.

Because prior knowledge is so important to reading comprehension, activities are designed to build the background knowledge that ELLs may be lacking. To build background knowledge, the teacher begins the unit by having the children map out their own local urban community. The teacher introduces vocabulary and language related to suburban communities when mapping her own suburban community. Once the maps are completed, teacher and students engage in activities comparing and contrasting their urban and suburban communities.

Once the children have compared their own urban community with the suburban community of their teacher, they are introduced to their first social studies text. This text offers pictures of urban and suburban communities and questions that are to be answered about each picture. Beginning with pictures rather than with a reading selection offers students an opportunity to begin to apply some of their new knowledge. The teacher has the children look at the pictures of the different communities and list what they notice about each type of community. The second text requires children to describe a picture of a Native American community, which is a community that the students have not had experience with. Their observations about the picture are documented on chart paper by the teacher. After they complete the activity, they move to answering multiple-choice questions about the picture in partners. It is only after this series of activities that children finally are introduced to the chapter in the social studies textbook on communities. The chapter is introduced through a choral reading, in which the teacher and children read aloud together. After each paragraph, the class as a whole clarifies definitions of unknown words and main ideas. Choral readings are particularly effective for the children who are emergent readers or who know very little English. We have observed that after multiple choral readings, these children volunteer to read alone even though they may be "pretend" reading. Additional scaffolding is provided by small-group work on the material already introduced, which is facilitated by junior high school students who volunteer once a week in the third-grade bilingual classroom.

When instruction is scaffolded, even reticent learners participate. The evidence that scaffolding is effective can be found in the work that children produce independently. Figure 4 offers an example of how one third grader has begun to apply vocabulary she has learned in social studies to a narrative account she wrote during a writers' workshop, which is part of the literacy block in late October.

Once children have developed prior knowledge of concepts and vocabulary related to communities, they are ready to begin looking at communities in different countries around the world. They begin with the Caribbean because many of the students are either born in Caribbean countries or have family living there and have prior knowledge that they can use during class discussions. By the end of the year,

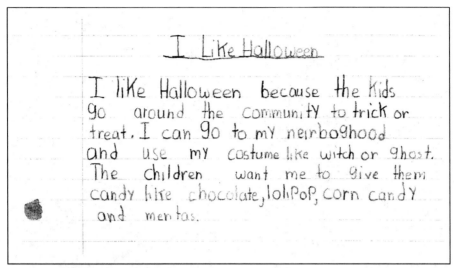

I Like Halloween

I like Halloween because the kids go around the community to trick or treat. I can go to my neirboghood and use my costume like witch or ghost. The children want me to give them candy like chocolate, lolipop, corn candy and mentas.

FIGURE 4. Sample of Student Work From Third Grade

children will have studied at least five communities in different parts of the world and will have graphed what they have learned using an attribute chart, which is a form of graphic organizer that scaffolds learning by displaying important information and concepts in ways that show how the information or ideas are related to each other and connect known information or concepts with new ones.

Building Content Vocabulary in English

In all of the bilingual classrooms, there are recent arrivals who are still developing basic interpersonal communication skills as well as cognitive academic language proficiency skills in the second language (Cummins, 1989). To achieve academically, children must develop the vocabulary of the second language to engage in learning processes, (e.g., comparing, inferring, mapping) and to understand abstract concepts (e.g., number sense, economy, climate). Often, they are not only challenged by specialized vocabulary but also by common words and known words used in ways that are new or confusing to them. For example, in the sentence, "A suburb is a large, medium-sized, or small community that is near a very large city," ELLs become confused by the use of multiple words related to size. When encountering text-embedded definitions of key words, ELLs often do not have adequate vocabulary to understand the definitions. For example, in reading the sentence, "The new community would need certain **natural resources**, or things in nature that are useful to people," most ELLs don't know what the word *nature* means.

As a result, we emphasize vocabulary development in all ESOL instruction. We use semantic webs, word walls, and personal dictionaries to support vocabulary development. Semantic webs are visual organizers that support vocabulary and concept acquisition. Webbing allows children to make personal connections that help them develop ownership over the content. Figure 5 offers an example of a semantic web from the second-grade social studies unit on the study of the local community. The ideas for these webs were first generated on chart paper with

FIGURE 5. Semantic Web in Second Grade

children sharing what they knew about their communities and the teacher documenting their ideas. Some of these webs then become displays, with pictures attached to words, and these displays provide contextual support for children when they engage in writing about what they have learned.

In additional to the semantic map displays, a word wall can be found in every classroom and word study is an integral part of language arts instruction. Figure 6 is a sample from a word wall in the kindergarten special education class. Children use the word walls as well as displays (such as the semantic maps) during writing. In later grades, children develop personal dictionaries to apply new vocabulary to their writing.

FIGURE 6. Word Wall in Kindergarten

The practices we have just described are examples of effective instruction in the transitional bilingual context. Sharing effective practices is celebrated in the PDS in a couple of ways. By participating in the study group, participants share their ideas ands suggestions with each other to help improve each other's practice. In addition, because of the special relationship between the school and the college, the PDS encourages school and college teachers to learn together and collaboratively serve as teacher educators. These opportunities would not exist if it were not for everyone's commitment to the PDS mission of sharing and disseminating information. In the following section, we share practical ideas about how to set up a PDS and promote teacher learning through a study group.

◈ PRACTICAL IDEAS

Initiate a Partnership With Collaborative Professional Development as a Focus

The work we have profiled in this chapter was supported by our participation in a study group initiated as part of our PDS partnership. Our PDS began with a strong emphasis on professional development because it served both school and college faculty. When selecting institutional partners, it is important to focus on compatibility of school and college missions, each institution's potential for supporting the other's accreditation needs, and the extent of commitment from school and college faculty. In 1999, the faculty in the Division of Education at Lehman designed a year-long selection process that resulted in the creation of PDS partnerships with two elementary schools and one middle school. Each PDS is governed by a 3-year, renewable charter agreement. Readers interested in more information on the selection process can find detailed descriptions in Lawrence and Dubetz (2001) and Dubetz, Lawrence, and Gningue (2002).

Focus the Partnership on Meeting Needs of Both Institutions

Once PDSs were selected, collaboration among our college and school PDS partners began with a set of planning sessions to prepare for the 1st year of the PDS network. The first collaborative planning session took place the summer before the 1st year of the PDS partnerships. Over 2 days, representatives from the college and schools co-constructed a draft of a charter agreement, goals for each partnership, and a governance structure. The planning began with college and school representatives exploring the similarities and differences between their institutional missions. Then, participants broke into site-specific groups and identified PDS goals and activities to be implemented in each partnership site throughout the year. These goals and activities were used as a platform to develop a PDS inquiry research agenda for each PDS. Our study group grew out of this agenda in an effort to meet one of the primary goals of the Lehman/PS 291 PDS: improving the scores of ELLs. Resources that offer detailed explanations of how to maintain a PDS partnership can be found on the Web site of the American Association of Colleges for Teacher Education (http://www.aacte.org). Additional resources include Clark (1997), Teitel (1998), and Teitel (2003).

Identify Liaisons to Facilitate Ongoing
Professional Development School Work

PDS partnerships are a labor-intensive endeavor. A critical aspect of maintaining a PDS is the identification of college- and school-based PDS liaisons. These individuals are responsible for maintaining the lines of communication among the different constituencies participating in the PDS: school and college faculty and students. The liaisons are members of a PDS executive council that serves as the governance structure for the entire PDS network. They coordinate PDS efforts, which include planning for field-based experiences for the teacher candidates, selecting cooperating teachers, facilitating professional development for college and school faculty, and studying the impact of the PDS on adults and children. PDS liaisons from all PDS sites meet monthly during the academic year and participate in annual evaluations in which they review and revise annual PDS goals. In the 3rd year of the PDS partnership, a formal self-study using the National Council for Accreditation of Teacher Education (2001a) PDS self-study process is conducted at each site.

The college-based liaison spends a minimum of 1 full day each week at the PDS and receives release time from college teaching responsibilities to undertake these responsibilities. The school-based PDS liaison is an individual who works full time in the PDS, meets weekly with the college-PDS liaison to undertake the responsibilities listed previously, and attends PDS executive committee meetings at the college a minimum of 1 day a month. This person also receives release time from the school principal to complete this work.

Decide the Focus and Structure of the Study Group

We found the study group to be an effective way for small groups of college and school educators with shared interests to examine practice over a sustained period of time. Unlike traditional staff development, study groups offer the flexibility to adapt to changing conditions. Our study group shifted its focus to social studies instruction when we learned about a change in district policy. To be effective, study groups should occur at a time that is convenient for members to meet and should have a focus. Ground rules for participation should be shared at the beginning, and we found it helpful to have a facilitator for the meetings. We also found it informative to have college and school faculty and student teachers represented in our study group. We provide a number of resources on study groups in the appendix to this chapter that offer specific guidelines for setting up and maintaining effective study groups.

❖ CONCLUSION

Effective content-based ESOL instruction focuses on meeting both content and language goals simultaneously. Our study group learned a lot about CBI through experimenting with a variety of strategies, some of which are profiled in this chapter. Together, we used our study group to improve our instruction in ways that (a) build on children's prior knowledge while promoting second language acquisition, (b) acknowledge that all forms of communication are accepted, and most important, (c) emphasize multiple approaches to learning. Our experience with study groups has been rewarding, and we hope that other teachers engaged in content-based ESOL instruction consider the study group as a tool for professional growth.

To undertake our inquiry, we depended on the support of our PDS partnership. Though study groups can be undertaken in schools without connections to institutions of higher learning, our work was strengthened by the diversity of our participants: teachers, college faculty, and teacher candidates all learned from the experience. Having a PDS research agenda motivated us to investigate our practice, and partnering gave us resources, both human and material, from the school and the university to sustain our work over a 2-year period.

We continue to challenge ourselves to find ways to better meet the needs of our ELLs. We are building on the practices we identified in this chapter and are encouraged by the results—our ELLs' scores on standardized tests and on the Language Assessment Battery (New York City Office of Testing, 1982) have improved every year for the last 3 years. Our PDS partnership is in its 4th year, and we plan to continue tapping its resources in our efforts to improve our practice and our students' learning.

❖ CONTRIBUTORS

Nancy Dubetz is an assistant professor in the Department of Early Childhood and Childhood Education at Lehman College, City University of New York, in the United States. She serves as a college PDS liaison to PS 291. She has her EdD in curriculum and teaching from Teachers College, Columbia University. Her research interests include the study of how PDSs affect teachers and the preparation of bilingual and ESOL teachers.

Hilduara Abreu was a bilingual second grade teacher at PS 291 in the Bronx, New York, when she participated in the bilingual teacher study group described in the chapter. Prior to this, she has been a bilingual kindergarten teacher and resource room teacher. She is currently the math coach for the school. She received her master's degree in bilingual education from St. John's University; her bachelor's degree is in computing and management.

Reina Alegria is a bilingual kindergarten teacher at PS 291. She received her MS in education from City College, City University of New York, and has been a public school teacher since 1992.

Mercedes Casado taught the bilingual special-education kindergarten class at PS 291 at the time she participated in the bilingual teacher study group described in this chapter. She is currently working on a master's degree in bilingual education at La Universidad Autonoma de Santo Domingo, in the Dominican Republic.

Asunción Díaz teaches a third/fourth-grade bilingual bridge class at PS 291. She has a MS in education from Mercy College. She has been teaching at PS 291 since 1998.

◈ APPENDIX: RESOURCES ON STUDY GROUPS

Clair, N. (1998). Teacher study groups: Persistent questions in a promising approach. *TESOL Quarterly, 22*(3), 465–492.

Clair, N., & Adger, C. T. (2001). Sustainable strategies for professional development in educational reform. In K. E. Johnson (Ed.), *Teacher education: Case studies in TESOL practice series* (pp. 29–49). Alexandria, VA: TESOL.

Clark, C. (Ed.). (2001). *Talking shop: Authentic conversation and teacher learning.* New York: Teachers College Press.

Dune, F., & Honts, F. (1998, April). *"That group really makes me think!" Critical friends groups and the development of reflective practitioners.* Paper presented at the annual meeting of the American Educational Research Association, San Francisco, CA. (ERIC Document Reproduction Service No. ED423228)

Grossman, P., Winebury, S., & Woolworth, S. (2000, December). *What makes teacher community different from a gathering of teachers?* Retrieved November 17, 2004, from http://www.ctpweb.org.

Murphy, C. U. (1999). Use time for faculty study. *Journal of Staff Development, 20*(2), 20–25.

CHAPTER 8

Teaching a Less Commonly Taught Language in a Social Science Classroom

Erin Fairlight Olsen and R. Kirk Belnap

◈ INTRODUCTION

The events of September 11, 2001, shocked Americans into reexamining their relationship with the rest of the world. Although the likelihood of Huntington's (1996) catastrophic clash of civilizations is debatable, there is little doubt about the value of Americans becoming better informed, particularly given that their votes affect millions beyond the borders of the United States. This chapter outlines a pilot course conducted as a partnership between the National Middle East Language Resource Center (NMELRC) and a local high school in which some Arabic was taught in a social studies class to help students better understand the people of the Middle East. This class was designed to raise awareness through history, current events, culture, and language of a region that has had a considerable impact in many domains. This course confronts stereotypes about the Middle East, replacing them with an appreciation and understanding of the throngs of peace-loving people who do not make the headlines. The course and its experiential curriculum have kindled in many of the students a desire to further study the region and its languages.

◈ CONTEXT

This course came about as a result of efforts to provide motivated high school students an opportunity to study Arabic. Initially, arrangements were made for a few interested students from nearby Provo High School in Utah to participate in Arabic courses on the Brigham Young University campus. The next step was to take Arabic to the high school. When the principal was approached, he welcomed the idea but observed that the impact, in terms of number of students, would be far greater if the course were one that would fill a requirement, such as social studies. The mention of social studies immediately brought to mind one of the ideal conditions for learning: timely and relevant content. A review of Utah's requirements and objectives for social studies courses confirmed that the Middle East would present an ideal constellation of perplexing and relevant issues on which a horizon-expanding course could be built.

A central goal of typical social studies curriculum requirements in the United States is to teach students the role each individual plays in a democratic society. These courses (sometimes titled *government* or *civics*) target real and meaningful participation by the students—participation that will lead the students to stand up for the rights that they enjoy and lead the world in valuing democracy and freedom for all of humanity (Wilson, 2000). Holdsworth observes that valuable forms of participation include "an active sharing by students in decisions about . . . key issues that determine the nature of the world in which they live" (1996, p. 26). Students must be exposed to questions that are worth pondering and that affect society. They must feel that they are an integral part of the world if they are to care and shoulder the responsibility to actively participate in such a way that they will make a difference in their society and in the world for years to come.

In the United States, the jolt of the September terrorist attacks spawned important conversations everywhere, including in schools. Questions, suspicions, and stereotypes about the Middle East pervaded public and private discourse. With a Eurocentric approach to history, most schools essentially had ignored the Middle East before 2001 (Short, 1996). Schools are now, however, far more receptive to filling this curricular gap, recognizing that some key world issues revolve around the Middle East and that students should be given the opportunity to address their confusions, curiosities, and fears concerning this area of the world. Deeper understanding and increased knowledge can potentially enhance resolution of conflicts and improve the lives of individuals and societies. In Europe, adult education classes in foreign languages are offered with the explicit goal of molding a united European political identity (Starkey, 1999).

The course described here diverges from the typical content-based language courses that have as their primary goal the promotion of more effective language learning. The goal is usually met by incorporating other subjects into the curriculum to aid in the teaching of language for use in those content areas. Traditional foreign language programs, especially at the postsecondary level, include language, history, culture, and current events. This course targets an audience that might never enroll in a foreign language class. The ultimate goal of this course is to encourage students to see the Middle East through the eyes of its people.

Eleven students (7 males and 4 females) participated in the pilot course during the fall 2002 semester. These students, ranging in age from 14–17, enrolled for a 1-semester social studies elective course entitled "Global Perspectives: The Middle East." (A course by this name had been regularly offered for the previous 10 years, but the course developed and taught with the sponsorship of the NMELRC had totally changed the focus of the course.) All but one of the students were from Christian backgrounds, with no previous knowledge of the Middle East or Arabic, and none had friends, teachers, or acquaintances from the Middle East. One student was of Sudanese and Islamic heritage and spoke Arabic as her first language at home. In an effort to expose her to another important Middle Eastern culture, she worked on learning Modern Hebrew with the aid of software designed for this purpose, while the rest of the class studied Arabic. All of the students had some previous experience in studying a foreign language, including Spanish, English (ESL/EFL), French, German, Norwegian, American Sign Language, and Chinese.

Erin Olsen, an author for this chapter as well as a course instructor, had taught Modern and Biblical Hebrew at Brigham Young for 2 years and taught this course as a volunteer under the supervision of the history teacher who normally teaches the Middle East course at the high school. At the time, the course instructor was a student in the second language acquisition/Arabic master's degree program at

Brigham Young. In addition to her passion for the languages of the Middle East and her love for the people of the region, her own personal history and experiences in the Middle East have led her to develop and teach the course described here. With NMELRC funding, she was able to develop the course and contribute to raising awareness, understanding, and appreciation of the region and its languages, cultures, and people.

◈ DESCRIPTION

Each day of class was a 95-minute block of time divided into thirds. Class began with students writing a journal entry addressing an issue in the news. This was followed by a discussion of their entries, what they had read in the newspaper, or what they had seen on the news (they were required to read or watch 2 hours of news every week). Because resources were limited, part of the students' assignment was to bring in magazine and newspaper clippings on the Middle East. The first task in reading an article was to identify the bias of the author or authors. The goal was to help students see events from a variety of perspectives, especially from the viewpoint of people living in the Middle East. Other resources implemented in the teaching of current events included video recordings of news programs, such as *Frontline* or *The NewsHour With Jim Lehrer,* as well as a variety of other videos. During the current events section of class, as many views as possible were presented. Students discussed issues and events and made up their own minds on the issues, often expressing widely varying opinions in their journals. For the second portion of the history class, few resources appropriate for teaching the Middle East to high school students were available. A college textbook was used to prepare for discussions of history and provide outlines to the students. The students were assigned to investigate the history and culture of two countries in the Middle East and then teach the class about these countries. All of the holidays of Judaism and Islam that occurred during the semester were celebrated. The instructor gave the historical background and significance of each of the holidays as the students ate food associated with them and asked questions concerning traditional observance. The final class project was to synthesize what they had read in newspapers and magazines, what they had seen on television, and what they had gained from classroom discussions and historical studies and then to debate their own solutions for peaceful existence in the region.

The final portion of class focused on learning Arabic. We chose Arabic; however, Hebrew, Persian, or Turkish could just as easily have been the language of focus. One student who was a speaker of Arabic focused on learning Hebrew. Whatever the language, it was important to include activities and discussion that result in a balanced approach, helping the students grapple with the complex issues of the Middle East.

The lack of appropriate materials hindered Arabic language learning efforts. Language textbooks and their audio- and videotapes are expensive for a high school budget. Even if sufficient funds were available, such books rarely introduce the necessary political or historical vocabulary, and even if they did, they would likely be too advanced for beginning students. At first, we had hoped to make some use of content-based instruction materials on the Middle East developed by Ryding and Stowasser (1997). These, however, proved to be far too advanced for the high school students who came to the course with no Arabic and little familiarity with the history of the Middle East. As a result, handouts were developed specifically for the course, and students used their notes to review the material covered. Despite the lack of materials, however, the language learning portion of the class proved to be very popular. A language curriculum complete with student workbook, audio component, and teacher instruction (intended for teachers with or without knowledge of Arabic) has now been developed. The meshing of current events, history, and language was a very exciting way to introduce students to the Middle East. Sample units of instruction are presented in the appendix to this chapter.

◈ DISTINGUISHING FEATURES

One of the most important strengths of this course was exposing students to complex issues and encouraging them to ask challenging questions. Often the topics and problems discussed in class required the students to write on topics that did not have clear answers or solutions. Journal entry topics included:

- What is a homeland?
- Do you value the home of your birth?
- Would you be willing to die to preserve this land?
- Is war sometimes necessary?
- What are some holidays or family traditions that you have participated in or want to participate in when you start your own family?
- What is a holy place to you?
- Why should you respect places that are holy to other people?
- Can land truly be holy?
- How would it change a society if the citizens were always afraid of being killed by violent factions?
- What are your thoughts on Islam? (This question was asked before we discussed Islam in class.)
- Write all of the questions that you can come up with about Judaism.
- What is your reaction to the hajj?
- Do you think that there is some place in the world that you are destined to visit at some point in your life?
- Are political assassinations OK?
- Should one elected leader be allowed to oust another elected leader?

Along with writing about these emotionally charged and challenging issues, we encouraged students to become comfortable with rationally discussing such issues. To facilitate discussion and community involvement, we invited guest speakers from the community to talk to the class. We also involved students in debates in the hope that students would search for solutions to problems in our world through dialogue rather than angrily jumping to conclusions and assuming the "other" is evil or foolish. Responses to student questionnaires and journal entries clearly demonstrate that students' perspectives on the Middle East evolved significantly as a result of the class.

Nine of the 11 students reported that they thought learning about the Middle East would help them in the future because they could help clarify misunderstandings about Arabs, Muslims, and Middle Eastern politics. We cannot be certain that teaching Arabic in the classroom inspired their learning of culture, but 10 of the 11 students stated that they thought the first goal in learning a second language should be to interact with native speakers of the language and to understand their culture and their perspectives on the world—a response that suggests integrative motivation for second language learning. According to Gardner and Lambert (1972), integrative motivation inspires participation and the desire to perpetuate the study of the second language. Seven of the students expressed the desire to continue the study of Arabic in the future. The 4 students that did not want to continue studying Arabic all said that it was too hard and confusing.

Time will tell whether students who have had this class will pursue the study of Arabic or some other Middle Eastern language. We are hopeful that this class will have an impact somewhat similar to the Arabic courses taught in Bountiful High School during the 1960s under the sponsorship of the University of Utah's Middle East Center. A number of the students that took Arabic at that time went on to serious study of the Middle East and careers in government and academe.

In the United States, students rarely begin the study of Arabic (or other less commonly taught languages) before their 2nd year of college. Students who begin language study earlier have significant advantages. The importance of starting language learning earlier emerged as a common thread mentioned by speakers from education, industry, and government at the Global Challenges and U.S. Higher Education Conference at Duke University in January 2003, which reviewed U.S. international education efforts and national needs to prepare for discussions connected with congressional renewal of the Higher Education Act. In his summary remarks, Patrick O'Meara, Dean of International Programs at Indiana University, noted that "early internationalization," creating "globally aware young people through the enrichment of curricula," requires new ideas for K–12 and undergraduate language and area studies education—precisely the goal of this course (O'Meara, 2003, p. 1).

◈ PRACTICAL IDEAS

As a result of its positive outcomes, this semester-long experiment has been refined and packaged for export to other high schools across the country (for more information, see http://nmelrc.byu.edu/). Some practical ideas for teaching similar courses are included here.

Choose an Interested and Knowledgeable Instructor

Raising students' awareness to the complex realities and the wonders of the Middle East through current events, history, and language can be achieved without large-scale structural adjustments or costly teacher education programs. The ideal instructor would be someone who has lived in the Middle East and is proficient in at least one Middle Eastern language. However, using the curriculum that has been developed, an open-minded social studies teacher with neither proficiency in a Middle Eastern language nor prior residence in the Middle East could teach this course and, if willing, acquire basic language skills that could significantly enrich the course. Another option is to enlist students from the Middle East as coteachers or teacher's assistants. Personal exposure to a mix of people from the Middle East is a cornerstone of the course and can be implemented in this way.

Include Guest Speakers From the Community

Teaching this course in a balanced way is a significant challenge, even for someone who has personal experience and respect for all parties involved in the conflict. To minimize the bias of the teacher, the curriculum at Provo High School was designed to include numerous presentations from guests within the community, including inviting the local imam of a mosque and the rabbi of a synagogue to participate in the celebration of religious holidays with the class or for question-and-answer sessions after the basic tenets of Islam and Judaism have been discussed. Visits of dynamic local specialists in history or political science also could be incorporated. College students from the Middle East and U.S. students who are using their language studies and knowledge of the Middle East to further their career goals are other possible guest speakers. Inviting people from the community helps to broaden the views of the teacher, the students, and the guests. The regular use of guest lecturers is an important component of the course and greatly enhances it, whether the lecturer is an area expert or an educator who sees an opportunity and wants to make a difference.

Include Thought-Provoking Topics and Questions and Allow Time for Exploration and Reflection

Because the primary focus of this course is to provide students with opportunities to grapple with complex issues, sufficient time must be allotted for students to individually explore a variety of perspectives in their journals and in discussions with their peers. We encourage teachers to open discussions with thought-provoking topics and questions that promote different perspectives. The greater the relevance, the more meaningful the course becomes and the greater the students' motivation to learn.

Also, having students bring in news reports, articles, or portions of radio or television programs to keep the discussion on current issues gives them an opportunity to direct the content of the class and feel it is both current and relevant. Indeed, we have emphasized in our language pedagogy the grounding of language instruction in vital topics and motivating students to learn a language in order to provide their own input and make a difference now and in the future.

◈ CONCLUSION

Student responses indicate that this Middle East class was successful in helping them to better understand the region and its people. Better-informed citizens are able to help family, friends, colleagues, and neighbors gain a deeper understanding of the

Middle East and its peace-loving people who yearn for a better world. The course was also designed to serve as a recruiting tool to encourage young students to continue studying the region and its languages to help produce a new generation of specialists who understand the Middle East and can thus more effectively explore solutions to address the challenges of the region. Time will tell if the course has these results as well.

The greatest distinguishing feature of the course is the potential it has for providing students with a different perspective on the Middle East and to use a language component as one means of raising awareness. Rooting out xenophobia and ignorance is a daunting task. However, even if one's reach (in terms of numbers of students) is limited, the leavening effect is incalculable. Recent political events have resulted in much increased interest in the Middle East and other parts of the world. The number of students reached through such programs could in fact be considerable. This course represents an innovative approach to giving more people (young and old) language learning experience, learning that is perceived by them to be timely and relevant. Widespread implementation of this type of curriculum could have long-reaching benefits for all. Clyne (1997) observed that "language is the most important medium of human communication. War, on the other hand, is probably the most important medium of non-communication" (p. 387). Education and tolerance can open pathways to peace, whereas ignorance and fear of other cultures can lead civilizations to violence.

◈ CONTRIBUTORS

Erin Fairlight Olsen is currently completing her master's degree in second language acquisition/Arabic and her TESOL graduate certificate at Brigham Young University in Provo, Utah, in the United States. She plans to obtain a PhD in international education and work on curriculum development in North Africa and the Middle East.

R. Kirk Belnap is director of the National Middle East Language Resource Center and an associate professor of Arabic at Brigham Young. He and his family have lived in Cairo, Jerusalem, and Tangier.

◈ APPENDIX: SAMPLE UNITS OF INSTRUCTION

Ultimate Cultural Goal	Current Events	History	Language
Begin to understand the role of women in the Arab world.	The parliament of Morocco passes a law that women will now hold one third of the seats. Journal: Do you think it is important for women to serve in the government?	Discuss female rulers in ancient history and the role of women in the Prophet Mohammed's life and his teachings on women.	New vocabulary: grandmother and other female kinship terms, parliament, government Review: Describing our homes using adjectives.

Continued on p. 118

Ultimate Cultural Goal	Current Events	History	Language
Understand Jewish aspirations for a Jewish state.	Discussion of the building of the fence to protect Israel from terrorist attacks. Journal: How will the fence affect Israel's relationships with its neighbors?	Discuss the Passover and Exodus from Egypt, entry into Canaan, and the establishment of the modern state of Israel.	Learn Hebrew Passover song.
Understand the role of the hajj in Islam.	Watch *Frontline* report on the hajj. Journal: What are your first reactions to the idea of a pilgrimage? Do you believe that there is some place that you are destined to go?	Discuss the historical significance of the hajj. When was the first hajj?	New vocabulary: Practice reading the Five Pillars of Islam in Arabic. Review: Numbers and dates in Arabic; practice telling time and asking one another's ages.
Understand different views on the separation of church and state.	Discuss the elections in Turkey and the nominee that wants to desecularize Turkey's government. Journal: What are the strengths and weaknesses of the separation of church and state?	Discuss Turkey's history: Brief review of Byzantine Empire onward. Discuss Ataturk and his secularization reforms.	New vocabulary: To vote, elections, government, capitol, reforms Review: Present tense forms.
Develop a feel for daily life in the Middle East through the eyes of a teenager from the region.	Have guest speaker. Journal: What was most surprising to you of all that our guest speaker said?	Jordanian guest speaker.	Guest speaker (Be sure students use greetings and ask all of the questions that they can in Arabic.)
Understand the different perspectives on the war with Iraq.	Watch excerpts from President Bush's UN address and discuss what his strong and weak points are. Journal: Is war sometimes necessary? When? Do you agree with war with Iraq?	Review the Gulf War and its results, such as the impact of UN sanctions against Iraq that have led to Arab sentiments of anti-war and, in some cases, anti-America.	New vocabulary: war, peace, to support, to oppose, to convince Review: Present tense of verbs and names of countries in Arabic (practice reading)

CHAPTER 9

Giving Them a Voice: Content-Based Instruction in an EFL Setting

Gabriel Díaz-Maggioli and Alicia Burbaquis-Vinson

◈ INTRODUCTION

Content-based instruction (CBI), as a framework for language teaching and learning, has not become a mainstream practice in English as a foreign language (EFL) settings. As opposed to English as a second language (ESL) situations, in most EFL settings, content is often merely an excuse to teach discrete grammatical items. In Latin America, more precisely, content-based initiatives have not proliferated at the same rate as they have in mainstream ESL environments. Despite this reality, the first content-based, partial-immersion elementary program recently has been established in Uruguayan public schools and, in its brief history, has opened up other avenues for CBI in EFL situations.

Uruguay, a country in South America, is roughly the size of the state of Pennsylvania, with a population of about 3 million. For many years, it was considered to be one of the Latin American countries with the highest educational level. However, during the past 20 years, it has sustained a succession of political and economic hardships that set its development back. One of the most direct consequences of those unfortunate situations was a weakening of the country's national educational system. However, since 1996, the country has been implementing a systemwide reform to target this problem. The main objectives of the National Educational Reform Movement (NERM) are enhanced accessibility, equity, and quality of education. Among its many initiatives, the National Administration of Public Education (ANEP) saw the need to offer a second language within the school day, to children who would otherwise not have the chance to access it. In 2000, the Elementary Schools Council of the ANEP became the host of an innovative bilingual education program, the first of its kind in Latin America. In this bilingual education program (BEP), children learn English through mathematics and science primarily, with other subject areas incorporated along the elementary-school cycle. In its short history, this program has turned into a very successful means of promoting the objectives of the NERM.

◈ CONTEXT

In Uruguay, elementary education is offered via two modalities: single- and double-shift schools. Single-shift school children attend classes from either 8:00 a.m. until

12:00 p.m. or from 1:00 p.m. until 5:00 p.m. and receive instruction exclusively in their native language. Given the many social problems experienced by the poorest populations, a new modality of school—double-shift schools—was developed in the early 1990s. These double-shift schools cater to the most challenged strata of the population and operate between 8:00 a.m. and 4:00 p.m. During this time, children receive breakfast, lunch, and an afternoon snack, and formal academic classes are interspersed with workshop sessions and recreation activities.

The children who attend these schools can be considered in danger of failing. Most of them come from single-parent homes located in poor urban areas. They may have been exposed to abuse and neglect, and parents tend to be unemployed. If these children did not come to school for an extended schedule, they would likely become street children. Given their socioeconomic disadvantages, these children have historically tended to perform poorly in academic subjects and seldom progressed beyond elementary school. Studies carried out until 1999 showed that the double-shift model managed to reduce the dropout rate—though not in a significant way—and that the sustained exposure to teaching stemming from the extension of the school day resulted in a moderate improvement in learning results. However, attrition rates in these schools continued to be higher than in other elementary schools around the country. Moreover, the atmosphere in the double-shift schools has been characterized as tense, given the many conflicts arising among students.

To improve the situation, the BEP program coordinator convened a group of second language (L2) educators to design the program 6 months before it was to start. This immersion team was in charge of designing the program standards, curriculum, and the professional development strategy. Members of this team were also responsible for the initial selection of teachers and for the monitoring of the experience during the 1st year of the program.

The basic arrangement of the BEP involved the L2 teacher introducing students to the language primarily through mathematics and science. The elementary school curriculum was restructured to accommodate a holistic approach to curriculum design. Teachers and the immersion team met frequently during the 1st year of implementation to design thematic units and align them with the mainstream elementary curriculum. Teachers made extensive use of manipulatives (e.g., snap-on cubes, solids, rods, pattern blocks, tangrams) and authentic L2 literature to deliver a hands-on, enriched curriculum where ongoing proactive assessment, cooperative learning, and differentiated instruction were the key instructional practices.

The success of the initial implementation of the BEP has caused the authorities to extend it to other parts of the country. Table 1 shows the number of immersion classrooms so far. In terms of the coverage of target population, Table 2 illustrates the acceptance of the program by a growing number of schools and families.

A key innovation brought about by the program was the creation of a resource center. Five of the teachers in the first cohort who did not take teaching positions developed specific materials for the immersion classrooms. Under the immersion team's guidance, they worked diligently selecting resources, designing classroom activities, and acting as communicators among the teachers in the classrooms. These teachers were also responsible for the creation of many of the manipulatives and other teaching resources needed for instruction. With their help, the implementation costs of the program were reduced significantly, because the lack of adequate funding posed an initial threat to the program's success. These teachers, together with those

TABLE 1. IMMERSION CLASSROOMS IN URUGUAY, 2001–2004

Number of Immersion Classrooms	2001	2002	2003	2004
1st grade	6	18	30	45
2nd grade	—	6	18	33
3rd grade	—	—	6	18
4th grade	—	—	—	6
Total	6	24	54	102

who were actually teaching in the program, were involved in modeling content-based strategies to new cohorts as the professional development agenda expanded.

To create the professional development model, the immersion team extensively reviewed the literature on teacher education and development. The result of this research was a 150-hour professional development program, which combined on-site workshops with online follow-up and a mentoring system for the supervision of novices.

At this stage, the teachers involved in the program have had no previous experience with either immersion education or CBI, having learned the second language mainly through audiolingual and/or pseudo-communicative approaches. Hence, it was anticipated that they would tend to dwell extensively on their "apprenticeship of observation" (Lortie, 1975) when beginning to make decisions in the classroom. The power of this apprenticeship became evident during the 1st semester. Mentors indicated that, after visiting the teachers, they could see good teaching in general but poor content-based teaching. In that respect, the observations of the mentors indicated that, given their previous experience with language learning, teachers tended to replicate many of the procedures they had been exposed to as students. They were language teachers, not content teachers. The follow-up professional development program gathered this information and targeted the problem in the midsemester meeting with the teachers. Mentors also went into the classroom and modeled effective content-based strategies for the teachers to observe. By the end of the 1st year, five out of the six immersion classrooms had become content-based language classrooms.

The expertise gained by these five teachers was instrumental in the professional development program for the second and third cohorts. During intensive 2-week sessions, these five pioneers contributed their insights and expertise on becoming a

TABLE 2. COVERAGE OF THE BILINGUAL EDUCATION PROGRAM IN URUGUAY, 2001–2005

Year	Schools	Teachers	Students
2001	5	6	180
2002	15	24	720
2003	25	54	1,600
2004	37	82	3,400
Projected for 2005	40	100	5,000

CBI teacher with prospective program candidates. They also shared videos of their classrooms and samples of students' work. In addition, the reflection in and on action that stemmed from the attempts to solve this problem (i.e., the lack of CBI in the classroom) served as fodder to the new generation of teachers undertaking their professional development as case studies of classroom situations were used extensively in further development sessions.

◈ DESCRIPTION

Program Design

The BEP is rooted in the conviction that the acquisition of a second language yields cognitive, academic, and attitudinal benefits to learners. The program was built taking into account the extensive research and best practices in L2 acquisition. At the cognitive level, the acquisition of a second language results in more mental flexibility, a greater capacity for concept formation, and diversity in mental operations (Bialystok & Hakuta, 1994; Vygotsky, 1962). At the same time, bilingual children seem to develop stronger metalinguistic awareness, which benefits the development of the native language (Díaz, 1985; Yelland, Pollack, & Mercuri, 1993). This improvement in higher mental processes results in enhanced academic performance (Garfinkel & Tabor, 1991; Rafferty, 1986), even in the case of children with special learning needs (Andrade, Kretschmer, & Kretschmer, 1989; Genesee, 1994). In terms of attitudes, research seems to indicate that early exposure to a second language experience fosters respect and appreciation of different cultures and diversity (Curtain, 1993; Met, 1991).

Children in the program receive instruction in English and Spanish. Two teachers work with each of the groups. One of the teachers covers curriculum areas such as social studies and language arts in Spanish—the children's native language. The other teacher delivers instruction in the target language mainly through mathematics and science in the first two grades, although other subject areas are integrated according to need and demand as children progress along the elementary cycle.

The program capitalizes heavily on techniques and procedures for teaching academic language that set it apart from other usual practices in EFL settings. First of all, the content-based nature of the procedures for curriculum development, teaching, and assessment depart radically from the mainstream EFL practices in the country. The reality of EFL in Uruguay indicates a strong emphasis on the teaching of grammar structures and a discrete approach to skills development. Even though hailed as communicative, the approach has yielded very few positive results. Hence, the incorporation of a content-based approach to teaching second languages has been received as a welcome improvement in the field.

Teachers working in the program are certified educators who have a teaching degree in elementary education and are also proficient in the second language (roughly a TOEFL of 550 or above). Teachers are expected to teach any content area of the prescribed elementary school curriculum—which is a national curriculum—via the second language.

Teachers must undergo a review of their qualifications and an oral interview in the second language. These two functions are performed by the immersion team.

Once selected, teachers attend a 150-hour professional development course that offers the necessary grounding for them to develop skills in implementing immersion education.

Curriculum and Materials

The curriculum of the program encompasses three fundamental standards: communication, culture, and connections. Standards-based instruction in the immersion program is based on the belief that standards help align the different levels of the curriculum. Basing the curriculum on standards helps create equal access to the curriculum, thus addressing the equity aims highlighted in the NERM. Likewise, standards "communicate high expectations to teachers, learners, and other stakeholders in the program, thus aiming at an improvement in a second crucial theme of the reform process: quality" (Burbaquis-Vinson, Brian, Brovetto, Casco, & Díaz, 2002, pp. 21–22). An important characteristic of this standards-based curriculum is that it allows the implementation of different kinds of assessment, both authentic and standardized. The information gathered from these different kinds of assessment allows the program to grow because it spots areas for further development and, at the same time, helps identify success stories that can be communicated to the rest of the community.

Insofar as materials are concerned, there are authentic materials in the form of children's literature in the second language and manipulatives to aid the development of mathematical, science, and linguistic concepts. Each classroom is furnished with a set of these materials to be used not only during the L2 hours but also throughout the school day, if needed.

Assessment of the program incorporated ongoing, proactive authentic assessment of student learning through authentic assessment tasks monitored by the teachers, class observation by mentors and school and system administrators, and a standardized mathematics and language arts test. An external evaluation unit designed and administered this test; its results are still being processed.

Other Resources

A key strategy in the success of the program is the resource center established in 2000. The resource center has been defined as "a clearinghouse for the development, organization and distribution of materials and other resources vital to the implementation of the program" (Burbaquis-Vinson, Brian, Brovetto, Casco, & Díaz, 2002, p. 51). The resource center fulfills a second important function in the program: It provides a physical space for educators to meet and expand their understanding of CBI. It offers continuing professional development opportunities as well as a network of information on educational opportunities for program participants and the wider TESOL community in the country. Topics covered in the resource center sessions include second language acquisition theory and practice, subject-area pedagogy (math, science, social studies, and other curriculum areas), professional development theory and practice, second language maintenance and expansion for teachers, and technology in the classroom.

◈ DISTINGUISHING FEATURES

Initial difficulties in the program's implementation arose from the apparent lack of qualified bilingual educators willing to participate. During the 1st year, 12 educators were selected to participate in the program. However, once the program began, the number of applicants soared, as shown in Table 3 (below). At present, of the 257 teachers who have completed the mandatory professional development program, 59 are teaching in immersion classrooms, 5 are working at the resource center, and the rest have been placed in a roster to opt for a teaching position during 2005.

Approach to Program Resistance

As is the case with any innovation, the BEP has encountered different forms of resistance since its inception.

Resistance at the Classroom Level

Perhaps the hardest obstacle encountered was the teachers' understanding of the nature of immersion education and CBI. Given their beliefs about teaching and learning, they insisted on spotting a linguistic structure and using subject-area contents to teach it. This approach severely limited the nature of the input provided to students and may be responsible for the limited intake identified in the first groups. To overcome this problem, a fluent system of communication among schools was implemented, and mentors carried out demonstrations of the approach in the classroom. An international expert on CBI and immersion education visited the country and did a 2-day seminar, which was followed by application and make-and-take sessions at the resource center.

The disruptive behavior of the students was another constraint at the classroom level. This situation was felt particularly at the beginning of the school year. Again, the immersion team provided support via workshops, study groups, and action—inquiries involving all the teachers. After the 2nd month of classes, most teachers had resolved the classroom management problems. The role of the school supervisors was also relevant in providing immersion teachers with enhanced awareness as to the sociocultural characteristics of the schools.

Resistance at the School Level

The biggest hurdle at the school level was to get the first language (L1) and L2 teachers to work cooperatively. Given previous innovations in the system, L1 teachers expected L2 teachers to receive certain economic privileges, such as extra compensation for second language proficiency. However, in reality, L1 and L2 teachers work under the same conditions. To foster cooperation and collegiality, L2 teachers attended the mandatory training that L1 teachers take on a yearly basis and

TABLE 3. TEACHERS WHO ATTENDED THE PROFESSIONAL DEVELOPMENT PROGRAM

1st cohort (2001)	2nd cohort (2001)	3rd cohort (2001)	4th cohort (2002)	5th cohort (2002)	6th cohort (2003)	7th cohort (2004)	8th cohort (2004)	Total
12	31	32	32	33	40	42	35	257

participated actively in the weekly planning sessions held at each school. They also volunteered to individually tutor students who were lagging behind. In Uruguay, most teachers work at a school for 20 hours a week, with the exception of those working in double-shift schools. The L2 teachers, given that they were to teach only half of the day, originally took up a 20-hour commitment. However, as the program developed, they were required to make a 40-hour commitment. Since the inception of this policy, problems have disappeared as L2 teachers have become an important part of the schools. They have proved instrumental in providing differentiated instruction opportunities in both Spanish and English for newcomers to the school as well as for those students who must repeat a grade because of their performance. L1 teachers have also developed a support system to coach children who have experienced difficulties in reading, writing, and mathematics.

Resistance at the System Level

The Uruguayan educational system is a highly centralized, hierarchical system. A supervisor who evaluates the administrators, teachers, and students oversees work at each school on a monthly basis. Resistance to the BEP came initially from the fact that, because classes were taught in a second language, most supervisors could not evaluate the teachers because they were not proficient in the target language. The immersion team extensively communicated the BEP vision to these authorities and published a brochure on the program and a set of guidelines in Spanish. In addition, the program coordinator accompanied inspectors in their school visits and served as liaison between them and the authorities. Because of this, all L2 teachers were evaluated according to the regulations. One recent innovation was the establishment of a mentoring system in which experienced immersion educators coach novices, thus providing a much-needed link between the L1 and L2 areas. Finally, the immersion team and the supervisors agreed on a lesson planning format in Spanish with the requirement that L2 teachers make explicit their content-obligatory and content-compatible language objectives.

Generally, it can be said that the incorporation of the BEP has proved to be a difficult task. Before the program was started, it was explained and advertised widely, with even the national media becoming involved. However, it became clear during the 1st and 2nd years of its implementation that there needed to be additional communication about the procedures and the results of the program. To aid this process, a document laying out the characteristics, procedures, and expected outcomes of the program was drafted and distributed free of charge to all schools and teacher education institutions in the country. Videos showing actual classrooms at work are used in 1-day workshops delivered by the immersion team. These workshops are used to make stakeholders aware of the benefits of the BEP while clearly addressing the hows and whats of a partial-immersion model that uses CBI as its main theoretical framework.

It should be noted that the parents' initial resistance was mainly overcome once the children began to communicate their enthusiasm about learning a second language to their families. Even though this resistance was minimal, it had to be addressed. To give parents a feel of what their children would experience, the program coordinator visited all schools during the 1st week of classes and conferred with parents, and, in some cases, even gave a demonstration of the concept of shapes and colors to parents who knew no English whatsoever.

Approach to Innovation

Rahman (personal communication, 2003) characterizes innovation as a process in which three constant variables interact:

- Simplification: The purpose of innovation is to make things easier.

- Speed: Innovations aim at speeding the system up so that it becomes more effective.

- Improvement: Any innovation needs to make things better.

He also suggests ways in which innovation can take place:

- Analyzing our core technology: What is it that we do? What is the core of our function? What is the core technology we are good at and how can we make this core function better?

- Remixing common elements: In the work that we do, we need to reformulate, reshape, and resimplify the practical use of our core functions.

- Filling unmet needs: In everything that we do, there is an element of work we have not addressed before that provides a niche for innovation.

- Process reengineering—or new ways to do things.

- Fusing technology: Taking two ways of doing the same thing and putting them together to bring about a third technology that simplifies, speeds up, and improves the process.

The BEP has tried to incorporate these aspects of innovation in a number of ways, including the following approaches.

Approach to Language

Willis (1996) explains that research on second language acquisition has identified three necessary conditions for the acquisition of language to take place. These three conditions are (a) exposure to extensive input of authentic language in use, (b) opportunities for learners to use that input in communicative settings, and (c) motivation to use that input. The BEP's content-based nature allows for all three conditions to take place. The program views language as a tool for communication and, as such, it promotes the active engagement of learners in language use. Following Krashen's (1987) characterization of the different stages of language acquisition, teachers in the program use different strategies to make the language salient to students embedded in mathematical and scientific concepts, which are age appropriate and cognitively appropriate.

Approach to Learning

No two people learn in the same way or at the same pace. The BEP recognizes these two facts and fosters the teachers' understanding of these variables by incorporating the concept of diversity at all levels of curriculum development and implementation. Teachers use cooperative learning extensively, but there are also chances for teachers to directly teach the content to learners. However, the teaching done by teachers has the characteristic of mediation, more than direct instruction. The theory of multiple intelligences has been used as a model for classroom organization, giving teachers the goal to plan their classes according to the different emphases students present. The mediating role of teachers also allows them to act as assessors of students on a daily basis. The feedback gained through the multiple assessment opportunities is used later on to plan lessons and further develop the curriculum.

Approach to Teaching

Perhaps the greatest contribution of the BEP is its approach to teaching. Education in many Latin American countries is characterized by the systematic implementation of a transmission model, where the all-knowing instructor teaches concepts to learners, who are, in turn, expected to practice those concepts and be able to repeat them, as if on cue, at the time of testing. The BEP incorporated a reconceptualization of the roles of teachers and learners in the classroom. The main teaching methods advocated maximizing the benefits of CBI, including cooperative learning, differentiated instruction, the natural approach, total physical response, brain-based learning, and task-based learning.

Approach to Professional Development

The preferred mode of delivery for professional development programs in this country is the intensive 3- to 5-day workshop, where teachers are expected to absorb the knowledge transmitted by the presenters for later translation into their classrooms. Given that teachers in the program had had no experience with immersion education practices, the immersion team felt that a reconceptualization of the approach to professional development was needed. The instructional design of the professional development program incorporated on-site, hands-on workshops taught using the concept of loop input (Woodward, 1993), follow-up application sessions in the resource center, year-long mentoring, and an online component.

In designing this program, the immersion team took into consideration two existing views of the process of supervision (Sergiovanni & Starratt, 1993). According to Sergiovanni and Starratt, one mode of supervision is bureaucratic, where teachers are subordinate to the decisions of authorities. This mode of supervision, which the authors call Supervision I, is the one in effect in the Uruguayan educational system. Whereas this mode of supervision is useful in establishing control over the teachers, it contributes very little to the professional development of the teachers in the program. Supervision II, on the contrary, places teachers in a superordinate position in terms of the system and regards them as contributing professionals, able to identify needs and chart their own development. The professional development model took both concepts of supervision into account, making use of Supervision I during the initial stages of implementation (on-site workshops, initial mentoring, online component) and applying the principles and practices of Supervision II during the follow-up application sessions in the resource center and in later stages of the mentoring process.

The initial 2-week intensive professional development program covered the following:

- Perspectives on teaching and learning: theories of learning, including behaviorism, constructivism, social interactionism, neuroscience, and brain-based learning

- Second language acquisition: L1 and L2 acquisition theories, including Krashen's monitor theory; Krashen and Terrell's natural approach (Krashen, 1987); and Cummins's (Cummins, n.d.) basic interpersonal communications skills and cognitive academic language proficiency skills model

- Second language teaching models: second language teaching methods, with a focus on immersion education, CBI, and curricular alignment in the immersion classroom

- Best practices in immersion education: learning styles theory, multiple intelligences, cooperative learning, differentiated instruction, total physical response, and management of immersion classrooms

- The local bilingual education program: its history and status, the program and curriculum standards, the standards-based model, and the language teacher and the learning community

- CBI: teaching language through mathematics, science, social studies, language arts, and other curriculum areas; integrated instruction; and thematic teaching

- Technology-enhanced learning and teaching (module delivered online): teaching and learning with and through technology

- Evaluation and assessment: Evaluation and assessment of learning, teaching, and tools for the immersion classroom

To allow for maximum involvement in the part of the participants, the immersion team followed the advice provided by Magestro (2000) on how to organize the contents of the session. Each workshop facilitator followed the 6-I professional development agenda (as detailed in the appendix) to plan and deliver their encounters with the teachers. In addition, the immersion team adopted a workshop session planning framework (see the appendix for a sample workshop plan). This framework allows participants to become active builders of their professional knowledge, and, at the same time, it provides ample opportunities for reflection and integration of new learning experiences.

Approach to Curriculum and Materials Development

Resource Center

The resource center was a key factor in helping reduce the cost of materials while providing a forum for networking, professional growth, and communication about the program. Just at the level of materials design alone, the production of this center has been instrumental in helping L2 teachers cope with the extra demands of teaching language and content.

Creation of Communities of Practice

In making an explicit and sustained effort to involve as many stakeholders as possible, the BEP has brought together families, teachers, students, and administrators in unprecedented ways. This is shown by the strong adherence of parents, teachers, and administrators to the model, as well as for the constant request from local education authorities and individual schools to become a site of the program. Likewise, L2 teachers have set the immersion experience in the Uruguayan context, which offers new insights into the possibilities for the teaching of content and language in the country. The wealth of knowledge constructed by these communities has placed student learning at the center of the educational debate.

Technology Integration

By incorporating new communication and information technologies as mainstream immersion practices, the BEP has opened the door to the application of these technologies in other areas of the educational system.

Incorporation of Other Languages in the Elementary Curriculum

Given its proximity to Brazil, the northern part of Uruguay presents a bilingual situation that has only recently been acknowledged. Historical and geographic factors contributed over the past 2 centuries to the development of a number of dialectal varieties of Portuguese, known as Portuguese dialects of Uruguay (PDU). Paradoxically, even when whole communities speak these dialects, instruction in schools is delivered through Spanish, which is, in fact, a second language for those learners. Schools in this area of the country have Spanish L1 speakers, Portuguese L1 speakers, and PDU L1 speakers. Research data show that attainment levels in those areas rank among the lowest in the country. As a result of the success of the CBI initiative in the BEP, a pilot, two-way immersion experience started in two schools in the north of the country in 2003. This pilot program differs slightly from the initial partial-immersion model in that both the Spanish and Portuguese teachers will undergo the same professional development and will apply the same core content-based procedures to their teaching to develop learners' communicative competence in both languages simultaneously while respecting the learners' L1 that is used in socialization settings.

◈ PRACTICAL IDEAS

The following is a working list of practical ideas and suggestions that were taken into consideration at the time of planning the BEP.

Prepare a Thorough Research Base for the Program

Be sure to share your research base for the program with all stakeholders. Illustrate theory with concrete examples, if possible, from the local reality.

Involve as Many Stakeholders as Possible at the Design Stage

Emphasize the need for a connection between the school and parents and the parents and learners as the starting point of any educational endeavor.

Agree on an Implementation Schedule That Is Realistic

Take into consideration the human and material resources available when developing an implementation schedule.

Prepare a Budget Congruent With the Needs and Expectations of Stakeholders

In many realities, resources are scarce, and there is a tendency to think of innovations as expensive and even irrelevant given the scarcity of funds. Be creative in developing the materials needed and share whatever is available.

Communicate, Communicate, and Communicate

Communicate throughout the design process. Communication in the BEP involved visits to prospective schools, meetings with parents, and evaluation sessions involving supervisors, principals, and teaching partners before starting the program in the schools. Participate in community-sponsored activities and recruit the help of the media in spreading the word about the program.

After the first stages unfold, communicate some more. Be aware that it is during the first stages of implementation where frustration levels tend to be at the highest. Hence, enable participants in the innovation to network and share what works and what does not.

Provide Extensive Professional Development for L1 and L2 Teachers and System Administrators

Initial and ongoing professional development encourages participation and self-reflection. Make sure that the professional development strategy is congruent with principles of relevance.

Assess Constantly, in Multiple Ways, and Proactively Apply Assessment Results

Do not fear change; foster it. It is from the lessons learnt that true progress begins.

Document Everything

This includes data, anecdotes, quotes, incidents, and so forth. Use these in promotional materials about the program. Systematize findings, and look for thematic threads that may contribute to the enhancement of the procedures implemented.

Promote Sustained Networking Among Program Stakeholders

Constantly promote the sharing of experiences, ideas, and resources in an attempt to build a grounded theory. Reach out to the community, and make the impact of the program salient.

Do Not Give Up, Even in the Face of Adversity

◈ CONCLUSION

In the 2 years since its inception, the BEP in Uruguay has accomplished a cultural change in the schools where it is being developed and resulted in increased learning gains for students, teachers, and the broader community. Attrition and dropout rates in the schools where the program functions have been reduced by 19% and 48% respectively, and high levels of satisfaction are evidenced by the number of teachers applying to teach in the program, as well as by the number of schools who want to become part of it.

Given the initial results of the program—stemming mainly from incidental data gathered so far—it appears that its impact will continue to be positive. On the one hand, the program has managed to bring together a number of educators who work at different levels in the system. This collective involvement of professionals has brought about a more fluid sharing of knowledge and expertise. On the other hand, more children are succeeding in the program than in any other educational innovation in the system. Finally, the incorporation of technology in the classroom has prompted an interest in the processes and practices common to technology-enhanced teaching.

The prospects for the expansion of the program to other double-shift schools look promising. Under funding from a grant by the World Bank, the BEP is expected to have reached 5,000 of the 50,000 elementary school students by the year 2006. This grant will allow for the purchase of materials, teacher development, and program monitoring. During 2004, a second external evaluation assessed the institutional impact of the program as well as the learning gains derived from its implementation. In short, the experience has demonstrated that, so far, there are clear advantages in the incorporation of a content-based language learning model at the elementary level. These gains have been noticed not only at the level of attrition and dropout rates but also at the level of school culture and contributions to the profession through the development of situated theories of learning and teaching.

Jose Pedro Varela, the 19th-century educator and reformer whose forethought guided the development of the Uruguayan National Education System in the 19th century, provided the vision for this program when he wrote:

> In order to establish the Republic the first thing we have to do is to educate the republicans. To foster the government of the people by the people it is necessary to awaken, to actively involve all citizens; in order for public opinion to be truly democratic we need to teach the citizens of the country in democratic ways; all the needs of Democracy, all the demands of the Republic can only be heeded through one means: educate . . . always educate" (as cited in National Administration of Public Education, 1999, p. 48).

⬦ CONTRIBUTORS

Gabriel Díaz-Maggioli is an educational supervisor, teacher educator, and current coordinator of the bilingual education program in Montevideo, Uruguay. During 2002–2003, he was a visiting Hubert H. Humphrey Fellow at The Pennsylvania State University.

Alicia Burbaquis-Vinson is the founder of the bilingual education program in Uruguay and served as coordinator from its inception through July 2003. She has taught extensively in immersion programs at the elementary level in Kentucky, United States, where she was also a teacher educator. Currently she is affiliated with the Kentucky Educational Television Network, where she produces and delivers a Spanish distance-learning program that utilizes content-based instruction.

◈ APPENDIX: SAMPLE WORKSHOP PLAN

Date:	Facilitator:	Group:

Aims of the session	Purpose of the session expressed in terms of the facilitator's input.	
Objectives of the session	Expected outcomes of this session, expressed in terms of what the participants should be able to do upon completion of this session.	
Resources	**Contents**	Articles, books, video, etc. (the "software")
	Process	Overhead projector, flip chart, etc. (the "hardware")

The 6-I Professional Development Agenda

Inspiration	A brief task/activity that serves as motivator to explore background knowledge and preconceptions
Input	A brief presentation of the main contents to be explored in the session
Illustration	A demonstration of the concepts in action followed up by participants' discussion
Integration	Loop activities/tasks for participants to experience the concepts firsthand
Inquiry	Reflection upon what has been learned/discovered. Time for participants to pose development questions.
Impact	Assessment of the learning and teaching in this session (self-assessment, peer assessment, assessment of facilitator, etc.)

Follow-Up
Next steps to be taken by participants (peer coaching? mentoring? etc.)

CHAPTER 10

Frilled Up Science: Developing Practices Within Collaboration

Sophie Arkoudis

⬦ INTRODUCTION

Since the late 1980s, educational policy direction in mainstreaming English for speakers of other languages (ESOL) education in the Australian state of Victoria has focused on the role of the ESOL teacher and the ESOL program to include whole-school approaches. Official documents continue to stress the need for "promoting colleagues' awareness of the language demands of all aspects of the curriculum, and assisting in developing teaching strategies throughout the school to promote Language Other Than English (LOTE) background students' language development" (Board of Studies, 2000, p. 5). Although this policy direction was welcomed by the ESOL profession in Victoria (Davison, 2001), it had signaled a change in the role of the ESOL teacher to include working with mainstream staff in the school. A major impact of this change has been that ESOL teachers need to develop skills in working with mainstream teachers, which can be a very complex process (see chapter 4 in this volume). This chapter will discuss how an ESOL and a science teacher work together in planning a unit of work for a Year 10 science class in an inner-metropolitan, multiethnic secondary school in Melbourne, the capital city of Victoria. It will explore the processes that are involved in maintaining and sustaining collaborative teaching practices in secondary school contexts.

⬦ CONTEXT

Jelford Secondary College was a large, metropolitan coeducational secondary school with an established ESOL program. The school had a large population of speakers of LOTE, as well as a large number of newly arrived ESOL students. At the time of the study, the school population was 734. Ninety-five percent of the students came from families in which one or more parent spoke a language other than English at home. The distinctive feature of the school was that it had a reputation in Victoria as one that worked hard to improve the educational needs of ESOL students. Teachers at this school were committed to teaching in an environment where most of their students come from LOTE backgrounds, and a significant number of students in mainstream classes were learning the English language as well as the subject content.

⬦ DESCRIPTION

The school was one of the largest ESOL secondary colleges in metropolitan Melbourne and one of a few ESOL schools in Victoria that had a separate ESOL faculty. ESOL teachers, in Victorian government schools, were usually part of the English faculty. At the time of the study, the school was facing a dilemma. The number of ESOL students in the school was increasing, yet the number of ESOL teachers remained the same. The reason for this was largely because of the change in the federal government's funding of ESOL programs.

According to the school's ESOL co-coordinator, approximately 25% of all students from language backgrounds other than English were targeted by the school's ESOL program. A high proportion of those students had been in Australia for less than 3 years. Most had spent 6 months in a nearby intensive English language center before enrolling at the school. At the time of this study, priority was given to the needs of the recently arrived ESOL learners, particularly the students at the elementary levels of language proficiency and the more advanced students in Years 10, 11, and 12 who were identified as needing ESOL support.

The organization of the ESOL program was typical of Victorian schools with ESOL specialist teachers involved in the direct teaching of ESOL students, and less than a quarter of the overall ESOL resources directed to support teaching in the mainstream (State of Victoria Department of Education and Training, 2003). Most of the support teaching was concentrated in Years 11 and 12—the final years of secondary schooling. Class sizes in direct ESOL classes ranged from 16 students in junior years to 8 students in Year 12. Year-level, rather than English language proficiency, determined how ESOL classes were grouped. This meant that there were mixed-ability groups with different English language levels in every ESOL class. ESOL classes were run parallel to English and humanities classes. ESOL was also offered as an elective in Years 7–10. It was possible for newly arrived students to have up to 15 periods of ESOL classes in their 1st year of schooling. Compared to other ESOL programs in Victoria, Jelford had an extensive ESOL program for recently arrived ESOL learners.

As a result of placing so many resources into the new arrivals program, there was little direct support available for non-English-speaking students who had been born in Australia or who had completed most of their schooling in the Victorian education system. These students had been learning English for more than 3 years and generally experienced problems coping with the English language demands of mainstream education (Davison, 2001). The school attempted to address the English language needs of these learners by arranging for ESOL and mainstream teachers to plan curriculum for the mainstream classroom together.

The school was committed to raising mainstream teachers' awareness of the language and learning needs of ESOL students. The whole school had participated in the "ESL in the Mainstream" course (Education Department of South Australia, 1991), which involved all staff in 10 sessions of professional development after school. This program offered mainstream teachers ESOL strategies that they could use in their classrooms. In addition, it encouraged mainstream and ESOL teachers to work together in planning for the mainstream classes. This further indicated the mainstream teachers' willingness to develop better ways of teaching the ESOL learners in their classroom and the administration's support for this.

◈ DISTINGUISHING FEATURES

One of the distinguishing features of this program was that ESOL and mainstream teachers involved in collaboration were allocated time to plan together. The teachers met 1 day a week for 1 hour. Involvement in this aspect of the ESOL program was voluntary.

Alex, the science teacher, and Victoria, the ESOL teacher, had worked collaboratively with each other and with other teachers for many years. At the time of the study, they were working together in planning for Alex's Year 10 class. In interviews conducted during the study, Alex said that he was willing to try new ideas in his science class and recognized that ESOL students needed some support in his classroom. According to Victoria, her aim was to offer Alex ESOL ideas and strategies that could become a part of his teaching style and therefore develop his own understanding of ESOL students' needs that he would be able to use in future classes. The nature of their collaboration was that they were both willing to engage in ongoing conversations about ESOL learners. This was not a one-time approach to professional development but rather an ongoing commitment by the teachers and the school.

The Planning Conversation Extract

For the purposes of this chapter, I will focus the rest of this discussion on the short extract from the teachers' planning conversation on genetics to illustrate the complexities involved in sharing pedagogical understandings. This extract was selected from a larger study (Arkoudis, 2000), and it highlights the process involved in developing collaborative practices. The teachers were planning a unit of work on genetics and discussed what they wanted to achieve in the planning conversation. Victoria suggested to Alex that he might want to ask the students what they already know about the topic. In the following extract, capital letters indicate where the speaker used higher than normal stress, ". . ." indicates a short hesitation of less than 3 seconds, and "==" indicates an overlap between the teachers' speaking.

25   Alex: But what I'm really wary of is umm is that disparity between science and humanities. I mean I wouldn't like to sort of say, well OK I understand the social implications of this but I'm not really going to APPLY myself to the understanding of the process, the causes, and the preventions and all of the other, that word rigorous (they both laugh)—it's ACTUALLY very hard to understand and do require you to think in a very disciplined way about what's going on, if you really are going to get the ultimate understanding of what's going on. So yes, I'm wary of it being, like SO MANY of the so-called girl-friendly things that happened in the seventies and eighties in science, but really ended up being, I think, just fairly trivial explorations of science. And I think the girls saw through these in the end, that really they were just being presented with FRILLED-UP science and not being exposed to some of the more DEMANDING aspects of the subject. I DON'T WANT TO GO DOWN THAT PATH TOO FAR, but I do want to motivate students in the beginning.

26 Victoria: The thing is with what students come though, I mean . . . you know with myself, I remember my understanding of genetics, I can imagine that this is quite common, that sort of umm sense of umm blending that idea of it sort of. . . you know. . . if you know . . . if you have black and white you'll end up with grey or kind of like sort of, which is a very naive notion, BUT in some ways I see that as, like to me, that sort of, just because I went through that, that's some sort of preliminary understanding that's necessary and it needs to perhaps be refined, but I'm interested just in how umm you work, I mean would students in Year 10 have those sorts of naive notions or do you think that they would by that stage they would have something more . . . developed . . . scientifically?

27 Alex: Well, it would be interested to know what you know NOW about that. That is I think (V. laughs) everybody's first, that melting pot idea, that averaging of mothers and fathers to make kids, is the most intelligence that == some people bring to the subject.

28 Victoria: == Yeah and at some stage, would scientists have had that understanding?

29 Alex: Oh, absolutely. . . . They certainly thought that. I mean it was basically that monk Gregor Mendel who when he did experiments on peas that sort of made it more PARTICULAR. You know, it isn't black, the fact is that it will act independently and sometimes one dominates the other and sometimes it doesn't. So that in the examples you know about, I mean YOU CAN GET a white petunia and a red petunia as part of the work requirement, umm not petunias they don't work like this but other flowers do, peas do, if you get a white pea and a red pea then you'll end up with a pink flower. And THAT'S what happens. I mean this is called incomplete dominance in genetics, but it's quite rare I mean the more USUAL thing that happens is that one will generally dominate the other. And see they also bring with them concepts like the fact that if you have a white person and a black person then the kiddies will be all black, wont they? Whereas if you had an Asian and a . . . you know, Caucasian person then the kiddies will all look pretty Asian. They bring that with them too, that there are certain indomitable genes or indomitable factors in inheritance and there are others that blend. So those two things they bring with them, they just don't have any sense about them. They don't know how to make any sense of that and part of my job is to try and say, OK, these two things do exist and how can we EXPLAIN them you know, in a theoretical sense?

30 Victoria: I mean I know who Mendel is but I don't know much about him. What motivated his research within the particular area?

31 Alex: Well, he was just in the church and in the church it was quite common to be naturalists. And when they weren't writing their sermons, they engage in gardening and in his case he loved to garden. He had an inquiring mind and was a naturalist and wanted to know about how to grow a better pea. He set up, not just a garden to grow peas, but you know

an experimental garden, and investigated the way things in peas that he wanted were being passed on. He pre-dated Darwin, his work was unknown by Darwin, unfortunately. And if Darwin had KNOWN about his work he would have been able to come up with a much better a much more plausible theory of inheritance by natural selection than he was ABLE to. He wouldn't have faced 50 years of isolation.

32 Victoria: Mmm do you talk to the kids about that?

33 Alex: No, I DON'T. It's too sophisticated.

34 Victoria: OH NO BUT THAT'S SUCH A I mean kids love injustice, you know. You know, here this person did ALL THIS WORK, and it could have helped and it was just disregarded. Now he is known as the father of, I don't know, things, but you know he has this sort of key role in the whole history of genetics. I just think, BUT TO ME that sort of stuff makes it very human and real and it moves it from beyond the study of this topic genetics to that sort of whole thing of scientific == discovery.

35 Alex: == Scientific shit. (he laughs)

36 Victoria: NO IT'S NOT SHIT. You know I think that's really interesting.

37 Alex: Are you, I mean you're an intellectual. You're a person who is you know

38 Victoria: I don't think so.

39 Alex: YES, YOU ARE. You are also a social scientist. You're a person who, I mean I DON'T THINK MANY of our students in Year 10 are much like you, if you know what I mean, their motivations are really much different from that. They like the BLOOD BIT, but I don't know whether they would like the social history aspect. I mean they MIGHT. I might be completely wrong, but I think that I could talk all day about the history side, but I SELDOM DO. I think I don't because they just don't like it much.

40 Victoria: Oh, I wasn't suggesting talking all day. I just thought that umm that somehow it makes it you know part of human endeavor and all that sort of stuff. I mean I just FEEL that all students, you know, connect with that a bit, and I wonder too with the different cultures that are represented in the group, that you know just the different educational backgrounds and things like that, I mean there could be some pretty fascinating things umm represented there too. Like you'd have, you might have some students that would have very umm . . . fundamentalist beliefs. I mean, how, I mean does that come up?

41 Alex: It does.

42 Victoria: How do you deal with that?

43 Alex: EVERYBODY in my class, given an opportunity, will tell me the very fundamental things, either from the point of view of Islam or the point of view of Christianity, about what really happened. And about you know us having nothing to do with monkeys whatsoever and . . . you know we are God's children. I ALWAYS SAY at the beginning, and we began a few weeks ago in talking about changing species, we were talking about evolution, that my aim was not to offend anybody, and that I was aware of the fact that there are lots of different explanations

about how we all came here. And that what I WAS DOING was giving what was the accepted scientific view of the MOMENT. A view that was changing, and changing according to the evidence that people are getting from experiments around the world. But . . . but principally I was not about offending people, and if ANYTHING I SAY offended, I'm sorry, and I would really like to talk about it, but I am not trying to push religion here, and I'm just sort of trying to give you a scientific viewpoint. And, that's, every single student in my class, WITHOUT EXCEPTION, has a fundamentalist Christian or Islamic view about the way we got here. AND THEY SEEM TO BE ABLE TO TALK TO ME ABOUT THESE OTHER IDEAS while still holding those. And that's what I mean about INTELLECTUALS, they you know they are able to hold both those things in their mind at once, PERFECTLY happy it seems to me.

44   Victoria: It's just as well or you might see yourself outcast. (They laugh)
45   Alex: That's true. Well, one's BORING OLD SCIENCE and the other one's FAMILY and FRIENDS and CULTURE. I mean they really don't put the two together at all. We should perhaps talk about how we're going to approach this. . . . Umm I've produced this little idea here, and WHAT I'VE TRIED TO DO THERE is indicate from my own perspective about how I think we should start, and as I mentioned before, it has to start with sex. It has to start with your understanding of how a new individual is formed. And, already we've discussed this and umm they understand that really everybody begins just as ONE CELL and that cell is a combination of cells from TWO PARENTS.

Discussion of Extract

Within the ESOL field, there has been a lack of conceptualization of how ESOL teachers can develop collaborative practices with mainstream teachers. The previous extract can offer some insights into how two experienced teachers work together when planning a unit of work. Harré's (1999) positioning theory has been used to analyze the planning conversation. Within positioning theory, Harré has provided a framework that allowed for a focus on the capacity of the teachers to position themselves and each other within their conversation (cf. Harré & van Langenhove, 1999). The framework was used to explore the mutual cooperation in the positioning and the reasons why this was occurring. This mutual cooperation is revealed through the teachers' perceptions of themselves and each other as they negotiate the science and ESOL curriculum. This, in turn, offered some insights into how the teachers work together.

Throughout the extract presented here Alex asserted his opinion. Victoria, on the other hand, appeared to defer to Alex. A simple interpretation of this could be that Alex, as the science teacher, was more powerful than Victoria. This would be a situation that ESOL teachers, who work with mainstream teachers, may be familiar with. It would appear that their subject disciplines defined their power relations within the conversation. Although this may be true to a certain extent, to accept only this interpretation would mean that ESOL teachers would have little, if any, influence in their work with mainstream teachers. The discussion needs to move beyond this interpretation to one that explores how teachers from different subject disciplines, whose views of teaching and learning are defined by their subject disciplines (Siskin & Little, 1995), can maintain productive dialogue.

As mentioned previously, Alex and Victoria have been working together for many years. Victoria was familiar with Alex's views about ESOL teaching. In the extract she used strategies to sustain the conversation, sidestep Alex's nonnegotiating stance, and open up some space in the conversation where ideas can move forward. Strategically, Victoria chose to take a noncombative stance in the conversation, thereby positioning herself as deferring to Alex. Alex, by virtue of being the science teacher, held the authority over the science curriculum. Victoria had to convince him that he needed to change his approach to science teaching. He did not want any of Victoria's suggestions to trivialize what he saw as important in science teaching. For Alex, science was a serious subject area, one that is perceived as important within the academic hierarchy of the secondary school (Reid, 1992). He had firmly positioned himself within his subject discipline, claiming responsibility for the content and not necessarily for the education of ESOL students if it meant "frilling up" his teaching of science. Alex did not feel that he had to justify his teaching to Victoria. At no point in the conversation had Victoria challenged Alex's authority over the science curriculum. This revealed the mutual positioning of Alex by both teachers, which allowed the conversation to move forward.

Victoria did not have the same claims as Alex over the science curriculum, but she exercised her power in managing the conversation. Howie (1999), using Harré's framework, refers to this as strategic positioning. Victoria wanted to achieve certain insights with Alex about the importance of accessing students' background knowledge of genetics. This was especially important as there were different cultural groups in the class, and therefore there may have existed different views on the origin of the human species. Rather than accepting Alex's views, Victoria engaged him in an exchange of information to keep the channels of communication open. She did not dismiss his views or challenge his perceptions. To do so would have resulted in the probable termination of the conversation, which was not what Victoria wanted to achieve. By the end of the extract, Victoria's deference to Alex and probing of his views resulted in Alex acknowledging Victoria's point about the importance of students' background knowledge in teaching genetics. She elicited Alex's responses to her questions and then supplemented and complimented his knowledge and experiences with teaching strategies that he could use in the classroom. This allowed opportunities for Victoria to explore different possibilities with Alex that led to some agreement at the end of the extract between the two teachers. In this way, Victoria demonstrated her positive positioning skills (Howie, 1999) and was powerful within the planning conversation. This, in turn, influenced future planning meetings as the teachers developed these new understandings further.

◈ PRACTICAL IDEAS

Accept That Unequal Power Relations Exist

ESOL teachers enter the mainstream teachers' domain and offer ideas about teaching language within their subject area. This is usually done within the school context where ESOL as a subject discipline is not afforded the same status as curriculum areas such as mathematics, science, and history. Accept the power dynamics, as Victoria did, and concentrate on developing strategies that offer productive conversation about catering for ESOL students in mainstream subject areas.

Be Aware of the Processes Involved in Maintaining Collaborative Practices

The diagram here (see Figure 1) can help to inform ESOL teachers' work with mainstream teachers. The knowledge quadrant represents the public and visible knowledge that the mainstream teachers express. This would involve the content of their subject area. The understanding quadrant represents the private pedagogic assumptions that teachers have about their subject area. This could include their ideas about what is good and effective teaching in their subject area as well as their view of themselves as effective classroom teachers. Although this view is privately held, ESOL teachers can challenge some of the assumptions and offer other teaching strategies. Through discussion of different ideas and strategies, mainstream teachers may begin to appropriate some of them into their own teaching. When the ideas are successfully tried out in class, there could be a shift in mainstream teachers' teaching experiences. When mainstream teachers have appropriated the new ideas, they are able to publicize them by presenting them as information. Once the information is discussed in public, then it becomes part of the knowledge base of the teachers. The movement around the quadrants can lead to developing the mainstream teachers' pedagogy to include ESOL students' learning needs.

Accept That Collaboration Is a Process of Ongoing Professional Development

The movement around the quadrants is not unidirectional. In the course of different conversations that Alex and Victoria engaged in as part of the larger study (Arkoudis, 2000), they moved backwards and forwards across the quadrants, sometimes spending a lot of time attempting to appropriate certain ideas, as in the frilled-up

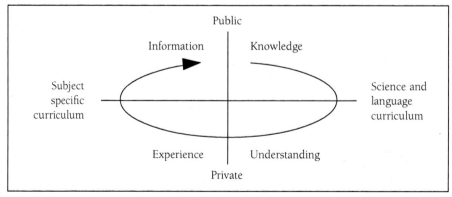

FIGURE 1. Mainstreaming ESOL: The Professional Development Project (Reprinted from Arkoudis, 2000, p. 241, with permission)

science extract. The aim would be for ESOL and mainstream teachers to be able to work in all four quadrants in their attempts to achieve shared understandings. This understanding could emerge over a period of time. The model allows the ESOL teachers to understand the nature of their work in developing collaborative practices.

Recognize That Developing Collaborative Practices Is Difficult

ESOL teachers need to acknowledge that there are genuine dilemmas and difficulties in attempting to bring together the somewhat different and competing perspectives of two teachers who come from different discourse communities. Whether ESOL teachers are involved in team teaching, support teaching, or professional development of educators from different fields, the essence of their work is in reconstructing the pedagogic understandings of teachers. This means that mainstream teachers will need to change or adapt their teaching style. The difficulty for the ESOL teacher is not so much about the strategies that can be recommended for teaching but in convincing the mainstream teachers that they may need to change.

Be Strategic in Your Work With Mainstream Teachers

ESOL teachers should have a plan in terms of what they want to achieve when working with mainstream teachers. Try to work out what issues you want to discuss in relation to ESOL students and what can remain for future conversations. It is important to maintain communication, as the main aim in collaborative work should be increasing educational opportunities for ESOL learners in mainstream classes.

◈ CONCLUSION

Policy makers in Australia, the United Kingdom, and the United States have assumed that collaboration between ESOL and mainstream teachers is a simple process of embedding the language curriculum into the mainstream subject curriculum. This discussion has highlighted the complex process of developing collaborative practices between ESOL and mainstream teachers. It has emphasized the important role of the ESOL teacher in this process. Notions of power as well as teachers' views of teaching within their subject discipline make the collaboration process an ongoing journey of professional development. The model in Figure 1 provides a way to conceptualize and appraise teacher learning within the professional development project implicit in collaborative practices. The model may assist ESOL and mainstream teachers to cross the rough ground that divides their subject disciplines and move toward shared understandings.

◈ CONTRIBUTOR

Sophie Arkoudis is a TESOL educator at the Department of Language, Literacy, and Arts Education, University of Melbourne, in Australia, and has vast experience in the secondary school sector. She has researched and published a number of articles in the area of mainstream and ESOL teachers' collaboration. She is currently the coeditor of the Australian journal *TESOL in Context*.

PART 3

Standards- and Content-Based Curriculum, Assessment, and Professional Development

CHAPTER 11

On the Road to "MECCA": Assessing Content-Based Instruction Within a Standards Framework

Margo Gottlieb and Timothy Boals

◈ INTRODUCTION

U.S. federal law mandating the inclusion of English language learners in statewide academic testing has been the impetus for a state initiative to create practical teacher tools for content-based instruction (CBI) at the local level. What is known as the Wisconsin Alternate Assessment for English Language Learners (WAA-ELL) has become much more than a requirement for school accountability.[1] WAA-ELL, as implemented in Wisconsin, is a statewide, performance-based assessment framework customized for beginner English language learners that results in an academic score on the same scale as the regular statewide testing program. Alternate assessment also assists English for speakers of other languages (ESOL) teachers in planning challenging, standards-based curriculum and promotes greater teacher collaboration schoolwide. Many Wisconsin ESOL and bilingual teachers contend that this assessment system, by providing them accessibility to academic content standards, has facilitated the integration of language and content as an ESOL or bilingual approach. In this chapter, we define this alternate assessment system, discuss its relationship to instruction, and describe its principal tools.

We begin with a brief background on the recent push for academic content standards and the inclusion of English language learners in assessments of academic progress. Next, the rationale for CBI and assessment becomes the backdrop to issues distinct to small states and Wisconsin's local context. We then share the conceptual framework of the model and its components and discuss the development process so that this framework could be adopted or adapted by states or local school districts.

Throughout the chapter, we highlight the distinguishing features and practical ideas from this model that ESOL teachers can modify and use. In particular, we believe teachers will recognize the value of content-based assessment and the importance of feedback of its results to other stakeholders.

---

[1] Alternate assessment traditionally has applied to students with disabilities. However, the No Child Left Behind Act (2001) allows the use of alternate assessment for English language learners if the alternate reflects the same rigorous academic standards and can produce valid, reliable, and comparable scores to the regular system.

❧ CONTEXT

Standards and Accountability

The No Child Left Behind Act (2001) has altered the accountability equation in schools across the country to include all K–12 students. Although most educators would agree that English language learners should meet, within a reasonable period of time, the same academic content standards as other students, the issue of creating fair, reliable, and valid assessments is not easily answered. Do we simply test students in English who were previously excluded? Can testing accommodations, such as additional time or bilingual dictionaries, adequately level the playing field? What is the role of academic assessments in students' native language, and what limitations might these assessments have? Are there other options for states that adequately adjust for linguistic and cultural differences (Boals, 2000; Kopriva, 2000)? Most important, what about the instructional implications? The driving force behind both the movement toward higher standards and accountability is being able to offer students more rigorous curriculum and more effective instruction. If that is the ultimate goal, how will inclusion of English language learners result in improved pedagogy? These are some of the questions states and localities have been forced to grapple with since the late 1990s. The answers reached thus far seem as diverse as the students for whom these accountability systems are designed to serve. Despite the disparity of opinions, the stakes for English language learners are extremely high as these policies influence what is taught, how it is assessed, and who ultimately succeeds or fails at school (Heubert & Hauser, 1999; Short, 1993; Wiggins, 1998).

As part of standards-based education reform, the vast majority of U.S. states adopted or created academic content and performance standards based on what educators believe all students should know and be able to do. Subsequently, academic assessments were selected or developed and aligned with the academic content standards. Before this push for state-defined standards, there were few, if any, statewide criterion-based assessments to judge what was being learned, by whom, and to what extent (August & Hakuta, 1997; Falk, 2000; Laturnau, 2001).

The notion that bilingual/ESOL teachers should teach, or at least support, the learning of content began before the present push for common academic content standards and subsequent high-stakes tests (Gottlieb, 2003). And yet, undeniably, the standards movement has encouraged educators to reexamine the extent and the manner in which content instruction is delivered to English language learners, not just those who have reached intermediate to advanced levels of English proficiency, but beginners as well.

Wisconsin's Approach

Wisconsin is no exception to these recent educational trends; educators adopted state academic content and performance standards in 1998. Under each academic content standard, more specific performance standards (known in many states as performance objectives) were written at three grade clusters and are benchmarked at 4th, 8th, and 10th grades. In the same year, the state also drafted alternate performance indicators (APIs), modifications of the state's performance standards especially designed for English language learners, in the areas of English language arts, mathematics, science, and social studies.

To create the APIs (observable, measurable classroom indicators linked to the state academic content standards), bilingual, ESOL, and content-area educators from around the state adapted each performance standard as well as drafted sample classroom assessment tasks specifically for English language learners. By July 2000, the compilation of all this information became available on CD-ROM. In addition, an accompanying alternate assessment guidebook was written to offer teachers a variety of classroom assessment tools and strategies to facilitate data gathering, analysis, and interpretation (Gottlieb, 2000).

District bilingual/ESOL program administrators decided to adopt one of the content-based rubrics, called MECCA (see the products section later in this chapter for more detail), as the statewide documentation form for measuring English language learners' academic progress. The end result, the WAA-ELL, provides for statewide accountability, locally controlled assessment, and CBI. Although the system is designed to produce reportable scores to the state's educational agency for those English language learners who cannot meaningfully participate in statewide academic testing, teachers are encouraged to use the standards-based instructional assessment with all learners as a means of providing ongoing academic feedback and guiding instruction (Boals, 2000).

Because alternate assessment for English language learners is both classroom and performance based, ESOL teachers have a practical set of tools, or "road maps," for content-based curriculum planning, instruction, and ongoing feedback of their students' progress. By having specific academic classroom performance indicators with sample assessment ideas, teachers can create (through backwards mapping) lesson plans with sheltered English instructional strategies to match the standards-based content goals. Thus, the academic content standards drive instructional planning, guide the teaching of content-based lessons, and assist ESOL teachers in moving English language learners toward a standards-based curriculum, even at the beginning levels of English language proficiency (Boals, 2000; Gottlieb, 2000).

◈ DESCRIPTION

The Wisconsin assessment initiative for English language learners is built around a conceptual framework that is anchored in the state's model academic content standards and their accompanying performance standards in the content areas (see Figure 1). Each component of alternate assessment is aligned to create a direct relationship between what is taught and how it is measured. In this section, we describe and illustrate the components of the assessment process that are bound to CBI.

Alternate Performance Indicators

The APIs are modifications of the state's performance standards that enable English language learners access to the model academic content standards and subsequent rich, challenging content-based curriculum. In this way, English language learners are afforded opportunities to demonstrate their academic growth in realistic and meaningful ways, and teachers, in turn, are offered options in the selection of appropriate instructional pathways that lead to student success. Additionally, the APIs are the first step in the recognition of English language learners and their teachers in

Wisconsin's Model Academic Content and
Performance Standards at Benchmark Grade Levels

Sample Alternate Performance Indicators (APIs) for

- Reading and Language Arts
- Mathematics
- Science
- Social Studies

Data Sources

Sample Alternate Performance Assessment Activities, Tasks, and Projects

Measuring Essential Communication in the Content Areas (MECCA) Rubric for

- Mathematics
- Science
- Social Studies

FIGURE 1. Components of Wisconsin's Alternate Assessment for English Language Learners

statewide accountability by facilitating the link between bilingual/ESOL support services and the general educational program.

Like the state's performance standards, the APIs are designed for English language learners at benchmark grade levels. The APIs are

- clearly stated
- observable and measurable behaviors
- applicable across diverse instructional settings and contexts
- amenable to a variety of student activities, tasks, and/or projects
- appropriate for the linguistic and academic range of the English language learner population
- fully aligned in depth and scope with the performance standard upon which they are based[2]

---

[2] Alignment was ensured by constructing the API from the original performance standard (scope) and comparing both to Norm Webb's 4-point depth of knowledge scale (depth). Dr. Webb was a consultant to the Wisconsin Department of Public Instruction in 2002.

Figure 2 identifies several performance indicators derived from the state's academic content standards and their corresponding APIs for science and mathematics (whose standards are marked by letter) across the benchmark grades (which are identified by the first numeral [the grade cluster] and the second numeral [the specific performance standard benchmarked to the grade cluster]).

This example shows the clear differences between the ways in which these standards-based indicators have been formulated. For English language learners, the APIs contain (a) plain language, yet the concepts remain in tact; (b) graphic support, as in Mathematics A.4.5; (c) appropriate materials and resources for English language learners, such as a picture atlas rather than a print-based atlas; and (d) active student performance, such as constructing a model in Science A.8.6. Throughout the state, individual school districts have the flexibility of selecting from this compendium of

Content Area	Performance Indicator for the General Student Population	Alternate Performance Indicator for English Language Learners
Science	C.4.2. Use the science content being learned to ask questions, plan investigations, make observations, make predictions, and offer explanations	1. Identify and use prior knowledge related to content to ask questions and plan investigation 2. Observe, predict, and explain based on experience/experiment
	A.8.6. Use models and explanations to predict actions and events in the natural world	1. Construct a model to explain an event in the natural world 2. Identify the cause and effect of temperature changes
Mathematics	A.4.5. Explain solutions to problems clearly and logically in oral and written work and support solutions with evidence	1. Give oral mathematical presentations with graphic support
	A.8.1. Use reasoning abilities to • evaluate information • perceive patterns • identify relationships • formulate questions for further exploration • evaluate strategies • justify statements • test reasonableness of results • defend work	1. Apply strategies, patterns, and relationships and show why they were selected to solve a problem 2. Provide a reasonable explanation of work

FIGURE 2. Examples of Wisconsin's Performance Indicators and Their Alternate Performance Indicators for English Language Learners

sample APIs as the basis for their instructional assessment or developing their own based on local academic standards.

Data Sources

The development and implementation of alternate performance activities, tasks, and projects are predicated on the collection of reliable and representative information. Thus, it is important to identify the sources of data to be used to provide evidence of English language learners' academic achievement. In general, teachers rely on several ways of gathering information including student work samples, tests, and direct observation. The reliance on a variety of data sources that reveal both the processes and products of student learning enables teachers to evaluate their students in a comprehensive and effective manner.

In CBI, irrespective of the content area, language plays a critical role for English language learners. Whether creating a hypercard presentation, constructing a relief map, manipulating Cuisenaire rods, or conducting a science experiment, English language learners must connect the content to language. Figure 3 shows methods of assessment in which the overlay of the language domains—listening, speaking, reading, and writing—onto content is categorized according to three major data sources.

As seen in Figure 3, there are numerous methods teachers can employ that simultaneously provide information on students' language and conceptual development. For example, in researching a science or social studies topic, students may watch a video (listening), search and maintain a log of topical Web sites (reading), take notes and summarize information (writing), and make a poster presentation of their findings (speaking). An accompanying product descriptor with each of the steps to the final product guides the students throughout this project and serves as a self-assessment tool at its completion.

Alternate Performance Activities, Tasks, and Projects

Alternate performance activities, tasks, and projects that require students to demonstrate learning in concrete ways are the centerpiece of instructional assessment. Sound performance assessment is authentic, drawing from the students' personal experiences and real-life situations, and has multiple avenues to pursue to reach a variety of solutions. It is content based when it deals with academic concepts and key principles, triggers higher level thinking and is thought-provocative in and of itself, encourages exploration of new ideas, and raises questions that leads to other content-related issues (Gottlieb, 2000). These characteristics of both instruction and assessment maximize students' opportunities to engage in lifelong learning.

In most classrooms, instruction includes varying degrees of student involvement (such as time on task) and comprehensiveness that, in turn, is mirrored in assessment practices. These instructional inputs generally manifest themselves in a combination of activities, tasks, and products. Figure 4 differentiates among the identifying features of these three instructional assessment formats.

In planning standards-based instruction and assessment, teachers need to select the format that yields the best results for their language and content goals and objectives. One major consideration is time. Projects often correspond to thematic units of instruction that may be a month in duration, student products from tasks

Domain	Data Sources		
	Student Work Samples	*Direct Observation*	*Tests*
Listening	Graphic organizers	Role play	Illustrations
			Matching
	Drawings or illustrations	Responses to commands	True/false
			Multiple choice
Speaking	Interviews	Anecdotal records	Student conferences
	Speeches	Interpretation through rubrics such as checklists, rating scales, and holistic scales	Student self-assessment
	Broadcasts		
	Debates		
Reading	Cassettes of oral reading	Read/think alouds	Informal reading inventories
	Reading response logs	Reciprocal teaching with peers	Running records
	Reading inventories	Literature circles	Cloze
	Semantic webs		Short response
	Learning logs	Miscue analysis	Student self-assessment
	Graphic organizers		End of chapters or units
Writing	Process pieces, including drafts		Dictation
	Student-authored books		Peer assessment
	Research reports		Student self-assessment
	Exhibits or displays		Fill in the blank or short answer
	Journals		Essays

Figure 3. Data Sources and Methods of Alternate Assessment for Listening, Speaking, Reading, and Writing (Adapted from Gottlieb, 1999, reprinted by permission)

may be a week long, whereas activities are usually confined to a class period. Figure 5 offers examples of content-based activities, tasks, and projects applicable for English language learners across bilingual/ESOL contexts and settings.

Overall, the design and use of content-based instructional assessment have been a particular challenge in the implementation of Wisconsin's alternate assessment initiative. In large part, teachers have remained steadfast to more traditional teaching techniques and structured pencil-and-paper products; in particular, they seem to

Activities	Tasks	Projects
Ongoing, formative in nature	Short-term, formative in nature	Long-term, summative in nature
One-step series of actions	Multiple steps, series of related activities	Complex series of interrelated tasks
Narrow focus and scope	Expanded focus and scope	Multidisciplinary, expansive focus and scope
Represented by a standard from a single content area	Represented by standards from one or more content areas	Represented by related standards across various content areas
Usually discrete and independent	Usually holistic and correlated	Global and interdependent

FIGURE 4. Distinguishing Features of Content-Based Activities, Tasks, and Activities

overrely on worksheets. When students are not encouraged to produce language beyond the phrase or sentence level or create original work samples, accurate assessment of their content knowledge is diminished. Through statewide professional development efforts and the compilation of content-based student exemplars across the curriculum, it is anticipated that teachers will move toward more authentic, engaged instruction. Consequently, the performance assessment on which it is predicated will be richer and the results will be a more accurate reflection of student achievement.

Documentation

Performance assessment requires teachers to interpret what students do and how they perform on given activities, tasks, or projects. Variability in teacher judgment yields inconsistency in scoring student work, which, in turn, produces unreliable results. Documentation in the form of a scale or rubric, with carefully defined criteria anchored in standards, guides teachers in reaching agreement in the analysis of assessment data. As part of its alternate assessment, Wisconsin has created two such documentation forms, which are discussed later in this chapter. In interpreting student work, agreement between teachers of 80% or greater is necessary in a standards-based system used for accountability purposes.

Besides establishing the basis for interrater agreement, a necessary quality of assessment, rubrics have other uses. In particular, they

- serve as a yardstick for measuring student performance to be shared with stakeholders, including parents and students
- identify the targets to be reached, the developmental steps along the way, and a shared set of goals for students and teachers
- attach meaning to traditional forms of assessment, such as numbers or letter grades, by specifying and describing student expectations

---

Content-Based Activities, Tasks, or Projects . . . Which Do You Think?

_____ 1. Creating an HIV/AIDS awareness brochure

_____ 2. Completing a science-experiment worksheet

_____ 3. Producing a process-writing piece comparing and contrasting a revolutionary figure from the United States and native country

_____ 4. Determining sales tax on advertised goods

_____ 5. Constructing an ecologically efficient model and describing its usefulness to peers

_____ 6. Watching a news broadcast and writing a summary of its political highlights

(Answers: 1. Project, 2. Activity, 3. Task, 4. Activity, 5. Project, 6. Task)

FIGURE 5. Sample Content-Based Activities, Tasks, and Projects

- promote articulation and continuity from one grade level to the next, from teacher to teacher

The planning sheet for instructional assessment, depicted in Figure 6, is intended for teachers and administrators who may wish to align standards (expressed here as APIs) with instruction and assessment (Short et al., 2000). By aligning standards with performance expectations and concrete classroom activities, educators gain a sense of how instruction and assessment become intricately interwoven.

◈ DISTINGUISHING FEATURES

The most outstanding feature of this statewide assessment initiative is its comprehensiveness. Few states, to date, have addressed the construct of alternate assessment of English language learners; those that have tackled it have concentrated on developing measures of English language proficiency directly correlated with the state's English language arts standards. Wisconsin, on the other hand, has recognized academic achievement as the main thoroughfare to success for English language learners; its alternate assessment system is derived from state academic content standards. The integration of language and content for English language learners at the state level through this system has become the driving force for CBI and assessment at the classroom level.

There are two distinguishing sets of features of this content-based assessment initiative: its inclusive development process and its products. The involvement of

Standards-Based APIs	Data Sources	Content-Based Activities, Tasks, or Projects	Performance Criteria as Defined in a Rubric

FIGURE 6. Alignment of the Components of Standards-Based, Instructional Assessment

multiple stakeholders at the state, district, and school levels from its inception has solidified the vision for this initiative and has affected its implementation. Equally important, the tools that have been created are useful in the collection and analysis of classroom data while concomitantly offering a statewide, standard reporting mechanism.

The Process

The state's commitment to its English language learners and the value of content-based alternate assessment has been far-reaching—from its initial gathering of K–12 bilingual/ESOL specialists for 4 days of intensive training and product development to offering professional development throughout the state to publishing guidelines, procedures, rubrics, and other instructional assessment tools on the department's Web site (Wisconsin Department of Public Instruction, 2004). To this day, the Wisconsin Department of Public Instruction continues to support the efforts of refining this alternate assessment system for English language learners.

As part of the initial process of developing the APIs from the academic content standards, there was broad representation of school district bilingual/ESOL administrators and teachers with content-area expertise. The use of a team approach for each content area facilitated the coalescing of philosophies and teaching strategies to produce a viable document. By engaging in this sustained exercise, participants became vested in the process that they subsequently could share or replicate with others.

Equally important, each content-area team developed a keen sense of the interrelationship among state standards, CBI, and assessment. Through their task of creating the APIs, identifying data sources, and designing alternate assessment activities, bilingual/ESOL specialists learned firsthand the necessity for alignment among the components. The integration of assessment into instruction enabled team members to dispel the notion that this system would be burdensome for teachers and indeed would yield useful information.

Related to the implementation process, teachers have reported increased collaboration and coordination of lesson planning and delivery of instruction as well as in data collection, analysis, and interpretation (Boals, 2003). Often bilingual/ESOL teachers need to rely on their mainstream colleagues to assist in the assessment of English language learners, especially at the middle school and high school levels. The use of a single, statewide rubric with defined criteria for interpreting student work allows for communication of student performance across content areas and classrooms. This common, standards-based metric becomes an equalizer in ensuring English language learners access to the general curriculum and a gauge for measuring their progress in content-area classes.

The Products

Within the Wisconsin framework, the Measuring Essential Communication in the Content Areas (MECCA), the standard rubric, is the centerpiece of performance assessment. It has two comparable forms: The holistic scale is used for statewide scoring, and the focused-analytic scale is intended for classroom use. These rubrics have been designed to capture the full range of academic achievement of English language learners. The focused-analytic scale has four components or dimensions of

English language learners' academic proficiency: (a) vocabulary, (b) language use, (c) conceptual development, and (d) cognitive involvement (see Figure 7).

These four areas are integrated in the holistic scale (see Figure 8). Each is presented along a developmental continuum that is defined by four performance levels that correspond to and are aligned with the state's designations: (a) minimal, (b) basic, (c) proficient, and (d) advanced.

MECCA serves a host of purposes. It

- documents English language learners' conceptual development across grade levels and content areas

- assists in determining the relationship between the students' language and academic proficiencies

- monitors students' academic progress over time

- informs instruction and provides feedback to stakeholders

- aids in educational decision making in regard to transitioning of support services and readiness for state assessment

- contributes to accountability for student learning

Depending on the instructional setting, MECCA serves to document the academic achievement of students' in their first or second language(s). The extent to which the first language is used as the medium of instruction for the designated content area is reflected in the students' work samples, which, in turn, are interpreted with the rubric. In recognition of the universality of conceptual knowledge, the measurement of academic content standards does not have to be confined to one language (as is also recognized in Title III of No Child Left Behind). Therefore, it is advantageous for those school districts that provide dual language or developmental bilingual education to assess in the students' strongest language(s).

MECCA is a useful tool for both ongoing, formative assessment at the classroom level (in its analytic version) and annual, summative assessment at the state level (in its holistic version). Along with the guidelines for implementation (Gottlieb, 2004), teachers are encouraged to use MECCA throughout the school year to help differentiate instruction to best meet their students' needs. An assessment window is set annually (just preceding state assessment) whereby teachers collect original student work on specified topics within each content area, interpret the samples with the MECCA rubric, reach high levels of interrater agreement, and report the designations to the state. The state designations of minimal, basic, proficient, and advanced serve as the basis for scoring the alternate assessment of English language learners.

◈ PRACTICAL IDEAS

How can bilingual, ESOL, and mainstream teachers extract some practical ideas from this complex system for their own personal use? In this section, we offer three suggestions that may serve as a starting point. Together, they illustrate how to plan, implement, and document content-based instructional assessment of English language learners.

	Vocabulary	Language Use	Conceptual Development	Cognitive Involvement
Advanced	Displays a deep understanding and use of content-specific, grade-level vocabulary.	Presents ideas and concepts with coherence and organization. Consistently uses language patterns associated with the content area with accuracy.	Represents the interrelatedness of content-area concepts with or without graphic representations.	Solves complex problems using a variety of reasoning strategies with clear evidence of abstract reasoning. Infers and synthesizes meaning to create and transform knowledge.
Proficient	Consistently uses content-specific, grade-level vocabulary.	Presents ideas and concepts but not always with coherence or organization. Uses language patterns associated with the content area, with few errors in usage.	Represents some content-area concepts (using graphic representation such as models, charts, tables, graphs, drawings, concept maps, displays, or illustrations) and some concepts without graphic support.	Solves concrete, content-based problems using a variety of strategies with some evidence of abstract reasoning. Creates meaning in familiar situations but does not transform knowledge to create new meaning.
Basic	Reproduces content-related and some content-specific vocabulary.	Sometimes uses language patterns typically associated with the content area, with obvious errors in usage that may impede meaning.	Reproduces some content-area concepts (using graphic representation such as models, charts, tables, graphs, drawings, concept maps, displays, illustrations, or other graphic support).	Reorganizes the presentation of content-related concepts on a limited basis to solve explicit problems with no apparent use of abstract reasoning.
Minimal	Primarily uses everyday language in place of content-specific vocabulary.	Uses limited, repetitious language patterns to communicate content, with errors that typically impede meaning.	Identifies some content-area concepts when associated with visual or graphic support.	May recognize concrete concepts but is unable to solve problems in the content area.

FIGURE 7. Measuring Essential Communication in the Content Areas: Focused-Analytic Rubric

Student Name: _____ Grade Level: _____ Date: _____
Teacher: _____

Content Area:
    Language Arts _____ Mathematics _____ Science _____ Social Studies _____
Evidence: Oral _____ Written _____ Graphic _____
Language of Assessment: English _____ Spanish _____
    Other (Please Specify) _____

Advanced	Represents the interrelatedness of content-area concepts with or without graphic representations. Displays a deep understanding and use of content-specific, grade-level vocabulary. Solves complex problems using a variety of reasoning strategies with clear evidence of abstract reasoning. Infers and synthesizes meaning to create and transform knowledge. Presents ideas and concepts with coherence and organization. Consistently uses language patterns associated with the content area with accuracy.
Proficient	Represents some content-area concepts using graphic representation (such as models, charts, tables, graphs, drawings, concept maps, displays, or illustrations) and some concepts without graphic support. Consistently uses content-specific, grade-level vocabulary. Solves concrete, content-based problems using a variety of strategies with some evidence of abstract reasoning. Creates meaning in familiar situations but does not transform knowledge to create new meaning. Presents ideas and concepts but not always with coherence or organization. Uses language patterns associated with the content area, with few errors in usage.
Basic	Reproduces some content-area concepts using graphic representation (such as models, charts, tables, graphs, drawings, concept maps, displays, illustrations, or other graphic support). Reproduces content-related and some content-specific vocabulary. Reorganizes the presentation of content-related concepts on a limited basis to solve explicit problems with no apparent use of abstract reasoning. Sometimes uses language patterns typically associated with the content area, with obvious errors in usage that may impede meaning.
Minimal	Identifies some content-area concepts when associated with visual or graphic support. Primarily uses everyday language in place of content-specific vocabulary. May recognize concrete concepts but is unable to solve problems in the content area. Uses limited, repetitious language patterns to communicate content, with errors that typically impede meaning.

FIGURE 8. Measuring Essential Communication in the Content Areas: Holistic Rubric

Use a Standard Rubric Across Classrooms

A standard rubric across classrooms will capture the academic performance of English language learners outside of standardized testing. In this chapter, we offer the MECCA rubric with its four performance levels as an overview for ESOL teachers' expectations for academic achievement. Teachers and administrators throughout a school district should become familiar with the parameters of the rubric's designations by matching its description with exemplars of student work at benchmark grade levels. The work samples represent a map of content-based instructional assessment, exemplify alignment with standards, bring to life the distinction among the performance levels, and attach meaning to the descriptors. Collecting, analyzing, and sharing representative anchor papers across grade levels, content areas, and performance levels provide an excellent opportunity for professional development of all teachers.

Incorporate Assessment Throughout the Curriculum

The delivery of instructional assessment in classrooms can easily be carried out by teachers through lesson or unit planning. The sample outline for a lesson/unit plan in Figure 9 shows how to incorporate the components of a content-based curriculum (that are also directly linked to MECCA) into planning, delivering, and assessing instruction. It recognizes the roles of language and content as well as thinking/reasoning with their links to standards, as represented by the APIs. In addition, student self-assessment is incorporated into the plan as a vehicle for gathering information on the students' views of learning.

To the extent feasible, it is preferable to design instruction around content-based themes and important, overarching ideas. In that way, multiple APIs and standards from various content areas may be simultaneously addressed. Students, in turn, can engage in more long-term tasks or projects where they can approach the topic from varying perspectives and explore it more in depth.

Content-based lessons and units are to take into consideration the students' language proficiencies levels, whether in their first or second language(s), and are to be differentiated accordingly. These distinctions may be reflected in the materials and resources selected or the types of groupings preferred to maximize student interaction.

Use an Individualized Student Record Plan

The individualized student record plan is an optional form where quantitative and qualitative assessment information may be blended to address the extent to which English language learners' have attained the standards-based APIs on an annual basis (see Figure 10). In it, bilingual/ESOL teachers are encouraged to set individual goals for their students for both language proficiency and academic achievement, with input from the student, family members, and other teachers. Serving as a yearly summary of each student's accomplishments, the comments/recommendations section specifies the type and amount of support services needed based on concrete evidence.

Sample Standards-Based Lesson Plan for English Language Learners

Grade Level(s): _____

Materials and Resources: _____

Language Proficiency Levels: _____

Teacher(s): _____

1. PLANNING

CONTENT AREA(S):

     Alternate Performance Indicators:

     Academic Concepts:

     Vocabulary:

Language Elements/Patterns:

Thinking/Reasoning Strategies:

---

2. DELIVERING

Instructional Assessment Sequence (Activities, Tasks, or Projects):

Timeline:

3. ASSESSING

Documentation of Assessment (Methods and Data Sources):

Rubric(s):

Other Forms of Documentation:

Student Self-Assessment:

FIGURE 9. Components of a Standards-Based Sample Lesson/Unit Plan for Content-Based Instructional Assessment

❖ CONCLUSION

In this chapter, we have described a comprehensive, systemic initiative undertaken by Wisconsin, a relatively small midwest state in the United States, for its English language learners in Grades K–12. Grounded in the state's model academic content standards for language arts, mathematics, science, and social studies, the alternate assessment system is designed to guide teachers in their implementation of content-based practices and to inform the state of English language learners' progress toward standards attainment through a uniform, content-based rubric. Most important, however, we illustrate how educators may readily integrate the constructs of language and content, language proficiency and academic achievement, and instruction and assessment (Boals, 2001; Saville-Troike, 1991).

GENERAL INFORMATION

Student's Name *First, Last*		Grade Level	School Year
ID No.	Date of Entry in Wisconsin School	Student's Native Language	
School District	School		

LANGUAGE PROFICIENCY

English Language Proficiency Level	Date(s) Administered	Test Administered
English Language Proficiency Level	Date(s) Administered	Test Administered

Language Proficiency Goals *Listening, Speaking, Reading, Writing*	**Standards/Alternate Performance Indicators Addressed**
1.	
2.	
3.	
4.	

ACADEMIC ACHIEVEMENT

Standardized Test Data or MECCA Score					Date(s) Administered
Language Arts	Reading	Mathematics	Science	Social Studies	

Academic Goals *Listening, Speaking, Reading, Writing*	**Standards/Alternate Performance Indicators Addressed**
1.	
2.	
3.	
4.	

TYPE AND AMOUNT OF SUPPORT SERVICES

Comments/Recommendations

SIGNATURES

Student Signature	Teacher Signature	Parent Signature
Date Signed _____	Date Signed _____	Date Signed _____

FIGURE 10. Sample Standards-Based, Individualized Student Record Plan

We recognize that in this age of educational accountability, teachers and administrators are closely examining viable options for complex issues. The statewide framework, although Wisconsin-specific, has applicability to teachers, school districts, and states throughout the United States. For this reason, we have presented specific tools teachers may incorporate into lesson planning for CBI along with an assessment framework.

Increased federal and local pressure has led stakeholders to pursue creative solutions for their burgeoning English language learners' populations. This model, based on sound principles of second language acquisition research, instruction, and assessment holds promise for the future of our students and profession.

In 2003, Wisconsin received a federal grant and became the lead state in a consortium dedicated to the design and implementation of sound assessment for English language learners at the elementary and secondary levels. The instructional assessment model described in this chapter served as the groundwork for our current thinking. As of December 2004, there are 10 states that have joined this effort.

◈ CONTRIBUTORS

Margo Gottlieb, PhD, is director of assessment and evaluation for the Illinois Resource Center in Des Plaines, in the United States. Since 2003, she has also been the lead developer of the Wisconsin, Delaware, and Arkansas Consortium, the original three states designing an enhanced assessment system for English language learners. In that capacity, she has spearheaded the development of the states' English language proficiency standards and, based on that model, is currently chairing the TESOL writing team that is revising the 1997 *ESL Standards for Pre-K–12 Students*.

Tim Boals, PhD, has a background in curriculum, language education, and Spanish language and literature. At the Wisconsin Department of Public Instruction, he coordinated the development of the first statewide performance-based alternate assessment system for English language learners in the United States and is now project director for World-Class Instructional Design and Assessments, a standards and assessment consortium that includes 10 states. He regularly publishes articles and presents topics related to best practice for instruction and assessment of English language learners.

CHAPTER 12

Mapping the ESOL Curriculum: Collaborating for Student Success

Ester de Jong and Genoveffa Grieci

✦ INTRODUCTION

With the increased accountability for English language learners has come a critical examination of how schools can provide English language services and grade-appropriate content and skills to these students. The challenge to ensure equal access to quality schooling becomes even more profound at the secondary level with its emphasis on content learning, high academic language demands, and increasingly, high-stakes testing that determines whether students will graduate from high school (Heubert, 2001; Lucas, 1997; Valdés, 2001).

Traditional English for speakers of other languages (ESOL) classes have not effectively bridged ESOL and standard curriculum classroom expectations, particularly in the case of pullout ESOL programs (Thomas & Collier, 2002). The types of language skills developed in these ESOL classes insufficiently match the language proficiency needed to successfully participate in standard curriculum content classes, such as math and science (Cummins, 2000; Echevarria, Vogt, & Short, 2000; Gibbons, 2002). Content-based ESOL has long been proposed as an alternative to language-focused ESOL classes because it can provide a more meaningful and effective second language learning environment (Snow & Brinton, 1997; Snow, Met, & Genesee, 1989) and can better prepare students for the language demands in the standard curriculum content classroom (Chamot & O'Malley, 1994). In a content-based ESOL classroom, the ESOL teacher uses content-related themes to teach second language skills. By embedding language learning in content, second language learners learn English by using it in a meaningful context with a real purpose for communication (Díaz-Rico & Weed, 2002; Gibbons, 2002). A content-based ESOL curriculum requires a realignment of traditional ESOL curricula to include academic language functions and language structures within the context of grade-level content-related themes (TESOL, 1997).

Setting end-of-course goals for ESOL classes is an important first step. It is not sufficient, however, to simply articulate content-based ESOL curriculum standards and expectations. To ensure students' systematic progress toward such expectations, teachers must also carefully sequence their day-to-day lessons (see, for example, Agor [2000] for high school classroom vignettes). One tool that supports the dual goal of setting clear benchmarks and providing ongoing feedback on the implementation of curriculum is curriculum mapping. A curriculum map consists of four components: essential questions, content, skills, and assessment. It is designed to coordinate curriculum experiences for students horizontally by subject and/or grade level as well as vertically across the grades (Jacobs, 1997). A curriculum map is a way to present "real-time information about the actual curriculum" (p. 2). One key feature of a curriculum map is the formulation of essential questions. Essential questions help select conceptual content in such a way that teachers and students focus on the big picture and the purpose of learning, thus supporting students' acquisition of a discipline's habit of mind rather than disconnected facts (Sizer, 1984; Wiggins & McTighe, 1998).

This chapter describes how the bilingual/ESOL program at Framingham High School in Framingham, Massachusetts, transformed its grammar-based ESOL curriculum into a content-based ESOL curriculum through a collaborative curriculum mapping process. This curriculum reform was initiated in response to changing school demographics as well as the implementation of state curriculum frameworks and high-stakes state testing. After describing the context and organization of the bilingual/ESOL program, the chapter outlines the evolution of the ESOL curriculum. Next, the process of collaborative curriculum mapping is highlighted as it supported the implementation of the revised ESOL curriculum. The case study concludes with suggestions for practice for teachers and teacher educators.

◈ CONTEXT

Demographics

Framingham High School (FHS) is the only high school in a quasi-urban district that enrolls close to 8,700 students in Grades K–12 (7% Black, 5% Asian, 17% Hispanic, and 71% White [the latter category includes native Portuguese speakers]). From September 1995 to September 2002, the number of children requiring bilingual/ESOL support in the district jumped from 634 to approximately 1,200 students. The district has a longstanding history of supporting linguistic and cultural diversity, which has had a positive affect on the quality of programming for English language learners districtwide (de Jong, 2002).

In 2002–2003, FHS enrolled 1,857 students in Grades 9–12. Students come from 20 different language backgrounds and are ethnically and economically diverse. The ESOL population has grown from a handful of students in the 1970s to more than 200 students in 2002 (see Table 1). The change in this population can be almost specifically attributed to the growth of the school's Brazilian student population. Whereas the proportion of Spanish-language speakers and low-enrollment languages (such as Russian, Korean, and Chinese) has been fairly constant, the Brazilian Portuguese bilingual program enrollment has tripled since the 1990s.

The Bilingual/ESOL Program Organization

The FHS program for English language learners includes a bilingual program for native Spanish or Portuguese speakers and a self-contained ESOL program for low-incidence students. The program has three ESL levels (beginner, intermediate, advanced), with each level further divided into a beginner (Level A) and an advanced level (Level B), resulting in six proficiency levels (see Table 2).

The language of instruction for the content classes is determined by the student's

TABLE 1. DEMOGRAPHICS FOR FRAMINGHAM HIGH SCHOOL AND THE
BILINGUAL/ESOL PROGRAM FOR 2002

	Total Number	Percent of Total
Total number of students	1,857	
Free/reduced lunch	360	19.4%
Bilingual/ESOL	256	13.8%
Special education	187	10.1%
Race/Ethnicity		
Asian	101	5.4%
Black, non-Hispanic	131	7.1%
Caucasian, non-Hispanic	1,423	76.6%
Hispanic	198	10.7%
Native American	4	0.2%
Bilingual/ESOL Program Enrollment at FHS		
ESOL program (low-incidence students)	34	
Bilingual Portuguese program	125	
Bilingual Spanish program	46	
Two-way bilingual program (native English and native Spanish speakers)	51	
Total Number of Students	256	

level of English proficiency and native language. To ensure proper placement, all students are assessed in English oral and literacy proficiency on the Language Assessment Scale (Duncan & De Avila, 1988) upon entry. Additionally, native language assessment occurs on an individual need basis, for example, students with interrupted schooling experiences are always assessed in both languages.

Additional Bilingual/ESOL Program Features

There are several program features that shape English language learners' experience at FHS. First, all ESOL/bilingual language and content classes count toward high school graduation. Moreover, similar to other academic programs in the school, the bilingual/ESOL program offers classes at two college-preparatory (CP) levels: CP1 (advanced) and CP2 (basic). This allows English language learners to be included in GPA-weighing policies at the high school. Second, native language maintenance is made possible through the offering of Spanish and Portuguese language arts classes (for native speakers). These classes, which are electives, meet the high school's world language requirement. Third, basic literacy classes are offered in Spanish and Portuguese for students with limited native language literacy and English proficiency.

TABLE 2. GENERAL ORGANIZATION OF FRAMINGHAM HIGH SCHOOL'S BILINGUAL/ESOL PROGRAM

	Newcomers*	Level 1A/B Beginners*	Level 2 A/B Intermediate	Level 3A Advanced	Level 3B Advanced
ESL	3 periods of ESL	3 periods of ESL	2 periods of ESL	2 periods of ESL	1 period of ESL and 1 period of standard English language arts
Math	L1 math (Spanish and Portuguese)	L1 math (Spanish and Portuguese)	ESL math**	Standard curriculum math	Standard curriculum math
Science	L1 science (Spanish and Portuguese)	L1 science (Spanish and Portuguese)	ESL science**	Standard curriculum science	Standard curriculum science
History	L1 history (Spanish and Portuguese)	L1 history (Spanish and Portuguese)	ESL history**	Standard curriculum history	Standard curriculum history
Bilingual Elective	Portuguese/Spanish language arts	Portuguese/Spanish language arts	Portuguese/Spanish language arts	Portuguese/Spanish language arts	Portuguese/Spanish language arts

Note. * Low-incidence newcomers and beginners take their content classes as ESL content classes, with the assistance of a native language tutor whenever possible. The school is currently experimenting with coteaching the ESL history and the ESL 3B classes.

** These classes are taught by bilingual or ESOL teachers.

This has been an important addition as the enrollment of this group of students continues to increase. Finally, the program offers newcomer classes for students who enroll during the school year and who have no or very limited proficiency in English. Newcomers attend these ESL classes for 1 semester to give them a boost and then enroll in the regular Level 1A/Beginner class.

FHS has a well-prepared and cohesive staff. There are four monolingual ESOL teachers, four native-Portuguese-speaking bilingual teachers, and five Spanish bilingual teachers (one native speaker and four nonnative Spanish speakers). All teachers are certified in ESOL or bilingual education and hold master's degrees in these areas. Furthermore, teachers who teach content classes also hold certification in those specific areas. For example, a teacher who teaches ESL and Spanish/ESL World Studies would hold three certifications: ESL, bilingual education, and standard curriculum social sciences. Out of the 12 teachers, 5 have been teaching in the program for 5 years or longer, 3 have been at FHS between 3 to 5 years, and 5 have been hired within the last 3 years. Finally, all bilingual teachers teach bilingual (native language) classes as well as ESOL classes. In this way, the bilingual and ESOL programs are closely interwoven.

A final important component of this bilingual/ESOL program is its commitment to parent involvement and access to bilingual support personnel, such as bilingual school psychologists, social workers, and guidance counselors. Several activities are organized throughout the year, including an evening for bilingual parents of new ninth-grade students and a "Program of Studies" evening for eighth-grade students and their parents.

◈ DESCRIPTION

In 1998, the ESOL curriculum at FHS underwent significant changes in response to new demands placed on the program. One of the major events that prompted a critical examination of the ESOL curriculum was the institutionalization of state testing to hold schools and school districts accountable for teaching the content and skills outlined in the state's curriculum frameworks. The Massachusetts Comprehensive Assessment System (MCAS) was administered for the first time in 1998. More importantly, the 10th-grade MCAS is a high-stakes test: As of spring 2002, all students, including English language learners, must pass the English language arts and math test to receive a high school diploma. The following section describes the change from a grammar-based to a content-based ESOL curriculum in response to this development.

Revising the ESOL Curriculum

The FHS bilingual/ESOL department head initiated a process of revising the ESOL curriculum in the summer of 1999 (see Figure 1 for a timeline of activities). The existing ESOL curriculum dated back to 1976 and, in accordance with the philosophy of language teaching at the time, had an almost exclusive focus on grammatical structures and vocabulary development. Each ESL level (beginner, intermediate, advanced) was divided into two traditional sections: one for grammar and syntax and one for reading and writing, thus artificially separating language skills. The lack of coordination between sections and across levels resulted in

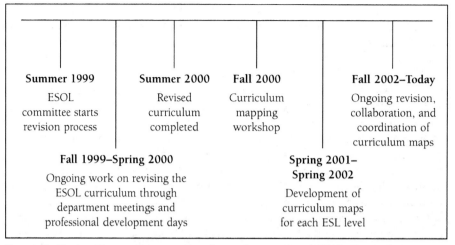

FIGURE 1. Moving From a Grammar-Based to a Content-Based ESOL Curriculum: A Timeline

significant overlap and repetition of skills and materials as well as gaps in students' development of English proficiency.

Over 2 years, the FHS bilingual/ESOL staff met during professional development days, summer workshops, and department meetings to critically examine the existing curriculum. An ESOL curriculum committee was established to define the expected language learning outcomes for each ESL level as well as to identify the vehicle for teaching these skills, considering the needs of their English language learners.

The committee used three key resources to determine ESOL curriculum outcomes: *ESL Standards for Pre-K–12 Students* (TESOL, 1997), the Massachusetts English Language Arts (ELA) framework, and a draft of the Boston Public Schools ESOL curriculum. (Boston Public Schools had already started to process of aligning their ESOL curriculum with the ELA framework.) After much discussion, the curriculum committee decided to focus on the ELA framework to determine the language proficiency expectations for each level in the program. It was hoped that this alignment would better prepare English language learners to pass the 10th-grade English language arts component of the MCAS after having spent most of their time in ESOL language arts classes. Outcomes were formulated both in terms of language functions as well as structural features and vocabulary.

In addition, the committee decided that the ESL classes should be thematically organized to support language learning and academic content preparation. The ESOL/bilingual teachers had expressed their concern with having to teach even the most basic academic language and vocabulary in English when the students moved from the Level 1 Beginner (native language content) to the Level 2 Intermediate (ESL content) (see Table 2). In addition, they questioned whether English language learners would be sufficiently prepared to compete with native English speakers in the standard content-area classroom when they exited the ESOL/bilingual program. A language-based ESOL curriculum was therefore no longer considered sufficient. This prompted the ESOL committee to explicitly connect the themes in the ESOL curriculum to high school math, science, and social studies/history content. The committee examined each content area's curriculum framework as well as the district's curriculum guidelines. They conferred with content-area colleagues to determine which topics could best be covered at each ESL level. Because there were two sections (A and B, as shown in Table 2) at each level, the topics were ultimately grouped into two general strands: math/science/technology and social studies/literature (see Table 3). As a result, the ESOL curriculum has systematically supported English language learners in acquiring the academic and English language proficiency they need to succeed.

The revised, content-based ESOL curriculum integrates reading, writing, speaking, and listening along with grammar, vocabulary, and thinking/study skills. In addition, it specifies key teacher resources and materials for each level. For example, the ESL 2A Math, Science, and Technology identifies the following science themes: nutrition, ecology, natural disasters, motion, space, and artificial intelligence. Within this theme, the teachers identify specific topics and vocabulary. For the ESL 2A science themes, this may include food groups, pollution, the water cycle, and velocity. Some of the materials listed for this theme are *Cause and Effect—Level 3* (Ackert, 1999) and *Time and Space* (Connelly & Sims, 1990).

The final step in the ESOL curriculum process was to explicitly coordinate within and across ESL levels as the revised curriculum was being implemented. Curriculum mapping was used for this purpose. After a workshop on curriculum mapping (see Appendix A for an outline of the workshop), the ESOL teachers collaborated on creating a curriculum map for their ESL level throughout the academic year, coordinating thematic content, English language skills, and assessment pieces. As of fall 2002, curriculum maps have been written for all the ESL levels.

◈ DISTINGUISHING FEATURES

Though the ESOL curriculum provides content themes and outcomes, it still does not function as an effective guide to daily lesson planning and the development of

TABLE 3. CHANGE IN ORGANIZATION FROM A GRAMMAR-BASED TO A CONTENT-BASED ESOL CURRICULUM

Old Organization	New Organization
ESL 1A/B Grammar and Syntax	ESL 1A Home, School, and Community
ESL 1A/B Reading and Writing	ESL 1B Experiences in American Living
	ESL 1A/B Social Studies
	ESL 1A/B Math, Science, and Technology
ESL 2A/B Grammar and Syntax	ESL 2A/B Social Studies and Literature
ESL 2A/B Reading and Writing	ESL 2A/B Math, Science, and Technology
ESL 3A Grammar and Syntax	ESL 3A Literature
ESL 3A Reading and Writing	ESL 3A Reading and Writing in Content Areas
ESL 3B Literature	ESL 3B Transition (Literature)

longer thematic units. Thus, the FHS bilingual/ESOL department has used curriculum mapping to support the implementation of the revised ESOL curriculum. A curriculum map structures the curriculum over time by asking teachers to describe their expectations and tasks on a month-by-month, unit-by-unit, or term-by-term basis.

After the workshop in the fall of 1999, using the revised ESOL curriculum as their basis, teachers developed a curriculum map for the ESL level that they were teaching. The most difficult part of the curriculum mapping process is often the formulation of essential questions. Nataly Reed, one of the ESOL teachers, participated in the curriculum mapping process from the beginning. Reflecting on her maps, she comments:

> [It was difficult] to get used to the idea of "Essential Questions" as opposed to more conventional comprehension questions. Two criteria of Essential Questions are that they be understandable and motivational at the students' level. However, there is a tension between the questions the teacher wants to consider and the questions, which students ask on their own accord.

The essential questions are significant because they organize the selection of content as well as materials, activities, and assessments. For example, the curriculum map for the ESL 3B literature class builds on the bilingual students' experiences with acculturation while including standard curriculum requirements for English language arts, as described here by Genoveffa Grieci, a teacher and one of this chapter's authors:

> The essential questions in my curriculum map center around themes of moving to a new place, living in two worlds, looking at the advantages and disadvantages that each world provides, and how these changes affect the individuality of each student. The literature that I have chosen addresses these same themes: short stories in *Changes, Life, Language and Literature*; Esmeralda Santiago's autobiographical portrait, *Almost a Woman*; F. Scott Fitzgerald's novel, *The Great Gatsby*; and William Shakespeare's comic play *Twelfth Night*.

Once developed, the curriculum map can be used to discuss ESOL curriculum content and to ensure that the academic language proficiency is developed systematically through oral communication as well as reading and writing. Figure 2 presents a section of a curriculum map for a Level 2A math/science/technology class focusing on Shackleton's expedition. Note that the ESOL teacher added two components to the traditional curriculum map in Figure 2. Besides the essential questions, content, skills, and assessment tools, the teacher also included the structures of language to be learned and links to the revised ESOL curriculum.

After identifying essential questions, content, skills, and assessment tools, teachers match their daily lesson plans with their curriculum map. For example, Heloiza Castellana's curriculum map for Level 2A/Intermediate includes a unit on making waves. Her map outlines the content and skills for this unit in the areas of academic language proficiency (cause/effect relationships, summarize), aspects of grammar (active and passive voice, sensory verbs), and study skills (use of the dictionary). For materials, she uses *Making Connections 3: An Integrated Approach to Learning English* (Kessler, Lee, McCloskey, Quinn, Stack, & Bernard-Johnston, 1996) as well as a PBS documentary on waves. Her assessments include journal entries,

Shackleton's Expedition

Essential Questions

Are leaders made, or are they born?

Of all the things that makes a good team member, what is teachable?

Was Shackleton's expedition a failure?

Content

National Geographic

NOVA: Shackleton

Encyclopedias and almanacs

Internet resources

Skills

To develop a thesis

To use documentation

To write an expository paper

To support a thesis with researched facts

To practice peer and self-review

To write a resume

To practice organized note-taking

Grammar

To use transitional adverbials

To use colons and semicolons

To use appropriate sequence of tense

Assessment

Research paper

Resume

Goal-setting rubric

Technology rubric

Alignment

Strand: Listening/Speaking

Standard 1:1–6; 2:1–4; 3:1–3, 5; 4:1–6; 5:1–3, 5–6

Strand: Reading

Standard 1:1–10; 2:1, 3–5, 8, 10–13; 3:1, 3–7, 9, 11–12; 3:10 (identify differences in complex sentences); 4:1, 2, 5, 7

Strand: Writing

Standard 1:1–3; 2:1–6; 4:1–4; 4:8 resumes

FIGURE 2. An Example of a Curriculum Map for Level 2A/Intermediate for May (Developed by Nataly Reed, ESOL teacher, Framingham High School; reprinted with permission)

class presentations, a narrative essay, and a role-play. From these resources, she has developed a lesson plan (based on Short, 1994), which uses the water theme to discuss drama (see Appendix B).

The FHS teachers regularly collaborate in pairs at each ESL level (e.g., Level 1A and Level 1B together) to compare their maps and share ideas, materials, activities, and assessment tools. Being able to discuss their practices from the curriculum maps allows them to avoid unnecessary overlap, reinforce key academic language skills that can be applied across subject areas, and identify any gaps that need additional attention. The teachers have taken full ownership of their curriculum maps and continue to be actively involved in a constant process of revision and refinement.

◈ PRACTICAL IDEAS

Curriculum Revision

Curriculum revision is a challenging process. Over the past 2 years, it has become clear that curriculum change takes time, careful planning, and requires administrative support.

Develop and Support a Common Vision

Program and school administrators, along with teachers, need to develop a common vision for transforming the ESOL curriculum. At FHS, the ESOL committee was pivotal in setting common goals and expectations. Administrative support was essential in securing access to monetary resources (i.e., for textbooks that aligned with the new curriculum) and in creating opportunities for professional development and curriculum planning workshops.

Prepare Teachers for Curriculum Revision

Teachers must have the necessary background knowledge and skills to revise and implement a new ESOL curriculum. Where expertise is less strong, professional development and planning opportunities with more experienced peers should be provided. For instance, the FHS bilingual and ESOL teachers were already experienced and highly qualified but needed extensive support in developing their curriculum maps.

Enable Collaboration

Teachers must be given common planning time within their regular schedule to allow for collaboration. The FHS teachers used district-supported workshop time, department meetings, and their planning time to achieve their goals.

Curriculum Mapping

Curriculum mapping emerged as an effective vehicle for translating the expectations for each ESL level outlined in the revised ESOL curriculum into lesson and unit planning and for coordinating content and skills among and across ESL levels. To be successful, districts and schools must support curriculum mapping.

Provide Professional Development if Teachers Are Unfamiliar With Curriculum Mapping

As part of this training, teachers must have the opportunity to examine and discuss a sample ESOL curriculum map because it can model the traditional components of a curriculum map (essential questions, content, skills, and assessment) as well as the use of essential questions to integrate ESOL curriculum standards (language structures and links to ESOL curriculum standards).

Use the Curriculum Map Purposefully to Guide Daily Lesson Planning

This requires collaboration with supervisors and other teachers to articulate how individual lessons are connected to the curriculum map.

Revisit the Curriculum Maps With the Whole Bilingual/ESOL Team

This should be done on a regular basis, and the maps should be modified as needed. Maps should be treated as dynamic, not static, documents to continuously inform programmatic and instructional decision making.

Support Teachers' Involvement in the Process

The collaborative curriculum mapping process at FHS also highlights the need to develop reflective teaching practices, build teachers' ability to collaborate effectively, and bridge the knowledge and skills of ESOL/bilingual teachers and those of standard curriculum teachers. The FHS bilingual/ESOL teachers were successful because they were willing to deepen their knowledge about content and language curriculum expectations for English language learners as well as those for standard curriculum classes. They had a reflective stance toward their own teaching practices and were open to change those practices. They possessed essential collaborative skills to work with each other and had the conviction that such collaboration was necessary; they owned the process.

❧ CONCLUSION

New accountability systems require bilingual and ESOL programs to critically examine the ways in which they prepare English language learners for meeting language and content standards. High-stakes testing has made it mandatory that English language learners have access not only to high levels of academic English but also to grade-appropriate content-area instruction. At FHS, this challenge was met by changing the ESOL curriculum and engaging in a collaborative process of curriculum analysis and implementation. First, bilingual/ESOL staff revised the traditional ESOL curriculum, which had a grammar and vocabulary focus. It was replaced by a content-based ESOL curriculum that included math/science/technology and social studies/literature themes aligned with the state's curriculum frameworks and district guidelines. Subsequently, the teachers used curriculum mapping as a tool to support the implementation and coordination of the new curriculum. This process became even more powerful because the bilingual/ESOL program staff approached curriculum mapping collaboratively. Teachers worked together within and across ESL levels on coherent, content-based units that reinforced key academic language proficiency skills for students, yet avoided unnecessary overlap and repetition.

The bilingual/ESOL teachers continue to refine their maps, increasingly also with student input. Anecdotally, the teachers have seen positive effects on the students' second language development and achievement in standard curriculum classrooms. One goal is to more formally document these trends. Another goal is to use the curriculum maps for collaboration across departments and school levels. For instance, some bilingual/ESOL teachers have started to share the curriculum maps with other departments, such as the English language arts department, to better match expectations for exiting English language learners. The school has also begun to experiment with classes that are cotaught by an ESOL and a standard curriculum teacher and that integrate native English speakers and English language learners. The curriculum maps are emerging as an effective tool to guide coplanning and teaching. Finally, the curriculum maps can also facilitate the transition from the middle to the high school. By discussing the expectations for each ESL level, eighth-grade English language learners can be placed more appropriately for their ninth-grade bilingual or ESOL classes. This can avoid an "ESOL ghetto" and a disjointed language and academic learning experience for adolescent students (Valdés, 2001).

This case study has shown how content-based ESOL as an integral part of a well-articulated bilingual/ESOL program can provide adolescent English language learners with essential academic language and content skills and how curriculum mapping can play an important role in ensuring the quality implementation of such a program. For adolescent English language learners to succeed, there must be optimal coordination within and across ESL levels, between bilingual and ESOL content classes, as well as between bilingual/ESOL and standard curriculum classes. Only through close collaboration can schools create effective learning environments for English language learners that encourage meaningful learning, avoid the fragmentation of curriculum content and skills, and promote success.

❖ CONTRIBUTORS

Ester J. de Jong, EdD, is an assistant professor in the School of Teaching and Learning at the University of Florida, Gainesville, in the United States. Her research interests include two-way immersion and other integrated approaches to bilingualism and second language learning.

Genoveffa Grieci is currently the department chair of the ESOL/bilingual program at Framingham High School in Framingham, Massachusetts, in the United States. She has been associated with the Framingham School District for more than 30 years, first as an ESOL student, then as an ESOL teacher, and finally as its department chair at the high school. Her immigrant experience has greatly influenced her as a person, teacher, and leader.

◈ APPENDIX A: CURRICULUM MAPPING WORKSHOP AGENDA

(This workshop used an ESOL curriculum map as an example.)

Curriculum Mapping

. . . a workshop looking at ways teachers can improve the curriculum in their classrooms through content, thinking processes, skills, and assessment . . .

1. Introduction or the need for calendar-based curriculum mapping
- What is mapping?
    a. Procedure for collecting a database of the operational curriculum in a school and/or district using the school calendar as an outline
    b. Overview of students' actual learning experiences, keeping in mind their learning characteristics, ages, stages of development, communities, aspirations, and needs
2. What information do we collect on the map?
    a. Content
    b. Thinking processes and skills
    c. Authentic assessment
3. Criteria for essential questions
    a. Realistic and easy to understand
    b. Distinct and substantial
4. Alternative assessment
    a. Student-generated work samples and projects
    b. Linguistic diversity and types of assessments
5. Timelines and guidelines
    a. Individual and departmental
    b. District and site-based curriculum councils
6. Mapping out a unit . . . let's get started!

◈ APPENDIX B: EXCERPT FROM A LESSON PLAN FOR "MAKING WAVES" UNIT

(Developed by Heloiza Castellana; reprinted with permission)

Level 2A Social Studies and Literature (Grades 9–12)

Integrated Instruction for a 90-minute class

Theme: Making waves

Lesson Topic: Reading a play

Objectives

Content Skills: To identify and describe the characters, the setting, the conflict, the action, and the resolution of a play

Language Skills:

Speaking/Listening: acting out the play

Reading/Writing: fiction/creative (play) writing

Structures: descriptive language (adjectives, nouns, and adverbs) and persuasion

Thinking/Study Skills: analysis of language formality level; preview map of ancient Greece and predict story content based on the title to establish schema

Key Vocabulary: tales, mortals, raging, jealousy, vengeance, mortals, dazzling, breeze, delightful, mighty, courtship, frighten, dwellers, terrified, watery, realm, persuaded, glittering, undersea, incredible, enrage, unpredictable, unreasonable, scowl, awful harsh, tiniest, untold, majestic, unfortunate, contented, prosperity, wrath, gratitude, loyalty, setting, conflict, action, resolution

Literature

Earth Shaker, Wave Maker, The Myth of Poseidon

Materials

Making Connections 3 (textbook), English language dictionaries available in the classroom

Motivation

Essential Questions: What is an emotional wave like?

Who is the ancient wave maker?

Presentation

Students look at the map of ancient Greece and think about the following questions: Why do you think the sea was important to the Greeks? What did their ships look like? How did sailors feel about wind and waves?

Teacher assists students in analyzing, taking notes, and sharing their thoughts about the life style of the Greeks with the class as a group.

Students brainstorm about the content of the story based on the title and the relationship they make with their background knowledge.

Students listen to tape-recorded play.

Teacher starts analytical process with whole group by discussing different points of the play (characters, setting, conflict, action, and resolution).

Practice/Application

Students work in small groups to find in the text descriptive language that characterizes the characters, the setting, and the situation. They also select expressions that indicate persuasion and resolution.

A student from each group writes the group's findings of a given point (i.e., characters, setting) on the board.

Teacher facilitates identification of parts of speech present on what students wrote on the blackboard, giving emphasis to descriptive and persuasive language.

Students work in groups to rehearse and act out the play.

Review/Evaluation

Follow-up practice sentences using parts of speech vocabulary from Earth Shaker Reading comprehension quiz

Extension

Tape-record acting out of student-generated scenes (using speaking rubric)

CHAPTER 13

Choosing Depth Over Breadth in a Content-Based ESOL Program

Martha Bigelow, Susan Ranney, and Ann Mickelson Hebble

◈ INTRODUCTION

The benefits of content-based instruction (CBI) for English language learners are maximized in programs that are able to explore content themes over an extended period of time. An advantage of working within a single theme is that students are able to build background knowledge within a given content area and use this knowledge not only to learn more about the topic but also to learn more English. In the CBI literature, this sustained feature has been formally added to the CBI acronym by Pally (2000), becoming sustained content-based instruction (SCBI). SCBI was transformed to sustained content-language teaching (SCLT) by Murphy and Stoller (2001). Although there are subtle differences in these conceptualizations, both have as their core the principle that holding a single theme constant over time will meet dual aims of teaching content and developing language skills in ways that are applicable to the learners' wider academic needs. A specific benefit, according to Pally (2000), is that by maintaining one theme throughout the academic year, students gain access through authentic materials and content-related projects to rhetorical and discourse patterns, both oral and written, that are needed to succeed in all of their classes. Additionally, SCBI solves the common problem in CBI of switching from one vastly different content to another, resulting in what Snow (2002) refers to as the "potpourri problem." This problem has been addressed in the CBI literature previous to SCBI by Stoller and Grabe's (1997) call for the "six T's approach" (theme, topics, texts, threads, tasks, transitions), meant to unify content. On the other hand, SCBI retains the benefits of CBI, which include integrated language skills, the contextualization of formal aspects of the language in highly meaningful and relevant content, integrated strategies, task- and project-based activities, and ample opportunity for cognitively demanding input and output (Grabe & Stoller, 1997; Snow, 2002; Stoller, 2002). Teaching language through content works well for all of these reasons, but mainly because academic language is learned through relevant and interesting instruction that requires accessing and producing challenging texts. When the content is sustained, the benefits of CBI are maximized through the continuous building on and recycling of linguistic and content knowledge.

◈ CONTEXT

This SCBI program is located at Murray Junior High School, which is a math and science magnet school located in the St. Paul school district in Minnesota, United States. A magnet school is a public school that has chosen to focus its curriculum in a particular way. Parents choose a magnet school for their children according to its curricular focus, rather than its location. Magnet schools, therefore, help to desegregate the district. The students at Murray come from a variety of language and cultural backgrounds, and, like most urban schools, the demographics of the student body change from year to year. Of the approximately 830 students who attend Murray, about 29% of the students are English language learners. Some of these English language learners are in English for speakers of other languages (ESOL) courses, and others are fully integrated into the mainstream classrooms. The ESOL department teaches approximately 100 students, or 12% of the school population. These students have a wide range of first-language literacy skills and second-language proficiency levels.

The ESOL program at Murray is small compared to other schools in the district, typically employing two or three teachers and with just two classrooms of its own. It can be characterized as a self-contained language arts class for English language learners. This means that the ESOL course gives seventh- and eighth-grade English credit to students but does not preclude advanced students from taking other English electives such as myths or Shakespeare. The program began in 1993, when Ann Mickelson Hebble, one of this chapter's authors, was hired to develop a new ESOL program for seventh and eighth graders. She had just graduated from a teacher education program at the University of Minnesota that emphasized the CBI approach and required students to develop extended content-based thematic units. The other authors, Martha Bigelow and Susan Ranney, currently teach in this program and learned about Hebble's distinct curriculum through her work with student teachers from the program. Drawing on her experience in this program, Hebble chose to ground all of her decisions from the very start in the notion that learning language through challenging academic content is best for English language learners in the K–12 setting. While searching for commercial curricula, she found that there were few materials specifically designed for this age group and none that she felt were suitable for her context. In retrospect, her dissatisfaction with mass-produced curricula was the beginning of a successful content-based ESOL program.

The program always has followed district and state standards and currently uses a new set of state standards specifically designed for English language learners (Minnesota Department of Education, 2003). Noteworthy is the fact that the standards include and differentiate between academic/formal language goals and social/informal language goals, similar to TESOL's (1997) standards. These standards are designed within a framework that includes levels of competence in listening, speaking, reading, and writing. In addition, the domains of purpose, audience and genre, communicative function, language features, and word knowledge and use are addressed. For the first time, the state ESOL standards are linked to the content-area standards in language arts and math and eventually will be linked to standards in science. This is an advantage for many types of ESOL programs and particularly for this program because it is already guided by language arts standards (Bigelow & Ranney, 2004).

◈ DESCRIPTION

Although many ESOL programs use content units that span days or weeks, the program at Murray has taken a larger view of sustained content by organizing instruction so that a single content theme spans the entire academic year. The particular themes vary from year to year, but in any given year, a single theme is developed into a yearlong curriculum that includes a wide range of English language learning experiences. Some of the themes that have been chosen over the years are listed in Table 1.

Thematic Instruction

The themes are rotated so that students in the program experience a new theme each year. Because students are typically in the program for only 2 years (i.e., seventh and eighth grade), teachers are able to repeat themes from earlier years. The curriculum also integrates language structures outlined by the district curriculum and the new state standards.

Skeptics may wonder why a particular content such as "Walls" warrants an entire year or question the validity of choosing a theme that does not precisely coincide with other content taught in the seventh and eighth grades. The answer is that the theme provides the context for the development of both academic English language proficiency and language arts skills. Students gain these skills because they are built on in-depth knowledge of a topic. The skills, therefore, are better learned

TABLE 1. YEARLONG THEMES FROM THE ESOL PROGRAM AT MURRAY

Title	Description
For the Birds	An examination of all things bird: songs, flight, mythology and folklore, symbolism, and survival.
Petroglyphs, Saguaros, and Gila Monsters: Life in the Sonora Desert	An exploration of desert plant and animal life, ancient and present desert peoples and cultures, and folktales from the desert.
Walls	A questioning into the concept of walls—interpersonal walls, intrapersonal walls, cultural/societal walls, familial walls, national and international walls.
In the News	A yearlong investigation of the newspaper and of all things current and new. Teaching of journalism as a genre, opinions, politics, and sports. Local newspapers provided resources, speakers, and tours.
Year of the Tiger	A closer look at this fascinating, feared species. An examination of the role the tiger plays in cultures and literature around the world. Research about other endangered species and conservation efforts.
Who Am I?	An autobiographical year, an investigation into all things related to identity: family, culture, likes, dislikes, opinions, style, taste.
Life Under the Sea	An investigation into the world of the ocean, its creatures, cultures, and mysteries.

and more easily and quickly transferred to other classes (Short, 1997), which is the goal of any ESOL program. Because of this urgent need for English language learners to perform at grade level as quickly as possible, the program at Murray stresses reading and writing skills, which are incorporated through theme-related activities such as research-related skills, creative writing, essay writing, and reading across multiple genres. Figure 1 offers a sampling of the reading and writing skills targeted in the program each year, regardless of theme.

The structure of the program is planned both at the level of the academic year and at the level of the week. This helps keep the conceptualization of the program

Reading-Related Activities	Writing-Related Activities
• Skimming	• Building complete sentences and paragraphs
• Scanning	• Capitalization
• Highlighting key words and information	• Punctuation
• Summarizing	• Verb usage
• Who, what, when, where, why, and how	• Various other grammar points
• Learning vocabulary in context	• Summaries
• Finding the main idea and supporting details	• Research skills
• Distinguishing fact from opinion	• Essay organization
• Fiction reading	• Thesis statements
• Nonfiction reading	• Supporting ideas using outside sources
• Knowing the elements of a story	• Opinion essays/research essays and reports
• Interpreting, inferring	• Note-taking
• Points of view: first person, second person, third person	• Graphic organizers
• Retelling	• Source lists
• Comparing and contrasting	• Story building
• Cause and effect	• Myths/folktales
	• Editing and revising
	• Sequencing
	• Book reviews
	• Dialogue between characters
	• Simile, metaphor
	• Analogy
	• Predicting
	• Analyzing information from outside sources
	• Synthesizing materials from a variety of source

FIGURE 1. Examples of Language and Literacy Skills Targeted Throughout the Year via the Thematic Unit

manageable and focused. The planning for the year flows around specific subtopics within the theme. Each new subtopic builds on and recycles the last. For example, in the yearlong theme "Life Under the Sea," the subtopics include geography of world's oceans and seas, the makeup of an ocean, sea creatures, myths and folktales of the seas, island/ocean peoples and cultures, and ocean careers.

To illustrate the theme work more specifically, we will describe some of the activities on this ocean theme. For the sea creature topic, students choose a sea creature to research after participating in several weeks' worth of instruction. They spend time in the class library and outside of class researching five areas: life cycle/anatomy, foods, ocean adaptations, habitat, and unusual facts. Students use Internet sources, content texts, periodicals, and encyclopedias, and they learn how to systematically take notes on note cards and compile a source list. When they finish collecting facts in each of the five areas, students organize that information in the form of a research essay. In addition, they design and present an art project (e.g., video, song, poem, poster, puppet show, or collage) in which they show the facts they collected in their five research areas using art instead of the written word. This type of process taps into the range of learning styles present in the class and provides an opportunity for the students of lower-proficiency levels to excel. The sea creature project meets Standards 3.2 and 4.2 of the Minnesota State Standards (see Table 2). Other examples of ways tasks align with skills in standards are also found in Table 2.

A Model for Integration

The process of developing content-based curriculum to meet standards and promote academic language development is complex. Figure 2 illustrates a way of conceptualizing the integration of content and language in CBI so that specific language goals are incorporated into the curriculum. Within the domain of academic content, Figure 2 identifies three general aspects of curriculum that promote language

TABLE 2. SAMPLE TASKS AND THEIR ALIGNMENT WITH SKILLS AND STANDARDS

Task	Sample Skills/Functions/Vocabulary	Minnesota Standards
Read a pirate myth	Fiction reading Elements of a story Predicting Points of view	Standard 3.2: The student will understand written English to participate in formal (academic) contexts.
Search the Internet for information on a sea animal's life cycle	Nonfiction reading Skimming and scanning for information Note-taking	Standard 3.2: The student will understand written English to participate in formal (academic) contexts.
Write a persuasive essay on an ocean, habitat, or environmental topic	Synthesizing material Interpreting and inferring Cause and effect Supporting ideas using outside sources	Standard 4.2: The student will produce written English appropriately to participate in formal (academic) contexts.

development: tasks and texts, language functions, and language structures. Tasks and texts include content learning activities and the written or aural texts that may accompany content instruction. Academic language functions are those functions that teachers and students accomplish during the course of classroom interaction that deal with academic content. Examples of language functions are explaining, persuading, hypothesizing, and comparing. Structures in this model refer to the specific grammatical and lexical forms needed to carry out the function and the academic task. The arrows in Figure 2 suggest that the teacher or curriculum developer may start the planning process from any of those three points of the triangle and then extend from there to the other two aspects. Whichever starting point the teacher takes, it is important to include the other two aspects to ensure content instruction that does not lose a language focus (Ranney & Bigelow, 2002). The curriculum at Murray aligns tasks and texts based on content (e.g., pirate myths) with specific academic language functions that are targeted in the state standards (e.g., predicting), and these are carried out through specific academic language structures (e.g., conditional sentences).

It is important to carry out an SCBI program in a way that keeps students engaged and does not result in students becoming fatigued by the theme-related work. The theme-related work in Murray's program is typically done on Wednesdays and Thursdays. Mondays and Tuesdays are "novel days," with the entire class reading a novel and participating in a variety of novel-based activities and projects. The teachers and students purposefully choose novels that are not related to the theme. This allows a single theme to remain exciting over time and avoids the potential for overload and boredom. Fridays are reserved for activities related to specific grammar points, spelling and vocabulary tests, standardized test practice, and sustained silent reading time. Spelling, vocabulary, and grammar are drawn from both the current thematic subtopic and the lessons related to the current novel. Teachers have noted

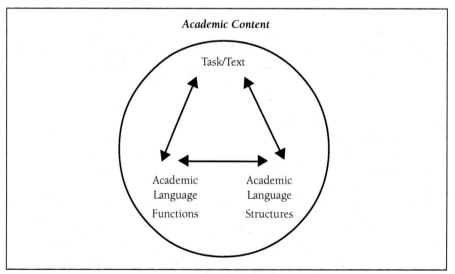

FIGURE 2. A Planning Model for Content and Language Integration in Content-Based Instruction

that traditional activities of classroom language learning such as these can be familiar and comfortable for many of the learners who have studied foreign languages in their home countries. In general, structuring the week in this way is a helpful scaffold for both teachers and students.

A central feature of the program is the extensive use of authentic materials. Because few ESOL materials are written for an extended content theme, the teachers at Murray turned to authentic materials. Both teachers and students consult a wide variety of sources while working on the theme. One of their primary sources is the Internet (see the recommended Web sites in the appendix). Using authentic materials such as those found on the Internet in SCBI encourages the development of a range of functional and academic literacies (Kasper, 2000). In addition to the Internet, teachers and students collect relevant books from the school and county libraries. They also gather authentic theme-related materials such as current newspaper articles, brochures, guides, maps (e.g., maps of the world's oceans), charts, or pamphlets. They request information from institutes, museums, botanical gardens, and ocean/coastal institutes. Teachers also seek out materials from the mainstream content-area teachers in the school.

These authentic materials are then used to work on developing academic language skills. For instance, students develop strategies such as previewing a document, unpacking its organization, looking for main ideas in topic sentences, and skimming and scanning for specific information or for finding the main idea. The authentic text creates a natural context for implementing these strategies because the text itself may be too long or too difficult to read in great detail. Although some teachers are tentative about using so many authentic materials with students of beginning proficiency levels, the teachers at Murray believe that it is their responsibility to ensure access to authentic texts for all students at all levels. How better can the students learn to cope in the mainstream classes than by using authentic texts? If the reading level of the authentic texts is too difficult for a particular student or group of students, the teachers use scaffolding techniques to help them gain access to the information in the text (e.g., lead students through using pictures and headings to find information), or they alter tasks for students with lower levels of proficiency (e.g., instead of reading the entire text, they would read the topic sentence or selected paragraphs). Authentic materials, in addition to being motivating, interesting, and essential to the learning of sophisticated content, can be used to meet a wide array of language learning objectives. This approach to materials development is sound in that it takes into consideration both authenticity of task and authenticity of text (Breen, 1985; Lee, 1995).

Beginning-level students participate successfully in the SCBI curriculum with additional support in terms of course work and modifications. Students who are recent arrivals or are still at the emergent literacy stage would be enrolled in an ESOL Level 1 class as well as an ESOL math class and an ESOL social studies class. This is in addition to an ESOL Level 2 theme-based class. The Level 1 class provides instruction in basic English skills and vocabulary development. At the same time, they participate in the Level 2 theme-based class as an additional hour of ESOL. The Level 2 theme-based class provides a vital cognitive challenge that may be absent in traditional beginning-level ESOL materials. In addition, it provides access to age-appropriate academic content through scaffolded instruction. For example, one activity in the Level 2 class is reading encyclopedia entries. Whereas the higher level students may comprehend the entire text on their own, the beginning students are given the task of listening to the text read aloud as they follow along. Next, they are asked to circle all the words they understand. Finally, students work in pairs to build their own phrases or sentences about the topic.

This approach to the ESOL curriculum ensures that students not only learn an enormous amount of information about a content topic, to the point of becoming experts in certain areas, but also gain valuable and necessary language and literacy skills that will support academic success in the future. Reading and language arts scores on district and state standardized tests have shown consistent gains each year, and the students have been well prepared for high school, as attested to by teachers from the high schools that graduates from Murray attend.

◈ DISTINGUISHING FEATURES

This SCBI program is different from other programs in that it teaches language through the focus on a single, yearlong theme with a clear and planned structure that meets state accountability standards. The teachers develop their curriculum to balance attention to content with attention to language development, which the CBI literature has identified as one of the most challenging aspects to the implementation of content-based language instruction (Met, 1994; Snow, 2001; Stoller & Grabe, 1997; Tedick, Fortune, & Walker, 2003).

High Interest to Students and Teacher

The ESOL program at Murray is based on a teacher-initiated curriculum but evolves and responds to the students' interests and needs. An important factor in this program's success is that all involved are given the freedom to pursue their interests. Teachers have the freedom to choose the theme and materials, and students explore their interests within that theme. This has much to do with supportive colleagues, administrators, and parents. Another essential feature of this program is that the teachers choose themes about which they feel passionate. The teachers' enthusiasm, motivation, and spirit of discovery serve to inspire the students' interest and that learning is indeed contagious. In this program, the themes originate from aspects of the teachers' own lives such as camping trips, national and international travel, and their own recreational reading. When an idea for a new theme emerges, however, the teachers always take care that the theme will be of interest to students of this age. In essence, teacher and student interests outside the classroom keep their energy high inside the classroom.

Teacher Roles

The role of the SCBI teacher differs somewhat from that of a teacher using a more traditional curriculum. Teachers are collectors and creators of the curriculum. They match appropriate materials to the task for which they are used. The teacher aids English language learners in their interpretation and creation of audience-appropriate academic texts. The teachers also facilitate cooperative group learning while allowing each student in the class to develop his or her own expertise. Teachers assess their students' language development formally and informally through the context of the content learning. At Murray teachers view themselves as directors or organizers of the curriculum, whereas students are held accountable for carrying out the tasks and projects.

Flexibility

The flexible nature of the SCBI program at Murray provides many advantages. Because most of the classes are multilevel, students can pursue individual interests and are able to find their niche in the classroom community, regardless of proficiency level. This results in information sharing across proficiency levels, which promotes cooperative learning and enhances the learning environment overall. Some teachers may have reservations about using CBI in classes with mixed proficiency levels; however, the experience of this program is that it is not only possible but also beneficial. The teachers also recognize that *level* is a relative term because although students are tested at the beginning of the academic year in all modalities, it is fairly impossible to place each student neatly at one particular level. A fundamental belief among teachers in the program is that heterogeneity is a strength and that this approach can be successful with all students. The teachers work toward transmitting this belief to their students by creating tasks that can be done at a variety of levels and by using texts for a variety of purposes. They find ways in which each student can become an expert in one particular area related to the theme. This lends itself to the most authentic kind of cooperative learning, where peers willingly seek and share information with each other. Because most of the classroom tasks are projects involving extensive reading and writing, each student completes the project at his or her own ability level and the subsequent assessment of the project is tailored to student's proficiency level. In conclusion, rather than considering the range of language proficiency and literacy levels as an obstacle, the teachers at Murray have found this situation to be well suited to the SCBI approach.

Authenticity and Coherence

The SCBI approach at Murray provides a coherent structure for the use of authentic texts, which are sometimes used haphazardly in language classes. Students can do different tasks with the authentic materials, depending on the texts themselves and the purpose for which they are used. Authentic materials give students practice understanding information presented in a variety of formats. By using authentic materials, teachers are giving students the opportunity to learn to distinguish between important and unimportant information, read by taking into account other points of view, and use the context provided by authentic texts for understanding. When students are exposed to sophisticated pictures, charts, or graphs, they learn how to interpret complex information. Therefore, the students are constantly immersed in the language and required to use it, and they become more confident readers. Engaging in this type of instruction focused on a sustained theme encourages the development of advanced skills and strategies that English language learners need to succeed in their content-area classes.

Sustained Content and Vocabulary

The use of sustained content also increases depth in vocabulary learning because vocabulary is best developed in context and with much recycling. Authentic materials provide a way of allowing students to increase the number of words they learn incidentally. Many new words that students encounter within a topic appear repeatedly throughout the year. This repeated exposure to vocabulary gives them the opportunity to develop full definitions of difficult words and permits students to master advanced, technical, or specific vocabulary related to their topic in both receptive and productive modalities (see Kibby [1995] for a discussion of the many layers of vocabulary acquisition). For example, the vocabulary that Murray's English language learners were exposed to through their research on underwater animals transferred easily to the later subtopics on underwater careers and sea folklore. An ordinary, content-based ESOL class may focus on similar tasks, structures, and functions, but the benefit of using a sustained thematic content is that it allows students of all proficiency levels to work at a much higher cognitive level and in more depth than would be possible if they dealt with topics about which they had little background knowledge.

◈ PRACTICAL IDEAS

There are several ways in which to tailor an SCBI program to a specific setting; however, the only way for such a program to succeed is if the teacher has the motivation and the desire to design his or her own curriculum and the conviction that this is a good way to meet the students' needs. We would like to offer the following suggestions to teachers and teacher educators who may wish to design or redesign curriculum to follow some of principles described in this chapter.

Choose a Theme That Fascinates You

This should be a theme in which you are not an expert. The teacher's enthusiasm and interest in the theme will sustain it. The fact that the teacher is not an expert brings him or her into the community of learners, providing more opportunities for true sharing of knowledge and learning.

Be Patient at the Beginning of the Process

When in the phase of collecting materials, it is easy to feel overwhelmed by imagining how so many materials will result in a cohesive curriculum. The process is very messy before it is neat. Nevertheless, once the theme is decided, search everywhere for anything related to that theme (e.g., discount stores, garage sales, book stores, flea markets, vacation sites, party supply stores, teacher stores). The Internet will be one of the most valuable resources for materials on any theme. Scholastic publishers also have many excellent publications for teachers. Do not eliminate materials because you think they may be out of the range of the students' language proficiency levels. You will be able to select and adapt them later in the process.

Plan in Advance

It is not unusual for the teachers at Murray to plan the themes for the program 2 years ahead. This gives ample time for the ideas to take form and to collect materials.

Don't Do It Alone

Collaborators may be other ESOL teachers in your school or in other schools if you are the only ESOL teacher in the school. Collaborating can foster a great deal of energy for the creative process as well as help with the work of curriculum development. Additionally, collaborating with teachers in other schools encourages the sharing of materials. Use the expertise in other departments in your school; this facilitates the gathering of materials. Working with other teachers can also serve to integrate the ESOL teacher in the school community while making others more aware of what occurs in the ESOL classes.

Remember to Think Across Disciplines When Choosing Content Materials and Projects

By drawing from the broader school curriculum, you can be confident that students will be exposed to a wide variety of academic discourses, which helps them with overall school success. Similarly, it is beneficial to choose a wide range of materials with different purposes, intended audiences, and levels of difficulty.

Realize That Most of the Work Occurs at the Beginning of the Creative Process

As the school year begins, the amount of curriculum development work is far less because the role of the teacher changes from focusing on gathering information to focusing on instruction.

Become Thoroughly Familiar With Your School's Standards

Keep a copy of the district, state, or national standards used in your district close at hand not only during the creative process but also throughout the year. Track which projects align with which standards for your own records, and be prepared to justify your approach. Being accountable to standards and outcomes needs to be an integral part of the curriculum and is important for maintaining the integrity of your program.

Develop a Plan That Outlines What Will Occur When

The teacher should keep track of what he or she plans to do during the week, month, and trimester/semester. Which days of the week will be the theme days? How long will the large projects take? To keep organized, outline the year around main projects that will address the standards and outcomes for the state and district and then build in the language points around the larger projects. Although the standards that need to be addressed should serve as parameters for the curriculum, it is also important to take into account the academic language and academic functions that will be targeted and develop them systematically in an iterative fashion (see Figure 2). However, if this is the first time with a new theme, the teacher needs to accept and understand that being only a few steps ahead of the students is normal and allowed.

Keep a Record of the Successes and Challenges

As the curriculum unfolds, note which materials and projects worked well for future reference. Likewise, teachers should keep an organized file of everything planned and everything created. This will save time when the theme is repeated.

Advocate for Yourself and Your Program

Administrators need to know what you are doing and may be able to give you extra planning time or allow some of the budget to be spent on theme-related materials. It is helpful to be able to purchase, for example, classroom sets of theme-related books that can be reused. Additionally, a strong advocate will convince an administrator that giving teachers the freedom to develop curriculum in this way, using all they know about best practices in language teaching, is not a risk but rather draws out the best performance from both teachers and students.

See the Process as a Way of Remaining Excited About Teaching

Although this process may appear to be extra work, it may be exactly what keeps an educator engaged in learning and teaching. The lack of repetition year after year is what the educators at Murray find so exciting about teaching this way. But also remember that once a theme has been developed, it can be repeated in future years with new subtopics, materials, and project ideas.

Help Preservice Teachers Develop the Necessary Skills for Content-Based Instruction

The previous list presumes a wide range of skills on the part of the teacher. For this reason, it is incumbent upon teacher education programs to offer experiences that will develop these skills. Preservice teachers need to practice content-based lessons and thematic-unit planning. In so doing, they learn to go through the process of choosing content and accompanying texts, designing content-related tasks, and matching these tasks with the academic functions and language structures and vocabulary that students need (see Figure 2), all while keeping the standards in the forefront. In addition, preservice teachers must practice using, interpreting, and adapting authentic materials for use in their thematic lessons/curriculum. In the Second Languages and Cultures Education Program at the University of Minnesota, students regularly do assignments that target these skills. It is the philosophy of the program that the ability to teach in this manner depends on good pedagogical skills as well as a solid grasp of English grammar. This is essential because of the frequent need to design meaningful, relevant lessons based on the linguistic needs of the students.

Part of any teacher preparation program includes student teaching or practicum experiences. It is very important for novice ESOL teachers to have the experience of seeing how CBI plays out in an actual setting, such as Murray. Being able to envision teaching this way is much easier after actually working in a classroom that is guided by the principles of CBI. The more teachers who enter the field with the skills needed to establish a CBI or SCBI program, the more confident they will be to design such a program or change an existing program. All of this depends on the involvement of the wider professional community and the availability of strong ESOL programs that are content based to student teachers.

◈ CONCLUSION

Teachers wishing to move into content-based language instruction need not be modest in their goals. SCBI can be used effectively with a range of proficiency levels, over an entire academic year, within standards, and with authentic materials. Teachers learn the content along with their students while guiding them through the process of learning to access academic knowledge and use academic language. This approach to teaching keeps teachers engaged professionally and deeply involved with their students' learning. The success of this program seems to hinge on the multiple ways the teachers have been entrusted to do what they believe is best for their students. In a climate of accountability, this may be a bold thing to say; however, the power of the teachers' belief and investment in their teaching approach and program design cannot be underestimated.

The program is always looking toward the future and contemplating what themes will excite both teachers and students. There will be new students and with them come new interests and language development needs. Currently, the program is adapting to a new set of state standards. None of these changes are problematic for this type of program because (a) it already has the students as central to the instruction; (b) the academic expectations are already high, resulting in only minor adjustments to meet new standards; and (c) a balance between already established language learning projects and the new theme is easily found because of the curriculum's flexibility.

The success of the program is apparent to both teachers and administrators, but it would beneficial to explore through research exactly how it works. For example, how does the sustained content impact students' language development over time? Research could track learners' spoken and written language production over the year as they engage in theme-related work. It would be useful to monitor how the complexity of the texts students choose changes as they gain more background on the theme. Because this program appears to be particularly successful with multilevel classes and learners, research on how it works for them would be helpful to other teachers who have similar classes.

At Murray, the teachers are committed to the value of a multidisciplinary approach to learning and the need for the ESOL class to be challenging and intensely interesting to their students. Through sustained content, the learning of language, literacy skills, and strategies are all made more palatable and possible. This program demonstrates the power of SCBI to provide academic rigor, motivation, and contextualized language instruction. The decision to choose depth of content over a curriculum favoring breadth of many topics has worked in this program.

◈ APPENDIX: RECOMMENDED WEB SITES

Enchanted Learning (http://www.enchantedlearning.com)

This Web site is supported by users with resources for teachers and students on common school-related topics such as animals, plants, astronomy, explorers, and inventors.

DesertUSA (http://www.desertusa.com)

This Web site provides information about deserts in the United Status, their animals, plants, minerals, and geology. *DesertUSA* is a monthly Internet-based magazine published by Digital West Media.

WhaleTimes (http://www.whaletimes.org)

At this Web site, students can learn about whales, seals, sea lions, and other sea life. It is produced by JakenMax Productions.

Learner.org (http://www.learner.org)

As part of the Annenberg Foundation, Annenberg/CPB produces this Web site for teachers interested in improving their teaching methods. It has many interesting instructional videos.

eNature (http://www.enature.com)

Produced by the National Wildlife Foundation, this Web site has field guides to plants, trees, animals, and insects. It is particularly good for information on birding.

Scholastic (http://www.scholastic.com)

Scholastic is a global children's publishing and media company. This Web site has useful links on many topics for children, families, teachers, administrators, and librarians.

Discovery (http://www.discovery.com)

This Web site has information about Discovery's programs, which generally relate to nature and travel.

National Geographic (http://www.nationalgeographic.com)

The National Geographic Society Web site has interesting information in a wide range of topics from history and culture to photography and geography. There is a particularly good link for children.

Public Broadcasting Service (http://www.pbs.org)

The Public Broadcasting Service Web site has links for children, parents, and teachers that offer activities related to its programming.

◈ CONTRIBUTORS

Martha Bigelow is an assistant professor in the Second Languages and Cultures Education Program at the University of Minnesota, in the United States. She has taught English as a second/foreign language in the United States, the Dominican Republic, and the Republic of Panama. Her research interests include processes of language teacher learning and instruction that serve secondary English language learners with limited formal schooling. She received her PhD from Georgetown University.

Susan Ranney teaches in the Second Languages and Cultures Education Program at the University of Minnesota. She has taught ESOL in the United States and Nigeria. Her research interests include sociolinguistics and grammar pedagogy. She received her PhD from the University of Minnesota.

Ann Mickelson Hebble is an ESOL teacher at Murray Junior High School in St. Paul, Minnesota. She started the ESOL program at Murray 11 years ago. Her interests include exploring techniques to effectively engage adolescents in language learning, particularly through content-based instruction, and best practices for the inclusion of grammar in content-based instruction. She received her MEd from the University of Minnesota.

CHAPTER 14

New Conceptual Tools for Content-Area Teachers: A Programmatic Approach to Content-Based Instruction

Annela Teemant

◈ INTRODUCTION

In the United States, a majority of English for speakers of other languages (ESOL) students are required to learn simultaneously a new language and important academic content. Although public school teachers have mastered effective strategies for teaching academic content (their typical task), many lack the knowledge and skills to effectively integrate a focus on second language learning (a new task) into content learning.

With the No Child Left Behind Act (2001), there is an increased focus on assessment-driven accountability for student learning and teacher use of scientifically validated practices. Consequently, this federal policy has important implications for the content and pedagogy of teacher preparation. In today's diverse educational milieu, what are needed are more effective teacher development (Darling-Hammond, 1997) and more cognitively complex teachers (Sprinthall, Reiman, & Thies-Sprinthall, 1996). In-service professional development programs with seat-time credit, minimalist workshops, or ad hoc courses are not capable of bringing about the type of teacher development needed to teach ESOL students to high standards. In addition, traditional, lecture-style preservice courses also fall short, leaving teachers on their own to determine how theory and practice connect (Goodlad, Soder, & Sirotnik, 1990). Lytle (2000) argues that innovative approaches to teacher education are needed.

In Utah, like in many other states, teacher educators with expertise in bilingual/ESOL education grapple with questions about content, sequence, and pedagogical practices that would effectively position mainstream teachers to both theoretically understand and pedagogically respond to the academic and linguistic needs of ESOL students. This chapter outlines the delivery system, content, and pedagogy embraced in Brigham Young University's (BYU's) programmatic approach to preparing K–12 mainstream educators. This chapter specifically describes the content-based instruction (CBI) course in BYU's Bilingual/ESL Endorsement Through Distance Education (BEEDE) program. Because the CBI course is designed to be a culminating course, this chapter captures a programmatic as well as a course-specific approach to CBI. It highlights five conceptual tools content-area teachers have for teaching language and content to ESOL students.

◈ CONTEXT

A profile of BYU's partnership districts, a description of BEEDE's delivery system, and an overview of the program's scope and sequence contextualize teachers' experiences in the BEEDE program as well as the CBI course.

Profile of Partnership Districts

Since 1984, BYU has partnered with five local school districts to form a university–public school partnership under the umbrella of John Goodlad's Center for Educational Renewal (Goodlad, 1994; Osguthorpe, Harris, Harris, & Black, 1995). One purpose of such partnerships is to ensure the simultaneous change, renewal, and growth of university teacher education and public school programs and practices.

Starting in 1994, one of the challenges the BYU–public school partnership took on was ESOL teacher preparation. ESOL-endorsed educators are scarce in Utah's highly yet newly affected rural districts, which span more than 2,000 square miles. In 2001, the ESOL student to teacher ratio was, on average, 51 to 1. According to the U.S. Office of Civil Rights guidelines, this ratio should have been 30 to 1. In this same year, the growth patterns in BYU's five partnership districts for ESOL students ranged from 54% to 1,332%. In all but one district, the growth statistic exceeded the state's ESOL growth estimate of 122%. These problems were exacerbated by the fact that Utah was ranked 51st in the nation in 2001 for average per-pupil funding. Conversely, Utah spent 44.8% of its state budget on K–12 public education in 2001, demonstrating the state's commitment to education. These financial restrictions limit districts' abilities to independently train their teachers to serve ESOL students.

Two thesis studies have shown that some teachers feel unprepared for second language learners (Guinn, 1996), whereas other teachers, in particular secondary teachers, do not want additional training (Christiansen, 1996). These studies, along with the tremendous growth of the ESOL student population, show a clear need for high-quality ESOL programs, capable of instilling teacher accountability for the ESOL population as well as the skills to educate these students to high academic standards.

Program Delivery System

Traditional, on-campus university courses failed to meet the increasing demand for preparing large numbers of teachers to teach ESOL students. The university experimented with a first-generation distance education format called EDNET (i.e., a two-way audio/video transmission from one professor site to multiple and distance district sites), which proved technologically unstable (Graham, Teemant, Harris, & Cutri, 2001). In addition, because these courses were designed by individual professors rather than programmatically, they were not sufficiently rigorous—in content or coherence—to change teacher thinking or practice.

The demand and urgency to qualify large numbers of teachers remained. A more accessible, flexible, and technologically stable distance-learning format was needed (Graham, Teemant, Harris, & Cutri, 2001) as well as content and pedagogy to promote substantive development in teacher thinking, reflection, and practices (Pinnegar & Teemant, 2003). Ultimately, the BYU–public school partnership collaboratively developed an innovative, video-based endorsement for preservice and in-service educators called the BEEDE program (Teemant, Smith, Pinnegar, & Egan, in press).

Design of Delivery System

Problems with technology were addressed by moving to a delivery system called ProfessorsPlus. The BEEDE program relies on Professors to develop high-quality video segments, CD-ROM materials, and instructional guides—the frozen elements of the system that capture and contextualize main teaching points. On-site facilitators are the Plus portion of the model—or the human element of the model. These facilitators are highly respected, ESOL-endorsed teachers who have master's degrees. Well trained to teach BEEDE courses, the facilitators are responsible for creating community, promoting active learning, scaffolding and evaluating performance, and ensuring application of course content to practice.

The ProfessorsPlus delivery system allows for flexibility and control. Courses are delivered at local schools at the convenience of participants using simple video technology. Additionally, this delivery system is also distinct in two other important ways: (a) It is built on a sociocultural theory of learning, and (b) it models sociocultural pedagogy (Teemant, Smith, Pinnegar, & Egan, in press). Therefore, the ProfessorsPlus model ensures that high-quality materials are consistently delivered in a sociocultural learning environment by highly qualified facilitators.

Design of Content

To improve teacher learning outcomes, the endorsement curriculum needed a foundation of research in teacher thinking (Munby, Russell, & Martin, 2001), sociocultural theories of learning (Dalton, 1998; Tharp & Gallimore, 1989; Vygotsky, 1978), and ongoing and reflective opportunities to consider theory against real-world practice (Korthagen, 2001). Six design principles guided development of the BEEDE program curriculum (Harris, Pinnegar, & Teemant, in press; Pinnegar & Teemant, 2003). Figure 1 briefly defines each design principle. The video segments, CD-ROM materials, instructional guides with their learning and homework activities, and portfolio components of BEEDE were developed to reflect a commitment to these principles.

Program Scope and Sequence

The success of the BEEDE program is evaluated by its capacity to build, extend, and demonstrate participants' abilities to improve the learning experience of ESOL students. Meeting the needs of all learners requires abandoning teacher-centered, behavior-oriented practices. Richardson and Placier (2001) argue that teachers' past experiences, knowledge, and practice exert powerful influences on their learning. Consequently, to change teachers' beliefs and practices, the content and pedagogy of the program must engage teachers in questioning their current practices, collaboratively building new ideas about practice, and analyzing what happens when practices change.

The overarching purpose of the BEEDE program is to advance the education of language minority students through teacher development. The program attends to the development of teachers in four ways. First, BEEDE develops teachers' cognitive

1.	**Pay attention to the adult learner**
	Use dialogue and social interaction to reveal and build on personal practical knowledge of teaching, which emerges out of who learners are and their current conceptions of teaching.
2.	**Develop learner autonomy**
	Support teachers in questioning practice from multiple perspectives to develop flexibility and cognitive complexity.
3.	**Juxtapose the practical with the theoretical**
	Systematically make visible to learners the theory of practice and the practice of theory through multiple and varied experience and exposure to diverse teaching events.
4.	**Ensure authenticity**
	Capture and present classroom practices in such a way that the immediacy, imperfection, nonverbal, and visual aspects of teaching are intact.
5.	**Develop problem representation**
	Use real-classroom teaching events to support learners in formulating their own problem statements and solution paths, increasing their cognitive complexity.
6.	**Develop multiple perspectives**
	Encourage varied theoretical explanations of teaching events to develop learner flexibility in attending to the content, context, pedagogy, and student layers of teaching.

FIGURE 1. Design Principles in Content and Pedagogy

complexity by holding them to high standards, developing their abilities to take multiple perspectives, teaching them about research-based practices, and instilling accountability for course learning. Second, BEEDE approaches teachers positively by assuming teaching competence, connecting to prior knowledge and experience, and showing how theory applies in practice. The focus is to support teachers in expanding what is good in their practice. Third, BEEDE courses develop a safe learning environment grounded in sociocultural theory. Every activity in every course provides an explicit model for using practices consistent with a sociocultural view of learning. Each week teachers gain experience with strategies that support the language development of second language learners. Finally, each course provides teachers with a conceptual tool for thinking about and educating second language students in mainstream classrooms. These conceptual tools can be applied in any teaching context.

The BEEDE program is holistically designed. Its curriculum packs courses with relevant content, provides strategic redundancy, and builds knowledge across courses so that what teachers learn in one course is built on in the next. Teachers take six 2-credit courses in the following order:

1. Foundations of Bilingual Education
2. Understanding Language Acquisition

3. Assessment of Linguistically Diverse Students

4. Developing Second Language Literacy

5. Content-Based Instruction

6. Family, School, and Community Partnerships

The 4-credit practicum, which is technically the seventh course, is fully integrated across each course; that is, either 1/2 credit or 1 credit, depending on the course, is counted toward the practicum. The practicum credits include major fieldwork and CD-ROM assignments in the program.

❧ DESCRIPTION

The CBI course, the fifth in the series, is the capstone course in the program because teachers are required to demonstrate and apply their learning from the program's first four courses (and related practicum activities) to develop their own classroom curriculum and practices. In this way, BEEDE gives attention to CBI throughout the program, with the specific CBI course providing time and space for teachers to enrich and act on their understanding of content. This section describes the learning process and three major goals that define BEEDE's CBI course.

Learning Process Rationale

All BEEDE courses reflect an understanding that learning is first social (Tharp & Gallimore, 1989; Vygotsky, 1978); however, in the CBI course, teachers form teacher working groups that are discipline specific. For example, teachers interested in pedagogical practices in mathematics for ESOL students work together throughout the course.

Teacher working groups promote ownership for learning (Clair & Adger, 2000) and create a safe space among peers where ideas and concepts can be discussed and debated openly. In the process, teachers contribute to each other's understanding and application of new concepts. Teacher working groups create opportunities for praxis; that is, action—teacher pedagogical practices—can be articulated and discussed because reflection—or theory—is evident and visible to teachers (Friere, 1994). Teachers are in dialogue with their own practice and with peers as they move between reflection and action. In this way, teachers are invited to become even more flexible, cognitively complex, self-monitoring, critical, and specific about how they will meet the needs of ESOL learners in their mainstream classrooms. Using the teacher working group as the processing mechanism, teachers are asked to achieve three main course goals.

Goal 1: Review Previous Course Learning

Teachers are asked to systematically review the main concepts of each previous course and develop their own holistic synthesis of learning. Using short video segments captured on CD-ROM, teachers can review these concepts at their own pace and as needed (e.g., *Teaching Alive Elementary Case*). Teachers are brought to a point where they understand their own beliefs and practices and can reconsider them against what the BEEDE program advocates. One assignment tied to this goal is called "Make the Case." This assignment asks teachers to provide evidence—make the case—to a district superintendent that appropriately educating ESOL students is or is not more than "just good teaching."

Goal 2: Reconsider Teaching Practices

Teachers engage in a series of CD-ROM activities that present authentic, not staged, best practices for ESOL students within various disciplines. These CD-ROMs represent a new class of hypermedia case studies, which allow teachers to study effective teaching in depth (Harris, Pinnegar, & Teemant, in press). (See the complete list of available cases at http://beede.byu.edu). Hyperlinks connect classroom video, audio perspectives, and text data for exploration. Such exploration and reflection positions teachers to expand, adjust, or change their own practices.

Goal 3: Applying Conceptual Tools to Curriculum Development

Teachers are asked to develop a curriculum unit plan for their classrooms that demonstrates their understanding and application of the five conceptual tools presented across the four preceding BEEDE courses. (See the next section for conceptual tool descriptions.) This means that teachers develop and then annotate their unit plan, demonstrating how their teaching attends to sociocultural context and teaching practices, learning goals for oral language development, appropriate assessment practices, and second language literacy development. Although the final curriculum unit plan is an individual assignment, teachers share, critique, and evaluate each other's work on an ongoing basis within their teacher working groups. This unit plan becomes part of the final portfolio display of professional growth.

◈ DISTINGUISHING FEATURES

Teachers make the primary difference in student achievement. To expand teacher knowledge is to invest in the development of children's full potential. Teachers need tools that are powerful enough to explain the complexity of their classrooms. The BEEDE program presents teachers with one adopted and four newly developed conceptual tools for mainstream educators. Use of these conceptual tools is first modeled in courses. In the CBI course, however, teachers are to use and apply these tools in the personal context of their curriculum and pedagogy. These conceptual tools comprise the distinguishing features of this CBI course and may also be used and applied in other programs.

Tool 1: The Five Standards of Effective Pedagogy

BEEDE courses model and educate teachers about a set of sociocultural practices established by the Center for Research on Education, Diversity, and Excellence (CREDE). CREDE's five standards for effective pedagogy (Dalton, 1998) focus on teacher and students producing together, developing language and literacy, connecting school to students' lives, teaching complex thinking, and engaging students in instructional conversations.

Tool 2: The Inclusive Pedagogy Framework

Inclusive pedagogy is a coherent and comprehensive framework for professional growth that supports teachers in educating special-population students. Inclusive pedagogy is defined by five characteristics: collaboration, guiding principles, essential policy, critical learning domains, and classroom strategies. All of these characteristics coexist in the daily life of teachers. Each characteristic is defined by a standard, goal questions that promote common understandings, and a "reflection for change" question that promotes united advocacy (see Figure 2). *Inclusive* is used to reflect common understandings, and *pedagogy* is used to remind teachers that every teaching act is an act of advocacy. The framework represents a process of investigating student, school, and community resources, considering beliefs and principles underpinning teacher practices, examining external policy that affects classroom practices and possibilities, focusing on the developmental needs of learners, and acting locally and pedagogically within the classroom to support student development.

Tool 3: Second Language Acquisition: Oral Language Development

Second language learners come to the mainstream classroom with a different trajectory for language learning than monolingual native speakers. A comprehensive understanding of second language acquisition is the most important knowledge a mainstream teacher can possess when teaching ESOL students. Three concepts and six principles of second language acquisition should guide mainstream teachers' work with ESOL students. These concepts are *communication* (principles: input and interaction), *pattern* (principles: stages of development and errors/feedback), and *variability* (principles: types of proficiencies and types of performances). Figure 3 provides an overview of these concepts and principles, as well as the implications for student and teacher work in the second language acquisition process.

Tool 4: Sociocultural Assessment Literacy

The BEEDE program seeks to develop teachers' assessment literacy from a sociocultural perspective. It argues for the importance of implementing a systematic and evidence-based assessment process: plan, collect, and record evidence; analyze and interpret evidence; and use information for reporting and decision making. From a second language perspective, teachers additionally must understand and use the following concepts and principles: *useful* (principles: educative and practical), *meaningful* (principles: relevant and accurate), and *equitable* (principles: open and appropriate). Figure 4 lists these assessment literacy concepts and principles, which become a tool in fine-tuning a teacher's ability to identify, assess, and meet the needs of ESOL students.

Tool 5: Second Language Literacy Development

Promoting literacy development is promoting academic development. BEEDE gives teachers a two-part, second-language literacy framework, which represents what mainstream teachers should know and do to support ESOL students' literacy and conceptual development.

	Standards	Goal Questions	Reflection for Change Questions
Collaboration	Meeting the needs of today's language minority students demands collaboration across academic disciplines, institutions, and school-home cultures.	1. Who are our language minority students? 2. What needs do language minority students have? 3. How can collaboration help me better meet students' needs and utilize their strengths? 4. What programs and practices exist to serve language minority students? 5. What does it mean to know in my discipline and classroom in contrast to other disciplines and classrooms?	How can I engage with other people in different disciplines and classrooms within my educational setting to support students' development as knowers?
Guiding Principles	Effective instruction for language minority students must be guided by theoretical and moral principles.	1. How does recognizing multiple perspectives inform my teaching and learning? 2. How can I develop and maintain high expectations for all students? 3. How does current knowledge about language minority students inform my instructional decisions? 4. How can accountability be instilled and promoted in my students and me throughout our educational lives?	How can I apply these guiding principles to my teaching and curriculum?
Essential Policy	Essential policy must be an integral part of advocacy for language minority students.	1. How do my content-area standards interface with standards addressing language minority students? 2. How can/do classifications both expand and limit my ability to advocate for language minority students? 3. What policies and legislation address the education of language minority students?	What are my moral obligations toward language minority students in my teaching?

Continued on p. 203

	Standards	Goal Questions	Reflection for Change Questions
Critical Learning Domains	Learning involves cognitive, social/affective, and linguistic development.	1. How can I influence students' ability to recognize, participate in, and master playing the school game? 2. How can I support students in a learning environment so that they are able to demonstrate what they know? 3. How do I teach in ways that support the language development of language minority students?	How can I demonstrate understanding of diverse learners' commonalities and uniqueness in critical learning domains in the process of teaching?
Classroom Strategies	Teachers must know the what and the why of effective classroom strategies for language minority students.	1. How can I adjust my planning to meet the needs and utilize the strengths of language minority students? 2. How can my teaching accommodate language minority students? 3. How can I diversify assessment practices to enable language minority students to demonstrate their knowledge?	What specific changes will I make in my own teaching to accommodate language minority students?

FIGURE 2. Inclusive Pedagogy Framework

Communication

How can I assist students in becoming successful communicators?

Six Defining Principles		Develop Flexibility in Examples of Student Work		Plan for Variety in Examples of Teacher Work
Input: How can I improve access to oral and written input?	C	• Activate and develop language skills and general, cultural, and content knowledge	P	• Recognize and build on students' language skills and general, cultural, and content knowledge
Second language acquisition requires access to comprehensible input; that is, written and oral input that is slightly beyond a learner's current ability level for language acquisition to take place.	O G N I T I V E	• Learn new structures and vocabulary • Develop flexible strategies for understanding	E D A G O G Y	• Contextualize language and learning • Move from concrete to abstract • Adjust teacher talk • Modify and elaborate speech and text • Avoid oversimplification of speech, text, tasks, or content
Interaction: How can I increase opportunities for meaningful interaction?	/ A C	• Take risks • Gain self-confidence • Create and sustain motivation for learning		• Create and maintain a safe environment • Respect multiple perspectives • Provide varied opportunities for authentic peer interaction
Second language acquisition requires interaction. Learners develop greater language proficiency through interaction with other people for authentic purposes, when they communicate to meet personal, social, academic goals and needs in a sociocultural reality.	A D E M I C	• Develop and work toward goals • Be aware of sociocultural factors' impact • Use formal and informal opportunities • Move from whole to part • Build a range of communication strategies • Learn new cultural ways		• Promote meaningful language use (not drills or worksheets) • Provide strategy instruction for skill-building • Teach nonverbal skills • Focus on meaning first • Model and teach strategies for repairing misunderstandings

Continued on p. 205

Pattern: How can I promote language and literacy development?

Six Defining Principles		Develop Flexibility in Examples of Student Work		Plan for Variety in Examples of Teacher Work
Stages of Development: How can I assess language and literacy skills? Second language acquisition is a patterned and gradual process of development characterized by specific stages, orders, and sequences of development that predict what aspects of language are learned earlier than other aspects.	L A N G U A G E	• Comprehend and discriminate sounds, words, meanings • Internalize rules and patterns • Move from unanalyzed to analyzed use of words/phrases/sentences • Avoid fossilization	L A N G U A G E	• Teach what is developmentally appropriate (Teachability Hypothesis) • Move students from comprehension to production • Create a rich linguistic environment • Understand and expect a silent period • Have appropriate yet high expectations • Plan opportunities for students to notice new features • Encourage communication • Use routines, models, visual, and nonverbal cues
Errors and Feedback: How can I use feedback to further language learning? Second language acquisition is a patterned but nonlinear process. As new features of language are learned, the learner's internal system is restructured, sometimes causing errors in production that look like backsliding or reveal a learner's testing of hypotheses. Errors and feedback are essential to this learning process.	L E A R N I N G	• Practice useful phrases • Integrate new and increasingly complex forms • Generate hypotheses • Transfer first language competence • Develop language skills simultaneously • Accept and respond to feedback on errors	D E V E L O P M E N T	• Recognize errors as students' hypotheses about how language works • Provide feedback with a focus on meaning and then form • Support transfer of native academic language skills to new language skills (Interdependency Hypothesis) • Integrate focus on reading, writing, listening, and speaking using appropriate scaffolding • Move students from comprehension to production • Allow multiple attempts and drafts • Collaborate with colleagues who can support student development

Continued on p. 206

205

Six Defining Principles	Develop Flexibility in Examples of Student Work	Plan for Variety in Examples of Teacher Work
Types of Proficiencies: How can I increase knowledge of language? Second language acquisition results in various levels of skill or proficiency with which a person can use language for a specific purpose, in a specific cultural or academic setting, with various individuals.	• Learn social language • Learn academic language • Learn sociocultural appropriacy • Use analysis and synthesis skills in understanding language • Build a repertoire of strategies for compensating • Develop awareness of self in sociocultural settings	• Teach language for social interaction • Model and teach socially and culturally appropriate classroom interaction • Teach academic language • Engage students in challenging curriculum • Assess students' L2 proficiency to ensure accessibility to instruction (Threshold Hypothesis) • Teach registers and genres • Teach standard English • Teach academic skills
Types of Performances: How can I expand use of language? Second language acquisition is marked by variability in performance as well as patterns because the very context, tasks, or language function (e.g., complimenting, requesting help) can affect the learner's ability to produce language with fluency and accuracy.	• Controlled/planned to automatic/spontaneous • Move between accuracy and fluency • Flexible learning strategies	• Provide varied opportunities for language use because features first appear in planned or monitored speech • Teach explicitly forms, functions, sentence structures, and vocabulary • Focus on fluency and accuracy • Hold students accountable for learning • Teach academic strategies for learning

(Spine labels: SOCIAL/AFFECTIVE · INDIVIDUAL DIFFERENCES)

Variability
How can I vary instruction to meet individual needs?

FIGURE 3. A Second Language Acquisition Framework for Mainstream Teachers

The first part of the framework extends teachers' understanding of communication, pattern, and variability. As an example, Figure 5 lists the new student and teacher work given for moving beyond oral language to developing necessary literacy skills.

The second portion of the framework delineates five ESOL curriculum guidelines that help mainstream educators promote second language literacy development. These guidelines are as follows:

- Teach to the next text using pre-, during-, and after-reading/writing activities that build vocabulary, background and cultural knowledge, and needed literacy skills.

Concept	Principles	Checklist Items
Useful for Stake-Holders	**Educative:** Assessment is educative when it supports learning, improves student performance, and supports effective instructional decisions.	Feedback: Does the assessment provide timely, actionable feedback to my students about the quality of their work and next steps for learning? Are scores and reports useful for stakeholders?
		Decisions: Does the assessment help me make instructional decisions that are beneficial for students?
	Practical: Assessment is practical when it is feasible and efficient within available resources.	Feasibility: Is the assessment feasible for me, given my students, workload, and resources?
		Efficiency: Does the assessment efficiently provide the information needed by me, my students, and other stakeholders?
Meaningful for Purposes	**Relevant:** Assessment is relevant when it emphasizes understanding important content and performing authentic tasks.	Content: Is the assessment content important? Does it reflect professional standards for the discipline?
		Tasks: Are the assessment tasks authentic? Are they coherent with my beliefs about learning and knowing? Do they elicit my students' best work?
	Accurate: Assessment is accurate when it produces valid results based on reliable evidence and expert judgments of quality.	Validity: Do the assessment results match my specified purpose for the assessment? Does the format of the assessment follow its function?
		Reliability: Are the assessment results consistent across tasks, time, and judgments?

Continued on p. 208

Concept	Principles	Checklist Items
Equitable for All Students	**Open:** Assessment is open when it is a participative process and discloses its purposes, expectations, criteria, and consequences.	Participation: Is the assessment process open to participation by interested stakeholders, including my students?
		Disclosure: Do my students understand the assessment: its purpose, what is expected, how it will be judged, and its consequences?
	Appropriate: Assessment is appropriate when it fairly accommodates students' sociocultural, linguistic, and developmental needs.	Fairness: Is the assessment unbiased in terms of my students' languages and cultures? Does it contribute to equal outcomes for my students?
		Impact: Are the personal and social consequences of the assessment equitable for my students?

FIGURE 4. Sociocultural Assessment Literacy: Concepts and Principles

- Provide for broad extensive reading to promote general vocabulary and literacy skill development.

- Support narrow reading of academic texts to give students repeated exposure to key concepts, ideas, and vocabulary.

- Focus on academic vocabulary, developing multiple activities with varied contexts to learn and communicate using key vocabulary.

- Use and produce both expository and narrative texts to build general and domain-specific vocabulary, awareness of text purposes, structures, and grammar.

◈ PRACTICAL IDEAS

From experience developing the CBI course and each of the BEEDE courses, several valuable lessons can serve as suggestions for others. These suggestions focus on pedagogy, curriculum, teacher development, and technology.

Model Teaching Practices

BEEDE is grounded in a sociocultural theory of teaching and learning. For teachers to understand and use sociocultural practices, they need to learn about and experience them. Modeling best teaching practices is essential for changing teacher beliefs and practices.

Teach Questions

There is a difference between being given questions to investigate and being given statements to learn. Questions allow teachers to evaluate their practices, settings,

Concept/ Principles			Develop Flexibility in Examples of Student Work		Plan for Variety in Examples of Teacher Work
Communication	Input	COGNITIVE / ACADEMIC	• Activate and develop language and literacy skills and general, cultural, and content knowledge • Read frequently from various texts • Understand and use language forms, meanings, and cueing systems • Learn academic and social language and vocabulary • Develop flexible comprehension strategies	PEDAGOGY	• Recognize and build on students' language and literacy skills and general, cultural, and content knowledge while avoiding oversimplification • Promote frequent reading to, with, and by students • Respond to student development and interests in text selections • Scaffold tasks and texts to build understanding of language forms, meanings, and cueing systems • Build metalinguistic awareness • Teach language and vocabulary needed in your class • Model and teach comprehension strategies
	Interaction		• Use literacy skills to communicate ideas • Connect texts to self, others, and the world • Use informal and formal opportunities to read and write • Read from the writer's perspective and write from the reader's perspective • Understand and use the writing process • Attend to audience, purpose, voice, organization, idea development, fluency, word choice, and mechanics in writing		• Scaffold frequent reading and writing in various genres to communicate ideas • Engage students in discussing texts and the reading and writing processes • Promote and articulate connections to texts • Develop students' attention to audience, purpose, voice, organization, idea development, fluency, word choice, and mechanics in writing • Involve parents in reading and writing to and with their child in their language(s)

FIGURE 5. Example of Student Work and Teacher Work in Second Language Literacy Development

curriculum, and dispositions. Questions can be applied to all classrooms. Questions invite discussion. When teachers learn a fruitful question, it can become a catalyst for promoting change in their thinking and practice.

Build Cognitive Complexity

The more nuanced teachers' understandings are, the more they understand what, where, why, and how ESOL students are the same as and different from other special-population students. In turn, they are more able to advocate for appropriate ESOL programs and practices. Engaging in cycles of learning, reflecting, acting, and sharing builds teachers' cognitive complexity.

Prepare Teachers for Technology

It is easy to underestimate how much preparation teachers need to feel comfortable and competent in using technology. Time invested in explaining, modeling, and experiencing the use of technology in the classroom or as homework will improve participants' learning experience.

⬧ CONCLUSION

Utah's need to qualify large numbers of teachers to educate a growing ESOL population was the impetus for BYU's development of the BEEDE program. The ProfessorsPlus delivery system, with its video segments, CD-ROM materials, and instructional guides, enabled delivery of high-quality "frozen" content to multiple and distance sites without compromising the need for building learner communities with trained facilitators. Most important, however, the collaborative effort led to programmatic planning of curriculum, with appropriate and strategic redundancy as well as cumulative learning opportunities. The CBI course described in this chapter reflects the benefits of programmatic planning: Teachers are positioned to more deeply consider, analyze, synthesize, and apply learning—and selected conceptual learning tools—to their own curriculum, pedagogy, context, and discipline.

⬧ ACKNOWLEDGMENT

Development of the BEEDE program has been a long-term collaborative process with many university faculty and public school colleagues. The following faculty have acted as codevelopers of the conceptual tools and courses: Dr. Stefinee Pinnegar (Department of Teacher Education), Dr. Ray Graham (Department of Linguistics), and Dr. Marvin Smith (educational consultant).

⬧ CONTRIBUTOR

Annela Teemant is an assistant professor of foreign/second language teacher education at Brigham Young University in Provo, Utah, in the United States. Her teaching and research focuses on the preparation of teachers to appropriately educate language minority students in public school settings.

References

Ackert, P. (1999). *Cause and effect.* Boston: Heinle & Heinle.

Agor, B. (Ed.). (2000). *Integrating the ESL standards into classroom practice: Grades 9–12.* Alexandria, VA: TESOL.

American Association for the Advancement of Science. (1998). *Blueprints for reform: Science, mathematics and technology education.* New York: Oxford University Press.

American Association for the Advancement of Science. (2001). *Designs for science literacy: Project 2061.* Washington, DC: Author.

Andrade, C., Kretschmer, R., & Kretschmer, L. (1989). Two languages for all children: Expanding to low achievers and the handicapped. In K. E. Muller (Ed.), *Languages in the elementary schools* (pp. 177–203). New York: American Forum for Global Education.

Andrews, L. (1993). *Language exploration and awareness.* New York: Longman.

Arkoudis, S. (2000). *The epistemological authority of an ESL teacher in science education.* Unpublished doctoral dissertation, University of Melbourne, Australia.

Arkoudis, S., & Davison, C. (2002). Breaking out of the billabong: Mainstreaming ESL in Australia. In E. Cochran (Ed.), *Case studies in TESOL: Mainstreaming* (pp. 53–67). Alexandria, VA: TESOL.

August, D., & Hakuta, K. (Eds.). (1997). *Improving schooling for language minority students: A research agenda.* Washington, DC: National Academy Press.

Baker, C. (2001). *Foundations of bilingual education and bilingualism* (3rd ed.). Buffalo, NY: Multilingual Matters.

Bawab, S., & Jakar, V. S. (2001). *Alice's wonderland of content-based TEFL.* Paper presented at the Annual TESOL Convention, St. Louis, MO.

Beatty, K. (2003). *Teaching and researching computer-assisted language learning.* London: Pearson.

Beaver, J. (1997). *Developmental reading assessment.* Parsippany, NJ: Celebration Press.

Berman, M. (2001). *ELT through multiple intelligences.* London: NetLearn Publications.

Bernache, C. (1999). *The impact of literacy development training on teachers' perceptions of middle school non-formally schooled or limited-formally schooled English language learners.* Unpublished doctoral dissertation, Berne University, New Hampshire.

Bettelheim, B. (1976). *The uses of enchantment.* New York: Alfred Knopf.

Biagetti, S. C. (2001). Teachers creating frameworks to understand their students' algebraic thinking. In U. D. Ranier & E. M. Guyton (Eds.), *Research on the effects of teacher education on teacher performance: Teacher education yearbook IX* (pp. 209–223). Reston, VA: Association of Teacher Educators.

Bialystok, E., & Hakuta, K. (1994). *In other words: The science and psychology of second language acquisition.* New York: Basic Books.

Bigelow, M., & Ranney, S. (2004). The new English language proficiency standards: Issues in curriculum and ESL teacher professionalism. *MinneTESOL/WITESOL Journal, 21,* 17–36.

Boals, T. (2000). Wisconsin's approach to academic assessment for limited-English proficient (LEP) students: Creating a continuum of assessment options. *MinneTESOL/ WITESOL Journal, 17,* 39–51.

Boals, T. (2001). Ensuring academic success: The real issue in educating English language learners. *Midwestern Educational Researcher, 14*(4), 3–8.

Boals, T. (2003). Using standards-based classroom assessments to influence practice in programs for English language learners (ELLs). Ann Arbor, MI: UMI Dissertation Information Service.

Board of Studies. (2000). *ESL companion to the English curriculum and standard Framework.* Melbourne: Curriculum Corporation.

Boyle, O. E., & Peregoy, S. F. (1990). Literacy scaffolds: Strategies for first- and second-language readers and writers. *The Reading Teacher, 44,* 194–200.

Bragger, J. D., & Rice, D. B. (1998). Connections: The national standards and the new paradigm for content-oriented materials and instruction. In J. Harper, M. Lively, & M. Williams (Eds.), *The coming of age of the profession.* Boston: Heinle & Heinle.

Bransford, J. D., Brown, A. L., & Cocking, R. R. (2000). *How people learn: Brain, mind, experience, and school.* Washington, DC: National Academy Press.

Breen, M. P. (1985). Authenticity in the language classroom. *Applied Linguistics, 6*(1), 60–70.

Brinton, D. M., Snow, M. A., & Wesche, M. B. (1989). *Content-based second language instruction.* New York: Harper & Row.

Bunch, G. C., Abram, P. L., Lotan, R. A., & Valdés, G. (2001). Beyond sheltered instruction: Rethinking conditions for academic language development. *TESOL Journal, 10*(2/3), 28–33.

Burbaquis-Vinson, A., Brian, N., Brovetto, C., Casco, E., & Díaz, G. (2002). *Bases para la adquisición de una segunda lengua por inmersión parcial en escuelas de tiempo completo* [Bases for the implementation of a partial immersion second language acquisition program in double-shift schools]. Montevideo, Uruguay: National Administration of Public Education.

Chamot, A. U., Barnhardt, S., El-Dinary, P. B., & Robbins, J. (1999). *The learning strategies handbook.* White Plains, NY: Addison-Wesley Longman.

Chamot, A. U., & O'Malley, J. M. (1987). The cognitive academic language learning approach: A bridge to the mainstream. *TESOL Quarterly, 21*(2), 227–249.

Chamot, A. U., & O'Malley, J. M. (1994). *The CALLA handbook: Implementing the cognitive academic language learning approach.* Reading, MA: Addison-Wesley.

Christiansen, D. K. (1996). *The preparedness, attitudes, and opinions of secondary school teachers concerning the education of limited English proficient students.* Unpublished master's thesis, Brigham Young University, Provo, UT.

Christison, M. A. (1996). Teaching and learning languages through multiple intelligences. *TESOL Journal, 6*(1), 10–14.

Clair, N. (1998). Teacher study groups: Persistent questions in a promising approach. *TESOL Quarterly, 32*(3), 465–492.

Clair, N., & Adger, C. T. (2000). Sustainable strategies for professional development. In K. E. Johnson (Ed.), *Teacher education* (pp. 29–49). Alexandria, VA: TESOL.

Clark, C. M. (Ed.). (2001). *Talking shop: Authentic conversation and teacher learning.* New York: Teachers College Press.

Clark, R. W. (1997). *Professional development schools: Policy and financing.* Washington, DC: American Association of Colleges for Teacher Education.

Clay, M., & Cazden, C. (1990). A Vygotskian interpretation of reading recovery. In L. Moll

(Ed.), *Vygotsky and education: Instructional implications of sociohistorical psychology* (pp. 206–222). New York: Cambridge University Press.

Clegg, J. (Ed.). (1996). *Mainstreaming ESL case studies in integrating ESL students into the mainstream curriculum*. Clevedon, United Kingdom: Multilingual Matters.

Clyne, M. (1997). *Undoing and redoing corpus planning*. Berlin: Mouton de Gruyter.

Cocking, R. R., & Mestre, J. P. (Eds.). (1988). *Linguistic and cultural influences on learning mathematics*. Hillsdale, NJ: Erlbaum.

Cohen, E. G. (1994). *Designing groupwork: Strategies for heterogeneous classrooms* (2nd ed.). New York: Teachers College Press.

Cohen, E. G., & Lotan, R. A. (1997). *Working for equity in heterogeneous classrooms: Sociological theory in practice*. New York: Teachers College Press.

Connelly, M., & Sims, J. (1990). *Time and space*. Englewood Cliffs, NJ: Prentice Hall Regents.

Crandall, J. A. (Ed.). (1987). *ESL through content-area instruction: Mathematics, science, and social studies*. McHenry, IL and Washington, DC: Delta Systems and Center for Applied Linguistics.

Crandall, J. A. (1993). Content-centered learning in the United States. *Annual Review of Applied Linguistics, 13,* 111–126.

Crandall, J. A. (1997). Language teaching approaches for school-aged learners in second language contexts. In G. R. Tucker & D. Corson (Eds.), *Encyclopedia of language and education* (Vol. 4, pp. 75–84). Dordrecht, The Netherlands: Kluwer.

Crandall, J. A. (1998a). *Challenges of content-based instruction for teacher education*. Paper presented at the Annual TESOL Convention, Seattle, WA.

Crandall, J. A. (1998b). Collaborate and cooperate: Teacher education for integrating language and content instruction. *English Teaching Forum, 36*(1), 2–9.

Crandall, J. A., Bernache, C., & Prager, S. (1998). New frontiers in educational policy and program development: The challenge of the underschooled immigrant secondary school student. *Educational Policy, 12*(6), 719–734.

Crandall, J. A., Dale, T. C., Rhodes, N. C., & Spanos, G. A. (1990). The language of mathematics: The English barrier. In A. Labarca & L. Bailey (Eds.), *Issues in L2: Theory as practice/practice as theory* (pp. 129–150). Norwood, NJ: Ablex.

Crandall, J. A., & Kaufman, D. (2002). *Case studies in content-based instruction in higher education*. Alexandria, VA: TESOL.

Crowley, J. (1986). *Yo amo a mi familia* [I love my family]. Bothwell, MA: The Wright Group.

Crystal, D. (1995). *The Cambridge encyclopedia of the English language*. New York: Cambridge University Press.

Crystal, D. (1997). *English as a global language*. New York: Cambridge University Press.

Cuevas, G. (1984). Mathematics learning in English as a second language. *Journal of Research in Mathematics Education, 15,* 134–144.

Cummins, J. (1989). *Empowering minority students*. Sacramento: California Association of Bilingual Education.

Cummins, J. (1994). Primary language instruction and the education of language minority students. In California State Department of Education (Ed.), *Schooling of language minority students: A theoretical framework* (2nd ed., pp. 3–46). Los Angeles: California State University, Evaluation, Dissemination, and Assessment Center.

Cummins, J. (2000). *Language, power, and pedagogy: Bilingual children in the crossfire*. Clevedon, United Kingdom: Multilingual Matters.

Cummins, J. (n.d.). *Dr. Cummins' ESL and second language learning web*. Retrieved February 11, 2005, from http://www.iteachlearn.com/cummins/

Curtain, H. (1993). *An early start*. Washington, DC: Center for Applied Linguistics.

Dalton, S. S. (1998). *Pedagogy matters: Standards for effective teaching* (Research Report 4).

Santa Cruz, CA: Center for Research on Education, Diversity, and Excellence. Retrieved January 1, 2005, from http://crede.org/products/print/reports.html

Darling-Hammond, L. (1997). *Doing what matters most: Investing in quality teaching.* New York: National Commission on Teaching and America's Future.

Darling-Hammond, L. (2001). Forward. In L. Darling-Hammond (Ed.), *Studies of excellence in teacher education* (pp. v–xi). Washington, DC: American Association of Colleges for Teacher Education.

Davison, C. (2001). Current policies, programs, and practices in school ESL. In B. Mohan, C. Leung, & C. Davison (Eds.), *English as a second language in the mainstream: Teaching, learning and identity* (pp. 30–50). Harlow: Longman Pearson.

Day, R. (1990). The value of observation in teacher education. In J. Richards (Ed.), *Beyond training* (pp. 43–61). New York: Cambridge University Press.

De Jong, E. J. (2002). Effective bilingual education: From theory to academic achievement in a two-way bilingual program. *Bilingual Research Journal, 26*(1), 65–84.

Díaz, R. M. (1985). Bilingual cognitive development: Addressing three gaps in current research. *Child Development, 56*(6), 1376–1388.

Díaz-Rico, L. T., & Weed, K. Z. (2002). *The cross-cultural, language, and academic development handbook: A complete K–12 reference guide* (2nd ed.). Needham Heights, MA: Allyn & Bacon.

Dixon-Krauss, L. (1996). *Vygotsky in the classroom: Mediated literacy instruction and assessment.* New York: Longman.

Dubetz, N. E., Lawrence, A., & Gningue, S. (2002). Formalizing a process for identifying urban PDS partnerships. *Issues in Teacher Education, 11*(2), 17–30.

Duncan, S. E., & De Avila, E. A. (1988). *Language assessment scales: Reading/writing.* Monterey, CA: Macmillan/McGraw-Hill.

Echevarria, J., Vogt, M., & Short, D. (2000). *Making content comprehensible for English language learners: The SIOP model.* Boston: Allyn & Bacon.

Edge, J. (2002). *Continuing cooperative development: A discourse framework for individuals as colleagues.* Ann Arbor: The University of Michigan Press.

Education Department of South Australia. (1991). *ESL in the mainstream: Teacher development course.* Adelaide: Government Printer.

Escamilla, K., Andrade, A. M., Basurto, A., & Ruiz, O. (1996). *Instrumento de observacion* [Observation instrument]. Portsmouth, NH: Heinemann.

Falk, B. (2000). *The heart of the matter: Using standards and assessment to learn.* Westport, CT: Heinemann.

Finocchiaro, M., & Brumfit, C. (1983). *The functional-notional approach: From theory to practice.* Oxford: Oxford University Press.

Fishman, J. A., Cooper, R. L., & Conrad, A. W. (1977). *The spread of English: The sociology of English as an additional language.* Rowley, MA: Newbury House.

Foreman, D. I, & Allen, S. J. (1990). *Maps, charts, graphs: Communities Level C.* Parsippany, NJ: Modern Curriculum Press.

Freeman, D., & Johnson, K. E. (Eds.). (1998). Research and practice in English language teacher education (Special-topic issue). *TESOL Quarterly, 32*(3).

Freire, P. (1994). *Pedagogy of the oppressed.* New York: Continuum.

Gallimore, R., & Tharp, R. (1990). Teaching mind in society: Teaching, schooling, and literate discourse. In L. Moll (Ed.), *Vygotsky and education: Instructional implications of sociohistorical psychology* (pp. 175–205). New York: Cambridge University Press.

Gardner, H. (1993). *Multiple intelligences.* New York: Basic Books.

Gardner, R. C., & Lambert, W. E. (1972). *Attitudes and motivation in second-language learning.* Rowley, MA: Newbury House.

Garfinkel, A., & Tabor, K. (1991). Elementary school foreign languages and English reading achievement. *Foreign Language Annals, 24* (5), 375–382.

Genesee, F. (Ed.). (1994). *Educating second language children: The whole child, the whole curriculum, the whole community.* Cambridge, United Kingdom: Cambridge University Press.

Ghosn, I. (1998). *Literature for language and change in the primary school.* Paper presented at the Annual TESOL Convention, Seattle, WA.

Gibbons, P. (2002). *Scaffolding language, scaffolding learning: Teaching second language learners in the mainstream classroom.* Portsmouth, NH: Heinemann.

Goodlad, J. I. (1994). *Educational renewal: Better teachers, better schools.* San Francisco: Jossey-Bass.

Goodlad, J. I., Soder, R., & Sirotnik, K. A. (Eds.). (1990). *Places where teachers are taught.* San Francisco: Jossey-Bass.

Goodman, Y., & Goodman, K. (1990). Vygotsky in a whole-language perspective. In L. Moll (Ed.), *Vygotsky and education: Instructional implications of sociohistorical psychology* (pp. 223–250). New York: Cambridge University Press.

Goodrich, H., Hatch, T., Wiatrowski, G., & Unger, C. (1996). *Teaching through projects: Creating effective learning environments.* Reading, MA: Addison-Wesley.

Gottlieb, M. (1999). *Guidelines for Wisconsin Alternate Assessment for ELLs.* Madison: Wisconsin Department of Public Instruction.

Gottlieb, M. (2000). *Standards-based alternate assessment for limited English proficient students: A guide for Wisconsin educators* [CD-ROM]. Madison: Wisconsin Department of Public Instruction.

Gottlieb, M. (2003). Large-scale assessment of English language learners: Addressing educational accountability in K–12 settings. *TESOL Professional Papers No. 6.* Alexandria, VA: TESOL.

Gottlieb, M. (2004). *Wisconsin alternate assessment for English language learners: Guidelines for educators.* Madison: Wisconsin Department of Public Instruction. Retrieved December 26, 2004, from http://www.dpi.state.wi.us/oea/ells.html

Grabe, W., & Stoller, F. L. (1997). Content-based instruction: Research foundations. In M. A. Snow & D. M. Brinton (Eds.), *The content-based classroom: Perspectives on integrating language and content* (pp. 5–21). White Plains, NY: Addison-Wesley Longman.

Graham, C. R., Teemant, A., Harris, M. F., & Cutri, R. M. (2001). The pedagogy and technology of distance learning for teacher education: The evolution of instructional processes and products. In L. E. Henrichsen (Ed.), *Distance-learning programs* (pp. 141–149). Alexandria, VA: TESOL.

Guinn, S. G. (1996). *Elementary teachers' perceptions of issues relating to LEP mainstreaming.* Unpublished master's thesis, Brigham Young University, Provo, UT.

Hall, J. K. (2002). *Teaching and researching language and culture.* London: Pearson.

Harper, C., & Platt, E. (1998). Full inclusion for secondary school ESOL students: Some concerns from Florida. *TESOL Journal, 7*(5), 30–36.

Harré, R., & van Langenhove, L. (Eds.). (1999). *Positioning theory: Moral contexts of intentional action.* Malden, United Kingdom: Blackwell.

Harris, R. C., Pinnegar, S., & Teemant, A. (in press). The case for hypermedia video ethnographies: Designing a new class of case studies that challenge teaching practice. *Journal of Technology and Teacher Education.*

Hedegaard, M. (1990). The zone of proximal development as basis for instruction. In L. Moll (Ed.), *Vygotsky and education: Instructional implications of sociohistorical psychology* (pp. 349–371). New York: Cambridge University Press.

Heubert, J. P. (2001). *High-stakes testing: Opportunities and risks for students of color, English-language learners, and students with disabilities.* National Center on Accessing the General Curriculum. Retrieved January 11, 2005, from http://www.cast.org/ncac/index.cfm?i=920

Heubert, J. P., & Hauser, R. (1999). *High stakes: Testing for tracking, promotion, and graduation.* Washington, DC: National Academy Press.

Hoffman, M., & Binch, C. (2003). *Amazing grace.* Minneapolis, MN: Sagebrush Bound.

Hofstra University TESL Program/Nassau BOCES. (2005). *ESL activities portfolio.* Retrieved January 8, 2005, from http://people.hofstra.edu/faculty/Tatiana_Gordon/ESL/

Holdsworth, R. (1996). What do we mean by student participation? *Youth Studies Australia, 15*, 26–27.

Holmes Group. (1990). *Tomorrow's schools: Principles for the design of professional development groups.* East Lansing, MI: Author.

Holmes Group. (1995). *Tomorrow's schools of education.* East Lansing, MI: Author.

Holten, C. (1997). Literature: A quintessential content. In M. A. Snow & D. M. Brinton (Eds.), *The content-based classroom: Perspectives on integrating language and content* (pp. 377–387). New York: Longman.

Hopkins, L. B. (1996). *Families, families.* New York: Sadler-Oxford.

Howie, D. (1999). Preparing for positive positioning. In R. Harré & L. van Langenhove (Eds.), *Positioning theory: Moral contexts of intentional action* (pp. 53–59). Malden, United Kingdom: Blackwell.

Huntington, S. P. (1996). *The clash of civilization and the remaking of world order.* New York: Simon & Schuster.

Hurley, S. R., & Tinajero, J. V. (Eds.). (2000). *Literacy assessment of second language learners.* Boston: Allyn & Bacon.

Interstate New Teacher Assessment and Support Consortium. (1992). *Model standards in science for beginning teacher licensing and development: A resource for state dialogue.* Washington, DC: Author.

Interstate New Teacher Assessment and Support Consortium. (2002). *Model standards in science for beginning teacher licensing and development: A resource for state dialogue.* Washington, DC: Author.

Jacobs, H. H. (1997). *Mapping the big picture: Integrating curriculum and assessment K–12.* Alexandria, VA: Association for Supervision and Curriculum Development.

Jakar, V. S. (2002). *Pickles and proverbs.* Paper presented at the First TESOL Eastern Mediterranean Conference, Middle Eastern Technical University, Ankara, Turkey.

Johnson, K. E. (Ed.). (2000). *Case studies in teacher education.* Alexandria, VA: TESOL.

Johnson, K. E., & Golombek, P. (2003). "Seeing" teacher learning. *TESOL Quarterly, 37*(4), 729–737.

Joyce, W. W., & Erickson, R. (1987). *Comparing communities.* Morristown, NJ: Silver Burdett Ginn.

Kagan, S. (1998). *Graphic organizers: A smart card.* San Juan Capistrano, CA: Spencer Kagan Cooperative Learning.

Kasper, L. F. (2000). Sustained content study and the Internet. In M. Pally (Ed.), *Sustained content teaching in academic ESL/EFL* (pp. 54–71). Boston: Houghton Mifflin.

Kauchak, D., & Eggen, P. (1998). *Learning and teaching: Research-based methods.* Boston: Allyn & Bacon.

Kaufman, D. (1996). Constructivist-based experiential learning in teacher education. *Action in Teacher Education, 18,* 40–50.

Kaufman, D. (1997). Collaborative approaches in preparing teachers for content-based and language-enhanced settings. In M. A. Snow & D. M. Brinton (Eds.), *The content-based classroom: Perspectives on integrating language and content* (pp. 175–186). White Plains, NY: Longman.

Kaufman, D. (2000). Developing professionals: Interwoven visions and partnerships. In K. E. Johnson (Ed.), *Case studies in teacher education* (pp. 51–69). Alexandria, VA: TESOL.

Kaufman, D. (2004). Issues in constructivist pedagogy for L2 learning and teaching. *Annual Review of Applied Linguistics, 24,* 303–319.

Kaufman, D., & Grennon Brooks, J. (1996). Interdisciplinary collaboration in teacher education: A constructivist approach. *TESOL Quarterly, 30*(2), 231–251.

Kessler, C., Lee, L., McCloskey, M., Quinn, M., Stack, L., & Bernard-Johnston, J. (1996). *Making connections 3: An integrated approach to learning English*. Boston: Heinle & Heinle.

Kibby, M. W. (1995). The organization and teaching of things and the words that signify them. *Journal of Adolescent & Adult Literacy, 39*(3), 208–223.

Ko, J., Schallert, D. L., & Walters, K. (2003). Rethinking scaffolding: Examining negotiation of meaning in an ESL storytelling task. *TESOL Quarterly, 37*(2), 303–336.

Kopriva, R. (2000). *Ensuring accuracy in testing for English language learners*. Washington, DC: Council of Chief State School Officers.

Korthagen, F. A. J. (2001). *Linking practice and theory: The pedagogy of realistic teacher education*. Mahwah, NJ: Lawrence Erlbaum.

Krashen, S. (1987). The input hypothesis. In J. Richards (Ed.), *Methodology in TESOL*. Boston: Newbury House.

Kucer, S. B., Silva, C., & Delgado-Larocco, E. L. (1995). *Curricular conversations: Themes in multilingual and monolingual classrooms*. York, ME: Stenhouse.

Lantolf, J. P., & Appel, G. (Eds.). (1994). *Vygotskian approaches to second language research*. Norwood, NJ: Ablex.

Laturnau, J. (2001). *Standards-based instruction for English language learners* (PREL Briefing Paper). Honolulu, Hawaii: Pacific Resources for Education and Learning. Retrieved January 1, 2005, from http://www.prel.org/products/pc_/standards-based.pdf

Lawrence, A., & Dubetz, N. E. (2001). An urban collaboration: Improving student learning through a professional development network. *Action in Teacher Education, 22*(4), 1–14.

Lee, W. Y. (1995). Authenticity revisited: Text authenticity and learner authenticity. *ELT Journal, 49*(4), 323–328.

Legutke, M., & Thomas, H. (1991). *Process and experience in the language classroom*. London: Longman.

Lichman, S. (2002, April). Showing different images with games. In *The Coexistence Chronicle*. Retrieved December 14, 2004, from http://www.coexistence.net/coexistence/library/V2Issue1.pdf

Lortie, D. (1975). *Schoolteacher*. Chicago: University of Chicago Press.

Lotan, R. A. (2003). "Group-worthy" tasks: When four heads are better than one. *Educational Leadership, 60*(6), 72–75.

Lucas, T. (1997). *In, through, and beyond secondary school: Critical transitions for immigrant youths*. McHenry, IL: Delta Systems/CAL.

Lytle, J. H. (2000). Teacher education at the millennium: A view from the cafeteria. *Journal of Teacher Education, 51*, 174–179.

Magestro, P. (2000). A tool for meaningful staff development. *Educational Leadership, 57*(8), 34–35.

Maryland School Performance Program Report. (2000). Upper Marlboro, MD: Prince George's County Public Schools.

Marzollo, J. (1993). *Happy birthday Martin Luther King*. New York: Scholastic Press.

McArthur, T. (1998). *The English languages*. New York: Cambridge University Press.

McArthur, T. (2002). *The Oxford guide to world English*. Oxford: Oxford University Press.

McGroarty, M. (1998). Constructive and constructivist challenges for applied linguistics. *Language Learning, 48*, 591–622.

Met, M. (1991). Learning language through content: Learning content through language. *Foreign Language Annals, 24*(4), 281–295.

Met, M. (1994). Teaching content through a second language. In F. Genesee (Ed.), *Educating second language children: The whole child, the whole curriculum, the whole community* (pp. 159–182). New York: Cambridge University Press.

Minnesota Department of Education. (2003). *Minnesota English language proficiency standards for English language learners.* Retrieved November 23, 2004, from http://education.state.mn.us/html/intro_eng_lang_learn.htm

Mohan, B. (1986). *Language and content.* Reading, MA: Addison-Wesley.

Mohan, B., Leung, C., & Davison, C. (2001). *English as a second language in the mainstream.* Essex, United Kingdom: Pearson.

Moll, L. (Ed.). (1990). *Vygotsky and education: Instructional implications of sociohistorical psychology.* New York: Cambridge University Press.

Moskowitz, G. (1978). *Caring and sharing in the foreign language class: A sourcebook on humanistic techniques.* Boston: Heinle & Heinle.

Munby, H., Russell, T., & Martin, A. K. (2001). Teachers' knowledge and how it develops. In V. Richardson (Ed.), *Handbook of research on teaching* (3rd ed., pp. 877–904). Washington, DC: American Educational Research Association.

Murphy, J. M., & Stoller, F. L. (Eds.). (2001). Sustained-content language teaching: An emerging definition. *TESOL Journal, 10*(2/3), 3–6.

Murrell, P. C. (2001). *The community teacher: A new framework for effective urban teaching.* New York: Teachers College Press.

National Administration of Public Education. (1999). *Una vision integral del proceso de reforma educativa en Uruguay* [A holistic view of the educational reform process in Uruguay]. Montevideo: Author.

National Board for Professional Teaching Standards. (1991). *Toward high and rigorous standards for the teaching profession* (3rd ed.). Washington, DC: Author.

National Council for Accreditation of Teacher Education. (2001a). *Handbook for the assessment of professional development schools.* Washington, DC: Author.

National Council for Accreditation of Teacher Education. (2001b). *Professional standards for the accreditation of schools, colleges, and departments of education.* Washington, DC: Author.

National Council for the Social Studies. (1994). *Expectations of excellence: Curriculum standards for social studies.* Silver Spring, MD: Author.

National Council of Teachers of Mathematics. (2000). *Principles and standards for school mathematics.* Reston, VA: Author.

National Research Council. (1996). *National science education standards.* Washington, DC: National Academy Press.

National Research Council/National Science Foundation (1996). *From analysis to action: Undergraduate education in science, mathematics, engineering, and technology.* Washington, DC: Author.

New York City Board of Education. (1998). *Early childhood literacy assessment system.* Monterey, CA: CTB/McGraw-Hill.

New York City Public Schools Office of Testing. (1982). *Language assessment battery.* New York: Author.

New York State Education Department. (n.d.). *The teaching of language arts to limited English proficient/English language learners: A resource guide for all teachers.* Albany, NY: Author.

Newman, D., Griffin, P., & Cole, M. (1989). *The construction zone: Working for cognitive change in school.* Cambridge: Cambridge University Press.

No Child Left Behind Act, 20 U.S.C. § 6301 (2001).

Nunan, D. (1992). *Research methods in language learning.* Cambridge: Cambridge University Press.

Olshtain, E. (2002). *A holistic view of professional development among teachers and school principals: An educational project in East Jerusalem.* Paper presented at MOFET Conference, Achva College, Israel.

O'Meara, P. (2003). *Wrap-up session: Global challenges and higher education.* Retrieved December 14, 2004, from Duke University Center for International Studies Web site: http://www.duke.edu/web/cis/globalchallenges/pdf/omeara.pdf

Osguthorpe, R. T., Harris, R. C., Harris, M. F., & Black, S. (Eds.). (1995). *Partnership schools: Centers for educational renewal*. San Francisco: Jossey-Bass.

Pally, M. (1999). *Content-based teaching and the use of film*. Presentation given at the English Teachers' Association, Israel, (ETAI) Summer Conference in Jerusalem, Israel.

Pally, M. (Ed.). (2000). *Sustained content teaching in academic ESL/EFL: A practical approach*. Boston: Houghton Mifflin.

Panofsky, C., John-Steiner, V., & Blackwell, P. (1990). The development of scientific concepts and discourse. In L. Moll (Ed.), *Vygotsky and education: Instructional implications of sociohistorical psychology* (pp. 251–270). New York: Cambridge University Press.

Peregoy, S., & Boyle, O. (1990). Reading and writing scaffolds: Supporting literacy for second language learners. *Educational Issues of Language Minority Students: The Journal, 6*, 55–67.

Perkins, D. N., Schwartz, J. L., West, M. M., & Wiske, M. S. (Eds.). (1995). *Software goes to school: Teaching for understanding with new technologies*. New York: Oxford University Press.

Peyton, J., & Adger, C. (1999). Immigrant students in secondary school: Creating structures that promote achievement. *TESOL Journal, 7*(5), 4–5.

Piaget, J. (1970). *The science of education and the psychology of the child*. New York: Basic Books.

Pinnegar, S., & Teemant, A. (2003). Attending to inquiry in the education of teachers: Enlisting frozen and human elements of distance education. *Teacher Education and Practice, 16*(1), 47–69.

Prabhu, N. S. (1996). Concept and conduct in language pedagogy. In G. Cook & B. Seidlhofer (Eds.), *Principle and practice in applied linguistics: Studies in honor of H.G. Widdowson* (pp. 57–71). Oxford: Oxford University Press.

Rafferty, E. (1986). *Second language study and basic skills in Louisiana*. Baton Rouge: Louisiana Department of Education.

Ranney, S., & Bigelow, M. (2002). *Linking language forms and functions to teach ESL through content*. Paper presented at the Midwest TESOL Convention, Minneapolis, MN.

Reid, W. A. (1992). *The pursuit of curriculum: Schooling and the public interest*. Norwood: Ablex.

Richards, J. (1998). *Beyond training*. New York: Cambridge University Press.

Richards, J., Li, B., & Tang, A. (1998). Exploring pedagogical reasoning skills. In J. Richards (Ed.), *Beyond training* (pp. 86–102). New York: Cambridge University Press.

Richardson, V., & Placier, P. (2001). Teacher change. In V. Richardson (Ed.), *Handbook of research on teaching* (4th ed., pp. 905–947). Washington, DC: American Educational Research Association.

Roberts, D. (1999). The sky's the limit. *Science and Children, 37*(1), 33.

Ruiz, O., & Cuesta, V. (2000). *Evaluacion del desarollo de la lectura* [Developmental reading evaluation or assessment]. Parsippany, NJ: Celebration Press.

Ryan, P. (2002). *When Marion sang*. New York: Scholastic.

Ryding, K., & Stowasser, B. (1997). Text development for content-based instruction in Arabic. In S. B. Stryker & B. L. Leaver (Eds.), *Content-based instruction in foreign language education*. Washington, DC: Georgetown University Press.

Saville-Troike, M. (1991). *Teaching and testing for academic achievement: The role of language development* (Focus Series, No. 4). Washington, DC: National Clearinghouse for Bilingual Education.

Sergiovanni, T., & Starratt, R. (1993). *Supervision: A redefinition*. New York: McGraw-Hill.

Short, D. J. (1993). Assessing integrated language and content instruction. *TESOL Quarterly, 27*(4): 627–656.

Short, D. J. (1994). Integrating language and content instruction: Strategies and techniques. In R. Rodriguez, N. J. Ramos, & J. A. Ruiz-Escalante (Eds.), *Compendium of readings in bilingual education: Issues and practices* (pp. 150–164). San Antonio: Texas Association for Bilingual Education.

Short, D. J. (1996). *Integrating language and culture in the social studies: A final report to the U.S. Department of Education, Office of Educational Research and Improvement.* Washington DC: Center for Applied Linguistics and the National Center for Research on Cultural Diversity and Second Language Learning.

Short, D. J. (1997). Reading and 'riting and ...social studies: Research on integrated language and content in secondary classrooms. In M.A. Snow & D.M. Brinton (Eds.), *The content-based classroom: Perspectives on integrating language and content* (pp. 213–232). White Plains, NY: Longman.

Short, D. J., Gomez, E. L., Cloud, N., Katz, A., Gottlieb, M., & Malone, M. (2000). *Training others to use the ESL standards: A professional development manual.* Alexandria, VA: TESOL.

Shulman, L. S. (1986). Those who understand: Knowledge growth in teaching. *Educational Researcher, 15*(2), 4–14.

Shulman, L. S. (1987). Knowledge and teaching: Foundations of the new reform. *Harvard Educational Review, 57*(1), 1–22.

Silver, S. (1997). Implementing inclusion in Pasco County. *The Messenger, 3,* 6.

Siskin, L. S., & Little, J. W. (1995). *Subject divisions: The subjects in question.* New York: Teachers College Press.

Sizer, T. R. (1984). *Horace's compromise: The dilemma of the American high school.* Boston: Houghton Mifflin.

Snow, M. A. (1997). Teaching academic literacy skills: Discipline faculty take responsibility. In M. A. Snow & D. M. Brinton (Eds.), *The content-based classroom: Perspectives on integrating language and content* (pp. 290–304). White Plains, NY: Longman.

Snow, M. A. (2001). Content-based and immersion models for second and foreign language teaching. In M. Celce-Murcia (Ed.), *Teaching English as a second or foreign language* (3rd ed., pp. 303–318). Boston: Heinle & Heinle.

Snow, M. A. (2002). *Content-based instruction: Looking back, looking forward.* Paper presented at the Midwest TESOL Regional Conference, Minneapolis, MN.

Snow, M. A., & Brinton, D. M. (Eds.). (1997). *The content-based classroom: Perspectives on integrating language and content.* White Plains, NY: Longman.

Snow, M. A., Met, M., & Genesee, F. (1989). A conceptual framework for the integration of language and content in second/foreign language instruction, *TESOL Quarterly 23*(2), 201–217.

Spolsky, B., Meir, D. B., Inbar, O., Orland, L., Steiner, J., & Vermel, J. (2001). *English curriculum.* Tel Aviv, Israel: Ministry of Education.

Sprinthall, N. A., Reiman, A. J., & Thies-Sprinthall, L. (1996). Teacher professional development. In J. Sikula, T. J. Buttery, & E. Guyton (Eds.), *Handbook of research on teacher education* (2nd ed., pp. 666–703). New York: Simon & Schuster Macmillan.

Stake, R. E. (1995). *The art of case study research.* Thousand Oaks, CA: Sage.

Starkey, H. (1999). Foreign language teaching to adults: Implicit and explicit political education. *Oxford Review of Education, 25,* 155–170.

State of Victoria, Department of Education. (1997). *ESL course advice for the curriculum and standards framework, S3-S4.* Melbourne: Curriculum Corporation.

State of Victoria, Department of Education and Training. (2003). *The ESL report 2002.* Melbourne: Department of Education and Training.

Stoller, F. L. (2002). *Content-based instruction: A shell for language teaching or a framework for strategic language and content learning?* Paper presented at the Annual TESOL Convention, Salt Lake City, UT.

Stoller, F. L. (2004). Content-based instruction: Perspectives on curriculum planning. *Annual Review of Applied Linguistics, 24,* 261–283.

Stoller, F. L., & Grabe, W. (1997). A six-T's approach to content-based instruction. In M. A. Snow & D. M. Brinton (Eds.), *The content-based classroom: Perspectives on integrating language and content* (pp. 78–94). White Plains, NY: Longman.

Tedick, D. J., Fortune, T., & Walker, C. L. (2003). *The complexity of integrating language in immersion teaching*. Paper presented at the Third International Conference on Language Teacher Education, Minneapolis, MN.

Teemant, A., Smith, M. E., Pinnegar, S., & Egan, M. W. (in press). Modeling sociocultural pedagogy in distance education. *Teachers College Record*.

Teitel, L. (1998). *Governance: Designing professional development school governance structures*. Washington, DC: American Association of Colleges for Teacher Education.

Teitel, L. (2003). *The professional development schools handbook: Starting, sustaining, and assessing partnerships that improve student learning*. Thousand Oaks, CA: Corwin Press.

TESOL. (1993, Winter/Spring). TESOL statement on the role of bilingual education in the education of children in the United States. *Bilingual Basics: The Official Publication of the Bilingual Interest Section*, pp. 1, 3, 5.

TESOL. (1997). *ESL standards for pre-K–12 students*. Alexandria, VA: Author.

TESOL. (2002). *TESOL/NCATE standards for P–12 teacher education programs*. Retrieved January 7, 2005, from http://www.tesol.org/s_tesol/seccss.asp?CID=219&DID=1689

Tharp, R. G., & Gallimore, R. (1988). *Rousing minds to life: Teaching, learning, and schooling in social context*. New York: Cambridge University Press.

Thomas, W. P., & Collier, V. P. (2002). *A national study of school effectiveness for language minority students' long-term academic achievement final report*. Center for Research on Education, Diversity & Excellence. Retrieved January 2, 2005, from http://www.crede.org/research/llaa/1.1es.html

Trueba, H. T. (1989). *Raising silent voices: Educating the linguistic minorities for the 21st century*. New York: Newbury.

Valdés, G. (2001). *Learning and not learning English: Latino students in American schools*. New York: Teachers College Press.

Vygotsky, L. S. (1934). *Myshlenie i rech: Psichologicheskie issledovaniya* [Thinking and speech: Psychological investigations]. Moscow and Leningrad: Gosudarstvennoe Sotsial'no-Ekonomicheskoe Izdatelstvo.

Vygotsky, L. S. (1956). *Izbrannie psichologichiskie issledovania* [Selected psychological research]. Moscow: Izdatel'stvo Academii Pedagogicheskih Nauk.

Vygotsky, L. S. (1962). *Pensamiento y lenguaje: Teoría del desarrollo cultural de las funciones psíquicas* [Language and thought: The development of higher mental functions]. Buenos Aires: Fausto.

Vygotsky, L. S. (1978). *Mind in society: The development of higher psychological processes*. Cambridge, MA: Harvard University Press.

Vygotsky, L. S. (1981). The genesis of higher mental functioning. In J. Wertsch (Ed.), *The concept of activity in Soviet psychology*. Armonk, NY: Sharpe.

Wang, M. C., & Walberg, H. J. (2001). *Tomorrow's teachers*. Richmond, CA: McCutchan.

Warschauer, M., Shetzer, H., & Meloni, C. (2000). *Internet for language teaching*. Alexandria, VA: TESOL.

Wertsch, J. (1990). The voice of rationality in a sociocultural approach to mind. In L. Moll (Ed.), *Vygotsky and education: Instructional implications of sociohistorical psychology* (pp. 111–126). New York: Cambridge University Press.

Wiggins, G. (1998). *Educative assessment: Designing assessments to inform and improve student performance*. San Francisco: Jossey-Bass.

Wiggins, G., & McTighe, J. (1998). *Understanding by design*. Alexandria, VA: Association for Supervision and Curriculum Development.

Williams, B. (Ed.). (2000). *Reforming teacher education through accreditation: Telling our story*. Washington, DC: National Council for Accreditation of Teacher Education.

Willis, J. (1996). *A framework for task-based learning.* Harlow, United Kingdom: Longman.

Wilson, S. (2000). Schooling for democracy: Issues on student participation. *Youth Studies Australia, 19,* 25–31.

Wisconsin Department of Public Instruction. (2004). *English language learners (ELLs): Standards and assessments.* Madison: Author. Retrieved December 26, 2004, from http://www.dpi.state.wi.us/oea/ells.html

Wood, D., Bruner, J., & Ross, G. (1976). The role of tutoring in problem solving. *Journal of Child Psychology and Psychiatry, 17*(2), 89–100.

Woodward, T. (1993). *Models and metaphors in teacher training: Loop input and other strategies.* Cambridge: Cambridge University Press.

Yalden, J. (1983). The communicative syllabus: Evolution, design, and implementation. London: Pergamon.

Yin, R. K. (1994). *Case study research: Design and methods* (2nd ed.). Thousand Oaks, CA: Sage.

Yelland, G., Pollack, J., & Mercuri, A. (1993). The metalinguistic benefits of limited contact with a second language. *Applied Psycholinguistics, 4,* 423–444.

Index

Information presented in tables and figures is denoted by *t* and *f* respectively.

 A

Abreu, Hilduara, 5
  "Supporting Sheltered Instruction in a Bilingual Program Through a Professional Development School Partnership," 95–110
Academic content
  curriculum promotion in, 183–184
  standards in, 145, 146, 147
Academic language
  development of, 23
  in sustained content-based instruction (SCBI) program, 179, 185
  in the content-based ESOL curriculum, 163
Ackert, 169
Activities
  as social studies topics, 101
  literacy-based, 101
  see also Thematic project(s)
Activities portfolio, 87
Agor, 163
Alegria, Reina, 5
  "Supporting Sheltered Instruction in a Bilingual Program Through a Professional Development School Partnership," 95–110
Alternate performance activities
  data sources for, 150
  instructional assessment of, 150, 151*f*, 152*f*
Alternate performance indicators (APIs)
  attributes of, 148–149, 148*f*

creation of, 146
data sources for, 150
definition of, 147
description of, 147
differences in formulation of, 149*f*
examples of, 149*f*
Amazing Grace, 87–88
American Association for the Advancement of Science, 1
Anderson, Mary, 87
Andrade, Kretschmer, & Kretschmer, 122
Andrews, 34
APIs
  see Alternate performance indicators
Arabic studies
  course in, 111
  resources, lack of in, 113
  sample units of instruction, 117*f*
Arkoudis, 135
Arkoudis & Davison, 48
Arkoudis, Sophie, 5
  "Frilled Up Science: Developing Practices Within Collaboration," 133–141
Assessment
  content-based instruction, 150, 151*f*
  documentation of, 152–153
  instructional implications of, 146
  No Child Left Behind Act, impact on, 195
  planning sheet for, 153*f*
  practical ideas for, 155, 158
  process description, 147–152
  rubrics for, 154–155, 156*f*, 157*f*, 158, 159*f*
  rubrics, uses in, 152–153
Assisted performance, instruction as, 81, 84–85, 88

U

V

W